Understanding the Power and the History of Amulets & Talismans

This book gives a fascinating history of amulets and talismans. It shows you how to construct these charms to fulfill your needs and desires. From the historical background provided, you can see that using amulets is no idle, superstitious whim, but rather a natural following of a traditional faith in the power of protective signs and symbols.

Reading this book will give a complete understanding of the meaning of amulets and talismans and of their place in today's modern society. Do amulets and talismans work? Are they really effective? Do they possess magical powers in themselves or do they draw such power out of the maker? The answers are all here, waiting for you.

Today's modern society, with its continual need to progress, its high pressures, stress, and constant competition, is one in which the amulet and the talisman can find a natural niche. We have come full circle from Paleolithic times when the world seemed overly complex. At that time, primitive people incorporated symbols representing the powers of Nature into talismans that they could use to protect themselves and give them the confidence to carry on. Today there is that same need in many people. Using modern talismans, we can bolster our courage and reinforce our confidence to fight the competition and run the "rat-race" of super-civilization.

Through its complete and detailed examination of the subject, the book puts religious and magical faith into true perspective, underscoring the utilitarian nature of charms in everyday life. They are not the exclusive preserve of ritual magicians, cabbalists, mystics, and priests, but the common tools of all of us; the birthright of those who would compete in a world growing ever more complex.

—Raymond Buckland
Author of *Buckland's Complete Book of Witchcraft*

About the Author

Migene González-Wippler was born in Puerto Rico and has degrees in psychology and anthropology from the University of Puerto Rico and from Columbia University. She has worked as a science editor for the Interscience Division of John Wiley, the American Institute of Physics and the American Museum of Natural History in New York, and as an English editor for the United Nations in Vienna, where she lived for many years. She is the noted author of many books on religion and mysticism, including the widely acclaimed *Santeria: African Magic in Latin America*, *The Santeria Experience*, *A Kabbalah for the Modern World*, *The Complete Book of Spells, Ceremonies, & Magic*, and *Dreams and What They Mean to You*.

To Write to the Author

If you wish to contact the author or would like more information about this book, please write to the author in care of Llewellyn Worldwide, and we will forward your request. Both the author and publisher appreciate hearing from you and learning of your enjoyment of this book and how it has helped you. Llewellyn Worldwide cannot guarantee that every letter written to the author can be answered, but all will be forwarded. Please write to:

Migene González-Wippler
c/o Llewellyn Worldwide
2143 Wooddale Drive, Dept. 978-0-87542-287-9
Woodbury, MN 55125-2989, USA

Please enclose a self-addressed, stamped envelope for reply, or $1.00 to cover costs. If outside the USA, enclose an international reply coupon.

The Complete Book of Amulets & Talismans

Migene González-Wippler

Llewellyn Publications
Woodbury, Minnesota

FIRST EDITION
Tenth Printing, 2007

(Previously part of the Llewellyn Sourcebook series, seven printings.)

Cover design by Gavin Duffy
Cover background images © by Digital Stock and Digital Vision
Llewellyn is a registered trademark of Llewellyn Worldwide, Ltd.

Library of Congress Cataloging-in-Publication Data
González-Wippler, Migene.
  The complete book of amulets & talismans / Migene González-Wippler.— 1st ed.
    p. cm.
  Originally published: St. Paul, Minn. : Llewellyn Publications, 1991.
  Includes bibliographical references and index.
  1. Amulets. 2. Talismans. I. Title. II. Title: Complete book of amulets and talismans.
BF1561.G66 2005
133.4'4--dc22
                                                          2005044497
ISBN 13: 978-0-87542-287-9
ISBN 10: 0-87542-287-X

Llewellyn Worldwide does not participate in, endorse, or have any authority or responsibility concerning private business transactions between our authors and the public.

All mail addressed to the author is forwarded but the publisher cannot, unless specifically instructed by the author, give out an address or phone number.

Any Internet references contained in this work are current at publication time, but the publisher cannot guarantee that a specific location will continue to be maintained. Please refer to the publisher's website for links to authors' websites and other sources.

Llewellyn Publications
A Division of Llewellyn Worldwide, Ltd.
2143 Wooddale Drive, Dept. 978-0-87542-287-9
Woodbury, MN 55125-2989, U.S.A.
www.llewellyn.com

Printed in the United States of America

Other Books by Migene González-Wippler

We fear . . .
We fear the elements with which
  we fight to wrest our food from land and sea
We fear cold and famine . . .
We fear the sickness all about us
We fear the souls of the dead
We fear the spirits of earth and air
We fear . . .

An Eskimo shaman to Knud Rasmussen,
Danish Explorer, ca. 1918

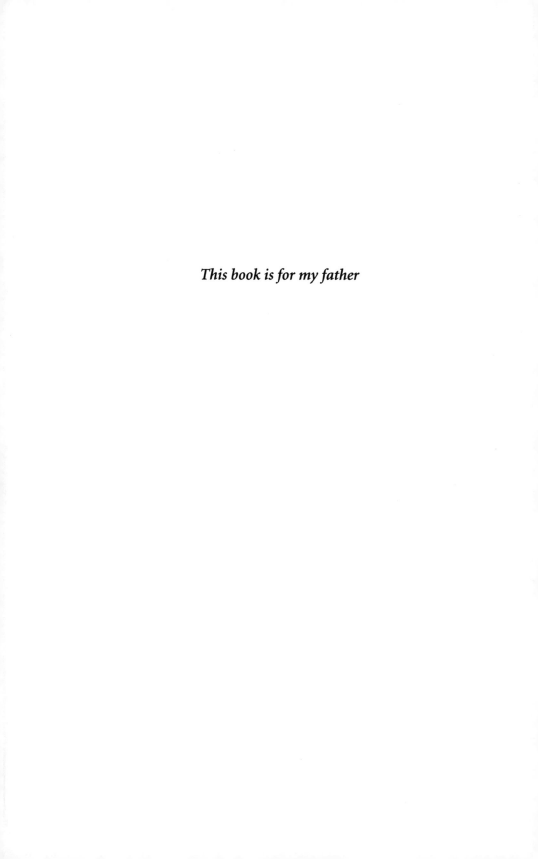

This book is for my father

CONTENTS

Introduction

LET'S FACE IT. WE ARE SCARED. WE WERE BORN SCARED. THE FIRST reaction a human has at the moment of birth is to let out one huge, frantic wail. There is no doubt in the minds of the people present at this blessed event that this tiny being's entrance into the world is made with the utmost reluctance. And why should it be otherwise? The average human fetus spends approximately nine months in the warmth and safety of its mother's womb, where its every need is met in blissful peace and silence. Suddenly, after being steadily conditioned to a life of total comfort, the fetus is brutally expelled from its cozy haven and banished into an unknown and threatening world. Gone are the warmth, the safety, the dreamlike state of quiet contentment. They are replaced by loud noises, cold air, hard surfaces, and constant physical discomfort. Small wonder the newborn child cries at birth. The child has come face to face for the first time with what will forever remain his or her worst enemy: fear.

Fear is our initial reaction to the threats of our environment. In a sense fear can be considered an overreaction of the preservation instinct. Because it invites caution, it can be at times of help to the individual. But if it is allowed to overpower the mind, it can be a terribly crippling affliction.

Primitive people learned the meaning of fear very early. Besieged by hunger, inclement weather, wild animals, disease, and natural disasters, their life was a constant struggle for survival. And they learned very quickly that to surrender to fear meant death.

In order to protect themselves against the dangers of their environment and to bolster their courage, they decided to enlist the aid of a formidable ally: the powers of nature. They began to anthropomorphize natural forces and to worship them. The sun, the

A common talismanic symbol representing the waxing and the waning phases of the moon connected by the stream of life.

The Seasons of the Year

Spring

Autumn

Summer

Winter

The symbols of the four seasons of the year are very popular in talismans for prosperity. They are very ancient and probably originate from alchemical sources. Each symbol is derived from one of the zodiacal signs associated with the four elements: Taurus for Spring and Earth; Leo for Summer and Fire; Scorpio for Autumn and Water; and Aquarius for Winter and Air. This last symbol is a mixture of the Aquarius and the Uranus symbology.

moon, the wind, the sea, and the earth itself with all its bountiful promises, became deities with supernatural powers that could be tapped through proper worship and sacrifice. Symbols representing these forces and their powers were among the first artistic efforts of primitive people. These symbols became known as amulets, talismans, charms and fetishes.

The purpose of magical symbols such as amulets was to concentrate power so that it could be used by human beings. These symbols represented all the supernatural qualities and abilities of the gods that humans needed to overcome the world around them. By holding an amulet or carrying it around constantly, primitive people felt secure and protected. This belief in the supernatural powers of the gods and their symbols became known as faith, the most potent weapon against fear.

Faith is the central promise behind both magic and religion, and firmly delineates the most important difference between both systems. In religion, humanity declares an undying faith in the powers of God. In magic, humanity declares an undying faith in its own powers. But the aims of both magic and religion are essentially the same—to protect us against the dangers that surround us, to give us self-confidence, and to assuage our fears, all through the power of faith.

Amulets and other magic symbols are used by both magic and religion for protective purposes, or for strength and self-assurance. The Star of David and the Christian cross provide the same feeling of comfort and protection to their religious-minded wearers as a rabbit's foot, a pentagram, or the Hand of Fatima provide to those magically inclined. The intention is the same: to attract good luck, to dispel evil, and to banish fear.

In our modern societies, we are no longer battling ferocious animals, intractable weather and the constant threat of starvation. The dangers we face are more sophisticated, but just as deadly. Air and water pollution, nuclear proliferation, the constant threat of war, disease, crime, drug and sexual abuse, inflation, unemployment, and natural and manmade disasters are the new fears that corrode our sense of well being and self-assurance. Tortured by an ever-growing anxiety about the future, besieged by worries and frustrations, humanity searches desperately for ways with which to relieve its anguish. Sometimes escape seems the only solution. Drugs, alcohol, mental illness, and suicide are some common forms

a.

b.

c.

a. and b. This famous symbol is known as Trinacria or Triskelion and is probably derived from three triangles. It was later developed into a figure consisting of a head surrounded by three legs, commonly associated with time and speed. Some authorities trace the three-legged Triskelion to at least thirteen hundred years before the birth of Christ. It is extremely valued as an amulet against the evil eye.

c. This figure is known as the Triquetrum and is used instead of the Triskelion whenever one desires to contain the forces of speed and time it represents.

of escape. Most of the time, however, faith seems the best way to exorcise fear.

Established world religions, no longer able to satisfy our growing spiritual needs, are beginning to lose ground to new religious sects, all of which vociferously claim to have the answers to society's ever-increasing problems. New techniques in meditation and self-awareness are being essayed in order to bring about higher states of consciousness. Ancient magical beliefs and practices are being revived all over the world. The aim is, as always, relief from fear and anxiety, and a return to the blissful state of peace and well-being that was the first experienced in mother's womb.

At the very core of all this religious and magical activity are the symbols we know as amulets and talismans. Every need, every want, every hope that ever dwelled in the human heart has been expressed in the form of an amulet or a talisman. These symbols are part of the language of the unconscious mind, and are an expression of our faith in ourselves and in the universal forces around us. We must believe in order to survive. Amulets and talismans help us to believe.

At this point we must stop and ask some very natural questions. Do amulets and talismans really work? Do they truly possess magical powers and have the ability to alter the circumstances surrounding our lives? The answer is yes, but only within the framework of our faith in them. Faith is the great miracle worker and the true power behind amulets and talismans.

PART I:

AMULETS

1 What is an Amulet?

THE WORD *AMULET* IS DERIVED FROM THE LATIN AMULETUM, WHICH, according to Pliny, is "an object that protects a person from trouble."* This is probably a perfectly valid definition, but our more discriminating modern intellectuals would prefer to redefine the term as "an object, either natural or man-made, which is *believed* to protect a person from trouble." (See Webster's Dictionary.) The word *believed* stresses the fact that it is the faith placed in the amulet that works for its owner, not just the actual powers of the amulet itself.

An amulet can be anything, a small seashell, a colored stone, a root, a diamond ring, or an old horseshoe. Its most important quality is its alleged power to safeguard its owner from harm and to bring him or her happiness and good luck. This "power" has been the subject of many theories and controversies among students of both the natural and supernatural phenomena. Some claim that amulets really have magical powers. Others insist that amulets are only psychological aids that help strengthen humanity's courage and self-assurance. Maybe there is some truth in both statements.

Magic, in its occult connotation, has been defined many times and in many contexts. Perhaps the most satisfying definition is the one that presents magic as any act of will that brings about purposeful changes in a person's environment. According to this definition all of us have, at one time or another in our lives, performed an act or acts of magic. Whether by means of prayers, magic spells, the use of amulets and talismans, or just plain will and determination, we are constantly trying to direct our lives along a specific course. Essentially, that is what magic is all about: controlling our lives and shaping our destinies. When we exceed the limits of human rights, and

---

* See S. C. Plinius, *Natural History,* (London, 1964).

1

attempt to control the lives of others, we are dangerously leaning toward "black" magic.

Magic, in one form or another, was our first attempt to control our environment. From early prehistoric times human beings arbitrarily attached special magical qualities to the objects and *events* that were the most important to them in their daily life.

A Shaman's rattle from the Northwest coast of North America. The body of the rattle is formed by a raven which is said to possess the secret of life. Its tongue contains the life spirit. The beaver stands on the stomach of a man who has just died, and receives the supernatural powers of the shaman.

(Courtesy of the American Museum of Natural History.)

They also concluded that a human being was dual in essence, that is, that he or she has a physical body and a spiritual alter-ego, or soul. This belief in a soul became a universal concept. The soul was conceived of as a vital force whose presence animates the body and whose absence stills it. Seen in this context, our spiritual nature or soul is the spark of life.

According to the 19th-century anthropologist Sir Edward Burnett Tylor, the attribution of spiritual qualities to plants and other natural objects resulted in what we call nature worship. This was the root of totemism, the deification of animals and plants, and of the use of amulets and talismans. From these beliefs was derived the high polytheism of primitive peoples, and their worship of the spirits of nature. Practices such as magical rituals and sacrifice were ways they invented to bring nature and life within their control, or at least within reach of their understanding. The belief in unknown forces beyond the realms of the physical world was mostly a response to what Max Weber called "the power of meaning." It was not that natural explanations could not be found for the phenomenon of their existence and that of the world around them. It was simply that magical and religious explanations were more emotionally satisfying.

MAGIC VS RELIGION

Primitive people tried by means of magical rituals and incantations to subdue the spirits of nature and subject them to their will. In this way they sought to achieve total control of their lives and of their environment. When they realized that their rituals and spells were not always successful, and therefore that their magic was limited, they attempted to propitiate the gods of nature through acts of worship and sacrifice. The difference between direct control and an appeal to higher beings marks the distinction between magic and religion.

In both magic and religion, we feel a compelling need to observe the tenets of our beliefs and to act in accordance with the nature and meaning of the universe as we believe it to be. This compulsive behavior is at the core of all true religious experience and gives rise to the various religious and magical practices that are an essential part of all human cultures. Attempts to control natural and supernatural powers, divination, sacrifice, taboos, prayers, rituals, and of course, amulets and talismans, are included in some of these practices. Although organized religion frowns upon magical practices, it makes use of a fair amount of magic in its own rituals, particularly in its use of amulets and other magical symbols for protective purposes. Typical among these are the Star of David in Jewish synagogues and the use of rosaries in the Roman Catholic Church. But even though magic is always differentiated from religion, they are both invariably treated under the heading of supernaturalism.

MANA

Supernaturalism expresses the belief in spirit beings placed in a hierarchical order that starts with the Godhead. It also postulates the existence of supernatural forces that do not emanate from any god or spirit but exist of themselves.

Supernatural forces may exist as personified power and as impersonal power. Personified power is an attribute of gods and spirits, and operates at their will or direction. Impersonal power is a force, usually invisible, that extends itself throughout the universe, and may only be found in certain objects and places. This force is known as *Mana.*

Mana may be a quality of both men and gods and of some natural substances. It may also be brought into operation by means of magic rituals and spells without the direct intervention of supernatural entities. Mana is simply power.

In Polynesia, where the concept of Mana was conceived, Mana was seen as both personified and impersonal power. In Hawaii the amount of Mana possessed by an individual was believed to be proportional to his social position. The higher his position, the greater the Mana he was believed to possess. There were also ways of gaining Mana, such as eating the eye of a fallen enemy. Mana was the essence of power and victory but it was also potentially dangerous. The king was believed to possess so much Mana that special precautions had to be taken so that his excess power would not injure the common people. A series of taboos or prohibitions were created in order to protect people from too much of this supernatural power.

Perhaps the best way to exemplify the power of Mana is by considering the quiet strength of trees. There seems to flow from every tree a kind of aura, like a controlled power, impassive yet very potent. A simple experiment will serve to show that this power, this Mana of the tree, can be used by us to replenish our own energies. Sometime, when you are walking down the street, feeling particularly tired, approach the first large, healthy tree in the vicinity. Lean lightly against the tree, take a deep breath and mentally "ask" the tree to share some of its energy with you. Wait a few minutes and then walk away. You will feel as refreshed and revitalized as if you had slept several hours.

In the same way as the tree has Mana, so do other natural things, such as stones, herbs, flowers, roots, and animals. The waters of the sea and the rivers also have Mana. When the Mana inherent in a natural object is particularly strong and positive, that object is considered to be a natural amulet. A four-leaf clover, a rabbit's foot, and a fox tail are all examples of natural amulets. They seem to be naturally endowed with an extra amount of Mana. And because one of the qualities of Mana is its ability to be transferred from one carrier to another, an amulet can pass its Mana on to you.

Mana is known by other names, such as personal magnetism. The healing power that is present in some people is an example of

Mana. When healers lay their hands on their patients, they are transfering Mana.

The power of Mana can be of either a positive or a negative nature. When the Mana is negative, the object or the creature that possesses it is believed to be noxious and injurious to all living creatures. Snakes, frogs, scorpions, ravens, and black cats are all traditional symbols of bad luck. When a person has this same negative power, he or she is believed to have the "evil eye."

Mana is then the natural power of the amulet. But even the power of Mana cannot rival the power of faith. Because only faith can make possible the transfer of Mana. When a person believes in the power of an amulet, the power of the amulet can work for him, making him feel strong and protected. When there is no faith, there is no link between the individual and the amulet, and therefore there can be no transfer of power. That is why I said at the beginning of this chapter that it is the faith placed in the amulet that works for its owner, not just the actual powers of the amulet itself.

SYMPATHETIC MAGIC

The term *sympathetic magic* comprises two magical categories, namely, *imitative* or *homoeopathic magic* and *contagious magic*. Imitative magic states that like produces like or that an effect resembles its cause. Burning somebody's wax image or stabbing it with pins is an example of imitative magic. The idea behind the magician's action is that the thing that is happening to the wax image will also happen to the person it represents. Likewise, objects bearing names similar to a desired condition or state may be used to bring about that condition. Thus, the well-known root of John the Conqueror is used as a powerful amulet to conquer and overpower. Am-

This is a typical voodoo doll. Its right side is always black and is used for evil hexes and for cursing a person. Its left side can be either red for casting love spells or white to get spiritual help. The doll's back is blue and is used for spells attracting good fortune. The eyes, the heart and the mouth are made using white and black threads.

monia, which sounds a little like *harmony*, is used to dispel trouble and bring about harmonious conditions. The root *satiricon*, which has a name with erotic connotations, is used to increase sexual power. The use of plants like myrtle and vervain, traditionally associated with love magic, is a form of calling toward a person all the magical attributes of these plants.

Contagious magic, on the other hand, states that things that have been in contact with each other will continue to act on each other long after that contact has been broken. According to this concept, it is possible to affect somebody in either a positive or a negative way if one can only acquire some object that has been in contact with this individual. Likewise, things that have been a part of a living creature still retain the essential characteristics of that creature. Thus a rabbit's foot is believed to be endowed with the swiftness and fertility of the rabbit, a lion's tooth is believed to possess its owner's awesome physical strength and proverbial valor, and a horseshoe is believed to possess the horse's strength, vitality, and swiftness.

VARIOUS FORMS OF AMULETS

There are two types of amulets: natural and manmade. A natural amulet is a combination of Mana and faith. The manmade amulet is simply a concentration of faith.

Of all the natural amulets, perhaps the one believed to be the most powerful is the *fetish*. This is an object believed to be the seat or the house of a spirit force. In Africa, fetishes are known by many names, such as ju-ju, gri-gri, wong, mkissi, and biang. A fetish can also be artificially made by the shaman or witch doctor. Many of the fetishes of the west coast of Africa are decorated with mirrors and then placed on

A horn amulet against the evil eye. It is also a virility symbol popular among Italian men.

various parts of the body for protective purposes. Mirrors were introduced into Africa by Christian missionaries and were promptly appropriated by the natives who saw in them the "white man's magic."

Most manmade amulets are representations of supernatural forces whose powers are invoked for protective purposes by the amulet's owner. An amulet can also be made to symbolize a desired quality or characteristic. In Italy, for example, the horn is a very popular amulet. It is considered to be a symbol of virility and sex appeal, as well as a sure protection against the *ietattura,* or the evil eye.

An amulet that is inscribed with special characters is known as a *charm.* Many of our modern slogans are charms in disguise. The peace and love signs, the smiling sun face, the outspoken demands for "Black Power" and "Ecology Now" are all good examples of charms because implicit in their symbology is the faith in their ability to turn hopes into realities. Even *Playboy*'s saucy rabbit's head is a magical symbol of sex and fertility.

"I love New York" is the slogan of that city, and is accompanied by the image of a bright red apple. The apple has always been one of the traditional fruits associated with Venus, and therefore it is a powerful love symbol.

Zodiac signs are also among the most popular of modern amulets. They appear on necklaces, bracelets, rings, and even key holders.

What all this means is that the belief in amulets is such an intrinsic part of the human psyche that we often use them without realizing what they are. Consciously, that is, because unconsciously we are expressing either a feeling or a need in the symbolic language of the mind.

2 The First Amulets

AMULETS ARE AMONG THE MOST COMMON OBJECTS UNEARTHED BY excavators at archaeological sites. These findings are not confined to any one place or period in history, and seem to indicate that the use of amulets can be traced to prehistorical times and to the various human families. Primitive people seem to have begun using amulets for protecting themselves from evil forces and for divining the future. They used amulets to enhance fertility, to gain strength, to overcome enemies, to protect family and property, and above all, to overcome the dangers of the evil eye. The power of these first amulets was *animistic*.

Animism, or belief in spirit beings, eventually developed into the first polytheistic religions. Primitive man conceived of his many gods as the possessors of awesome magical powers that were often concentrated in amulets and other magical symbols. It was believed that the gods created the power of magic so that they could help themselves and man. This belief persisted in the highly sophisticated priesthoods of Sumer, Babylonia, and Egypt, and formed an intrinsic part of the mystery religions. The gods were believed to be the first magicians, who passed on the benefits of their magic to the people through the priests.

The Egyptian Ankh, a symbol of life.

All the gods had made their own amulets as concentrations, as well as representations, of their powers. All the Egyptian gods were depicted holding an *ankh* in their hands. The ankh, also known as the *crux ansata*, is a symbol of life and was considered to be a very powerful amulet by the ancient Egyptians. It was also believed to be an ancient fertility symbol, as it originally represented the male and the female genital organs. The gods bestowed the ankh on

9

Egyptians who had led good lives, thus ensuring that those individuals would live in the afterlife for one hundred thousand million years.

Symbols of life have always been some of the most popular of all the religious amulets. The eighth letter of the Hebrew alphabet, *cheth*, is worn by many people as a life symbol. The Kabbalistic meaning of the letter is "enclosure," which is an accurate description of the womb and its life-giving powers.

Cheth, the eighth letter of the Hebrew alphabet, is another symbol of life, very popular among both Jews and Gentiles.

Hundreds of thousands of clay tablets in cuneiform script were unearthed in early excavations in western Asia, especially in the site of ancient Nineveh. This particular tablet tells the Gilgamesh epic, which has a perfect parallel with the Biblical story of Noah's ark and the deluge.

The Babylonian creation epic gives a fascinating example of the use of amulets among the Babylonian gods. When the goddess Tiamat, the personification of evil and the mother of all things, rebelled against the other gods, Marduk (the son of Ea) was the god chosen to destroy Tiamat. Marduk armed himself with many invincible weapons, but his greatest protection was an amulet made of red stone in the form of an eye, which he carried between his lips. He also carried a bunch of herbs in one hand to repel Tiamat's evil magic. But Tiamat was also well protected by an equally powerful amulet known as the Tablet of Destinies, or "Duppu Shemati." She made the mistake of giving her amulet, which symbolized a concentration of all her powers, to her son Kingu, whom she also called her "only spouse." Kingu, the commander in chief of all her forces, set out to destroy Marduk with the help of the tablet, but Marduk's magic proved stronger. He defeated Kingu and his demonic hordes and took from him the Tablet of Destinies. He stamped it with his seal and fastened it on his breast, thus claiming as his own all of Tiamat's magic powers. He then smashed Tiamat's skull and split her body into two parts. From one part he formed the vault of heaven and from the other, the World Ocean, or abode of Ea. From Kingu's blood Ea created humanity to serve the gods. For this reason humanity is tainted with evil and is always tempted to perform evil acts. The great number of clay tablets dating from Babylonian times that have been found with magical inscriptions in cuneiform purporting to dispel spirits are proof of the Babylonians' belief in the power of amulets against evil.

The traditional battle between the forces of good and evil is also echoed in Ethiopian religious legends. In the "Book of the Mysteries of Heaven and Earth" there is a detailed account of Satan's rebellion against God. Twice during the battle the divine armies were repulsed and overthrown. But the third time God sent with them a Cross of Light upon which the names of the Three Persons of the Holy Trinity were inscribed. When Satan saw the cross and the three names, his courage forsook him, he lost his strength, and the angels of God hurled him and his hordes down into hell's abyss. From very early Christian times the Ethiopians have regarded the cross as the most powerful amulet.

The Jewish rabbis and the Christian fathers frowned severely upon the use of amulets because they were considered a sign of distrust in the powers of the Almighty. All things magical also awoke feelings of profound disquiet in the minds of the founders of

Judaism and Christianity because they tended to strengthen humanity's belief in its own powers. The founders feared that a person who had faith in himself would not need to have faith in God. A false reasoning, but one that made the early churches condemn the use of magic in any form. Nevertheless it is clear that the practice of magic is finely interwoven in many of the rituals of the Christian churches, and the use of amulets is an integral part of Christianity as a whole.

A revival of the use of amulets began soon after the close of the fourth century. At this time Christians began to make amulets connected with their religion. The first amulet was the cross, as well as the crucifix, which shows an image of Christ on the cross. Pictures of the Virgin Mary, Jesus, and all the great saints and archangels also were believed to be powerful amulets against the forces of evil. Relics of the saints and the Christian martyrs, extracts from the Scriptures inscribed on parchment and metal, vials of sacramental oil and holy water—all became imbued with magical powers. With the invention of paper, the use of these religious amulets became more common. The Church, however, does not consider them amulets, but simple expressions of religious faith.

DIVINATION

The insatiable desire to know the future has always been deeply rooted in humanity. Amulets were also designed for divination purposes. Some amulets were believed to bring to their owners premonitions or dreams that could reveal all things to come. Others could be used as oracles, but they also possessed miraculous powers that were God-given. Among these latter were Urim and Thummim, the holy oracle of Israel. Urim and Thummim, meaning "light and perfection," were probably two small pebbles, or plaques or bits of wood, which were cast as dice. This may be inferred from the fact that they were kept in a small pouch by the high priest, who wore it at the back of the *breastplate of judgment* (Exod. 28:30; Lev. 8:8).

The oracle of Urim and Thummim was consulted according to Moses' strict directions, and was carefully controlled by him and the priests of the Levites. Their inquiry took the form of a semi-religious ceremony, and only the priesthood was allowed to conduct it. Urim and Thummim was the only form of divination accepted by the ancient Hebrews. But although the practice of magic was forbidden, the use of amulets persisted in the mezuzah, or sign on the doorpost; the phylacteries, or frontlets that were worn between the eyes and on the arm; and the tzitzith, or fringes worn on the prayer shawls.

Astrology and geomancy are two forms of predicting the future that can be traced as far back as the time of the Chaldeans. All the geomantic and astrological symbols we know were believed to possess magical powers. They are still used in our modern times as amulets for good luck or to dispel evil. Likewise all the symbols used in other forms of divination are believed to be imbued with magic and are considered to be potent amulets. The reason for this belief may be that divination symbols or objects are often used to reveal the future. This power remains in the object and can later be used for protective purposes.

BABYLONIAN AND ASSYRIAN AMULETS

The Sumerians, and later on the Babylonians, occupied Mesopotamia for several thousand years starting around 3000 B.C. They were a very magically minded people and practiced all forms of magic in their daily lives. They lived in constant fear of evil spirits and used innumerable charms, spells, and incantations to protect themselves against these evil forces. Chief among their protective devices were all types of amulets, most of them designed as deterrents against the evil eye.

The most archaic of these amulets date to approximately 2500 B.C. and are mostly in animal form. The frog, a symbol of fertility, was a popular amulet usually depicted in glazed clay. The bull and a pair of fish were also symbols of fertility and virility, as were the ram, the sow, and the horse. Lions were symbols of strength and were commonly used to overcome enemies. When figures of animals were used as amulets, they were often engraved on their bases with protective designs believed to bolster the amulet's power.

Cylinder-seals were also popular amulets. They were made of precious or semiprecious stones, such as jade, jasper, agate, topaz, lapis lazuli, and amethyst. Each kind of stone was believed to possess the power to protect its owner against evil and to bring him good luck, of its own special kind. For example, a seal made of lapis lazuli was believed to "possess a god and the god will rejoice in him," while a seal made of rock crystal would make a man prosper in all his affairs and bring him wealth.

Babylonian cylinder-seal amulets.

The cylinder-seal was used both as an amulet and as a seal. When used as a seal it was pressed against wet clay, and when the clay dried, the name of the owner and the seal's design was inscribed on the clay tablet. These were used during business transactions and for the signing of contracts. When the seal was not being used as a signature, it was carried around by its owner as an amulet.

Cylinder-seals were sometimes engraved with prayers and religious scenes. The most common scene found on the amulets is the one depicting Gilgamesh and Enkidu "fighting beasts." To create this type of amulet, a metal engraver cut the outline and a drill was then used to produce indented parts. Limestone was one of the most popular materials used to make the seals.

Other forms of amulets used by the Sumerians and Babylonians, and later on by the Assyrians, were prophylactic figures of gods, men, animals, and reptiles. Some of the most famous of these amulets are human figures with wings and lion heads made of terra cotta.

The Assyrians were fond of burying the figures of dogs of many colors under their houses. The belief behind this custom was that the spirits of the dogs would prevent any malicious or evil person or spirit from entering the house. Usually ten dog figures were buried, five on each side of the house.

In Ur of the Chaldees, the place of birth of the patriarch Abraham, statues of gods were kept at the entrance of each room of the house, each statue encased in a small box accompanied by bits of food, such as grain or small birds. The figures were generally made of unbaked clay and covered by a thin layer of lime, on which details of form and dress were etched in black ink.

Of all the evil spirits most feared by the Babylonians, the most dreaded one was a she-devil who attached herself to pregnant women and to young children. Her name was Lamashtu or Labartu and she was the daughter of the god Anu. Lamashtu is depicted in plaques of metal and stone. To thwart her evil powers the Babylonians used special stones in the form of cylinders. These stones were tied to various parts of the body by means of cords of different colors, and sometimes they had to remain in their position for as much as one hundred days.

Around the time of the downfall of the Assyrian Empire, after the destruction of Nineveh (612 B.C.)., the cylinder-seals were replaced by cone-seals. These were made of sard, carnelian, and agate, among other stones, and served as sealing tablets as well as amulets. Chalcedony was one of the most popular stones used for this type of seal, and upon its surface were inscribed symbols of the gods Marduk, Nabu, and Shamash; mythical beasts and wing demons; and men standing by the sacred tree. Also very popular were scenes from the Epic of Gilgamesh. In one of these chalcedony cone-seals one can see the figure of a man on horseback battling a winged monster. It could very well be the foundation of the legend of St. George and the dragon.

EGYPTIAN AMULETS

The Egyptian word for amulet was *mk–t*, which means "protector." Another word used to denote an amulet was *udjau*, meaning "the thing which keeps safe," or the "strengthener." The Egyptians believed that many of the substances of which their amulets were made possessed magical properties that could be absorbed by their wearers. The most powerful amulets were those inscribed with the names of one or more of the gods, or those that had been blessed by a magician and thus possessed some of the magician's spiritual powers.

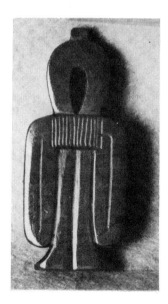

To the left is the ankh, the Egyptian symbol of life. To the right is the Tjet, an amulet representing the generation organs of Isis, which was said to bring to the wearer the powers of the blood of Isis.

The Egyptian Trinity. From left to right, Horus, Osiris and Isis. At their feet the
scribe Ammon and his wife Aul. (*Musée du Louvre, Paris.*)

The oldest Egyptian amulets date from the Neolithic period. They are mostly fertility symbols made of flint in the form of various animals, such as the crocodile, the hippopotamus, the cuttlefish, and a double-headed lion. The latter represented the sun gods of sunrise and sunset. Flint arrowheads were also used as amulets at this time. But the oldest amulet used by the Egyptians was undoubtedly the ankh. As we have already seen, the Egyptian gods all possessed this symbol of life, thus ensuring their immortality. When the Egyptians embraced Christianity in the first century, they still kept the ankh as a religious symbol and it often appears on tombs of that period, next to the Christian cross. The ancient Egyptians made the ankh from various materials, such as wood, wax, metals, and different colored stones. The ankh was closely associated with the sexual organs and was a symbol of life, but no one knows its true meaning.

The vast wealth of Egyptian amulets found during archeological excavations is largely of a funerary nature. That is, these are amulets placed in tombs for the protection of the dead. But it is probable that these same amulets were also worn by the living. Among the principal funerary amulets were:

1. *The Scarab.* This was the symbol of the god of creation to gather life and strength by the living. Models of the scarab, which was a type of dung-eating beetle, were also placed on the dead to effect their resurrection. These were known as "heart scarabs," and were mostly made of black basalt, green stone,

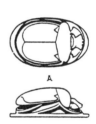

ROYAL EGYPTIAN SCARAB
In this illustration, (a) shows the top and side views of the scarab, and (b) the underface with the name of Men-Ka-Ra inscribed within the central cartouche.

or hematite. Huge models of scarabs were also made to be placed at the entrance to temples and to commemorate special events. Scarabs were made of practically every conceivable material and were sometimes used as seals. Amuletic scarabs varied in length from half an inch to two inches. They came into vogue around the XIth or XIIth dynasty and lost their popularity around 550 B.C.

The engraved base of a scarab amulet. (*Egyptian Museum, Cairo.*)

2. *The Djed.* This amulet was believed to give strength and flexibility to the back, for both the living and the dead.

3. *The Tjet.* This amulet represented the sexual organs of the goddess Isis and was supposed to bring the powers of Isis' blood to its owner. It was commonly made of some red material such as red jasper, red glass, red wood, and carnelian. Some Tjets made of gold or gilded stone have also been found. This amulet is commonly seen in the hands of statues and on many sarchophagi, as it prepared the dead to enter the Judgment Hall of Osiris.

4. *The Urs.* These were headrests or pillows. They were usually

made of wood, ivory, and various types of stones when they were intended for funerary use. They were then placed under the mummy's neck to lift up its head in the netherworld. As amulets, they were made of hematite and were seldom inscribed.

5. *The Ab or Heart Amulet.* The Egyptians believed that the heart contained the soul of Khepera, the self-created god, and was therefore immortal. It was also the source of all life and thought, and was believed to be connected with the *Ka* or double of man. The *Ab*, which was also the seat of the *Ba* (or soul of the physical body), was made of many kinds of red materials, such as carnelian, red jasper, red wax, and red porcelain. It was inscribed on the breast of the mummy to replace its heart, which was placed with other viscera in Canopic jars by the mummy's side.

6. *The Ner–t or Vulture.* This amulet was made to commemorate the wanderings of the goddess Isis as a vulture in the papyrus swamps of the Delta. It was usually made of solid gold and inscribed with chapter 157 of the Book of the Dead. The amulet was supposed to give its wearer all the strength and fierceness of the goddess Isis in her vulture form.

7. *The Usekh–t or Pectoral.* This amulet was made of gold and was inscribed with chapter 158 of the Book of the Dead. It was commonly tied to the mummy's head and was supposed to protect its chest and neck.

8. *The Uadj or Papyrus Scepter.* This amulet was made of mother-of-emerald in the shape of a papyrus shoot. It was inscribed with chapter 159 of the Book of the Dead and was supposed to give its owner, dead or alive, the qualities of youth and virility and constant growth. It was sometimes sculptured on a small rectangular tablet made of neshmet stone.

9. *The Udjat.* This was also known as the "Eye of Horus." It was worn for good health, protection, amd general well-being. The twin Udjats represent the eye of the sun and the eye of the moon, known also as the two eyes of the sky god Her Ur. One legend states that the eye of the sun god Ra was once blinded

by the powers of evil during the course of an eclipse. But the god Thoth healed Ra's eye and restored it to his face. This is the symbol of the Udjat. In the Book of the Dead there is a spell that compels Thoth to bring the Udjat to the dead during his journey to the kingdom of Osiris, god of the dead. The Udjat as an amulet was made of gold, silver, copper, wood, wax, various semiprecious stones, and faience glazed in many colors. This is perhaps one of the most important Egyptian amulets, and it is probable that it was also used to repel the evil eye.

The left eye of Horus, a symbol of the moon god. Lapis lazuli engraving on a gold bracelet.

10. *The Ahat or Cow Amulet.* This amulet was made in the form of a cow wearing the solar disk, with plumes between her horns. It was commonly made of gold and tied to the mummy's neck. The Egyptians be-

The right eye of Horus, a symbol of the sun god. Lapis lazuli on chalcedony, framed by the vultu re and the cobra goddesses that represented Upper and Lower Egypt. From a pectoral found in the tomb of Tutankhamen. *Egyptian Museum, Cairo.*

lieved that when this amulet was placed under the mummy's head, it would emit heat and keep the mummy's body warm until it arrived at the palace of Osiris.

11. *The Frog.* This amulet carried with it the protection of the goddess Hequit, who presided over conception and birth. It was a fertility symbol and was commonly made of gold, hard stone, steatite, and faience. Heqit was believed to have been present

when Isis resuscitated Osiris, and to have fertilized their sexual union. To this day many women of Central African tribes eat frogs so that they may have large families.

12. *The Nefer.* This word means good, beautiful, and pleasant. As an amulet the Nefer was commonly made of carnelian, sard, or some red semiprecious stone. There were also many Nefers made of fa-ience. It represented a lute or some sort of stringed musical instrument, and it was supposed to give its owner good luck, joy, youth, and physical strength.

The Nefer amulet was used by Egyptians both in life and death. The living used it to at-tract strength, happiness and good luck.

13. *The Ba.* The word *ba* means "strength" and represents the heart, soul, or vital forces of man. As an amulet the Ba was made in the form of a man-headed hawk wearing a beard. The Ba was believed to visit the body after death, and the Egyptians left narrow slits in the grave so that the soul could pass through. The Ba amulets were made of gold inlaid with semiprecious stones, and were placed on the mummy's breast, possibly with the idea of preserving it from decay.

14. *The Sma.* This amulet was a symbol of the lungs and was made of dark basalt or some similar black stone, and placed on the folds of the mummy's swathing. It was believed to give the mummy the power to breathe.

15. *The Aakhu.* This amulet was a symbol of life after death and rep-resented the sun rising in the east. It was made of red stone or red glass, and it was believed to give its owner the power of Horus or Ra.

16. *The Shuti.* A representation of the two feathers that are seen on the heads of Ra, Osiris, and Amen-Ra. These feathers symbol-ized light and air. The amulet was made of gold and semipre-cious stones.

17. *The Shen.* A symbol of eternity and the all-embracing power of the sun god. It was used as an amulet to prolong human life.

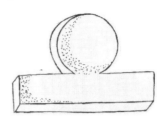

The Shen was a symbol of eternal life and was often seen in the hands of the gods.

18. *The Ren.* This was a name amulet. In some inscriptions the name of a king was enclosed in the Ren, which seemed to be a piece of cord with a knot tied on one end. In this way the name of the king, which was also regarded as his soul, was protected from evil. This belief was also extended to the names of the gods and of all human beings. The Ren is also known as a *cartouche.*

The Djed, or Osiris' backbone, in gilded wood. From the tomb of Tutankahmen. The king's throne name is inscribed in the middle pillar, enclosed within a Ren or "cartouche." *Egyptian Museum, Cairo.*

19. *The Serpent's Head.* This amulet was made of red stone or red faience and was believed to protect against the bite of the cobra and of all other venomous snakes. It was worn by both the living and the dead, who were always in danger of being attacked by the snake of the Tuat, or underworld.

20. *The Menat.* This was an amulet of virility, fertility, and sexual power. It was believed to preserve in the dead the desire and the ability to engage in sexual activities. It consisted of a necklace or collar to which was attached a pendant of distinct phallic characteristics. This amulet was worn by all the gods and goddesses, particularly Isis, Hathor, Ptah, and Osiris, who were particularly connected with the reproductive organs according to the Egyptians. Needless to say, it was very popular with the living, as well as the dead. It was made of lapis lazuli or bronze or copper, and it was suspended over the back of the neck so that it could exert its aphrodisiac qualities on the spinal

column, which was the seat of sexual desire according to the Egyptians.

21. *The Ladder.* Also known as *maq–t,* this amulet provided the dead with the ability to ascend to the floor of heaven, i.e., the sky. This amulet was made in stone and wood and placed in the tomb near the mummy. The Hebrews also conceived of a ladder that reached from earth to heaven, as exemplified by Jacob's dream.

22. *The Two-Fingers.* Also known as *dejebaui,* this amulet represented the index and middle fingers and was made of black basalt, green stone, or obsidian. It was placed among the mummy's swathings to symbolize the two fingers of the god who helped Osiris ascend the ladder to heaven.

23. *The Head of Hathor.* This fertility amulet had two forms. In one, it took the form of a cow's head; in the other, that of a woman's head with cow ears. They were both inscribed on plaques and scarabs, and worn as pendants.

24. *The Kef-Pesesh.* This amulet was made of iron ore and placed among the mummy's swathings. It was believed to restore the mummy's ability to move its jawbones, which was usually lost during the process of mummification.

25. *The Steps.* Also known as *khet,* this amulet was made of white or greenish faience, and symbolized the steps where the god Shu stood when he separated the earth from the sky.

26. *The Uraeus.* A representation of the sacred cobra, known also as *Naja haje.* It was a symbol of sovereignty and was worn on the headdress of all the kings and queens of Egypt. Most commonly the Uraeus, or cobra, was next to a vulture head on the headdress. Both symbols represented the goddesses who protected Lower and Upper Egypt, respectively. Tutankhamen's funerary mask shows the young king's headdress with the two royal creatures on the front. The vulture's head, a representation of the goddess Nekhbet, is made of solid gold and is amazingly lifelike. The cobra's head and hood are inlaid with lapis lazuli, carnelian, faience, and colored glass. On the front of the cobra's hood is the symbol of the goddess Neith, which it represents.

The famous death mask of the boy-king Tutankhamen, showing the Uraeus or cobra head, next to the vulture head. The two creatures symbolized the goddesses who protected Upper and Lower Egypt and usually appeared on the formal headdresses of all Egyptian kings. (*Egyptian Museum, Cairo.*)

Pectoral showing the Eye of Horus or Udjat, resting upon the bark that will take the dead to the judgment of Osiris. The scarab and the falcon, holding a Shen on each claw, are also part of the pectoral. The overall symbolism of the piece is eternal life. Materials used include gold, chalcedony, carnelian, turquoise, obsidian and various colored glass stones. From the tomb of Tutankhamen. (*Egyptian Museum, Cairo.*)

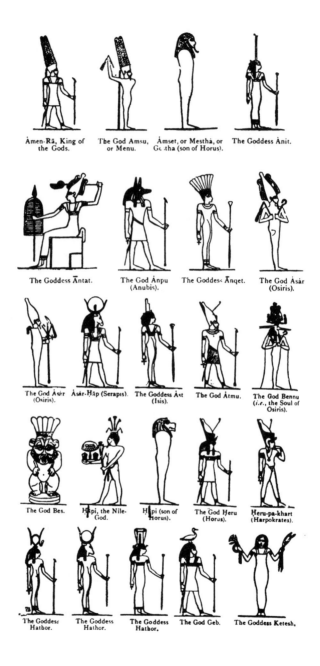

Amuletic figures of Egyptian gods and goddesses.

Amuletic figures of Egyptian gods and goddesses.

27. *The Pectoral Tablet.* This amulet had the form of a funerary chest, and its cornice was decorated with drawings of feathers. Pectorals were often composites of various magical symbols, all of great magical powers. They were placed on the mummy to protect it from evil and to guarantee the swift passage of the dead to the kingdom of Osiris. One of the many pectorals found on Tutankhamen's mummy was made in the form of the falcon sun god, Horus. This exquisite pectoral is made of chased gold inlaid with lapis lazuli, turquoise, carnelian, obsidian, and light blue glass. The falcon holds in each talon the Shen and the ankh, symbols of eternity and life, respectively. Its purpose was obviously to provide the king with eternal life.

Like the Babylonians and the Assyrians, the Egyptians shaped many of their amulets to resemble animals believed to have magical powers. Among the most popular were the bull (Apis), the ram, the crocodile, the lion, the cat, the smaller apes, and the jackal, whose head appears on figures of the god Anubis. Also commonly used were amulets in the form of birds, such as the ibex, the vulture, the hawk, the heron, the swallow, and the goose. Reptiles and insects were also used, particularly the cobra, the viper, the scorpion, the turtle, the grasshopper, the frog, and of course, the scarab or dung-feeding beetle.

The largest class of Egyptian amulets were those made to depict the various gods and goddesses and lesser divine beings. Some of these were protective in nature and were kept in the mummy chamber of the tomb to keep evil spirits at bay. Of these funerary amulets, the two usually placed in the tombs were wooden figures of the god Osiris and of the god Ptah-Seker-Asar, also an aspect of Osiris. The god amulets worn by the living were made of stone so that they might be strung on a thread and worn as a necklace. On the same string, the Egyptians wore animal amulets and magical symbols such as the ankh, the Nefer, and the pectoral. This necklace was believed to have magical powers even when it was made of stone beads, because stones were supposed to be especially protective, and to bring good luck to their owners.

During the early dynastic period, the Egyptians placed next to the mummy several figures of men and women called *Shawabtis* or *Shabtis*. These figures were made of hard stone, limestone, faience, sandstone, and other materials. They sometimes represented the

A Shawabti or Shabti figure, placed in the tombs to serve the mummy in its long voyage to the judgment of Osiris. This Shawabti is made of guilded wood and comes from the tomb of Tutankhamen. (*Egyptian Museum, Cairo.*)

HIEROGLYPHIC ALPHABET

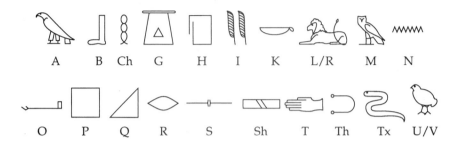

| A | B | Ch | G | H | I | K | L/R | M | N |

| O | P | Q | R | S | Sh | T | Th | Tx | U/V |

GREEK ALPHABET

Αα	Ββ	Γγ	Δδ	Εε	Ζζ	Ηη	Θθ	Ιι	Κκ
A	B	G	D	E	Z	Ee	Th	I	K

Λλ	Μμ	Νν	Ξξ	Οο	Ππ	Ρρ	Σσ	Ττ	Υυ
L	M	N	X	O	P	R	S	T	U

Φφ	Χχ	Ψψ	Ωω
Ph	Ch	Ps	ō

The Egyptian hieroglyphic alphabet and the Greek alphabet. After the finding of the Rosetta Stone by Napoleon's troops, a comparison between the Egyptian and the Greek version of the same historical account allowed scholars to decipher hieroglyphics for the first time. This particular Egyptian alphabet was prepared by the late E.A. Wallis Budge, probably one of the greatest Egyptologists who ever lived.

The prayer-spell inscribed on heart scarabs. It is perhaps the oldest complete prayer in the world. The ancient Egyptians used it for more than 3,000 years.

deceased, or servants who accompanied him in his long journey to take care of his needs. Spells were written on the figures to compel them to obey the dead. Kings had hundreds of Shabtis buried with them.

Of all the inscribed Egyptian amulets that have been discovered, those that appear in the Book of the Dead are the most numerous and were probably the most important to the ancient Egyptians. The hieroglyphs that appear in this venerable book are all magical in nature and were all intended to benefit the dead on their passage to the netherworld.

The life of the ancient Egyptians was so suffused with magical beliefs that many books would have to be written, and indeed have been written, about that aspect of their lives. The amulets we have so far discussed in this section form but a small part of the great wealth of magical symbols used by this very wise and extraordinary people.

HEBREW AMULETS

The Hebrews inherited much of their magic from the Sumerians and the Babylonians, and also from the Egyptians. The legend of Moses states that he was raised in the house of Pharaoh as one of Egypt's royal princes. Esoteric tradition teaches that all the princes of the house of Egypt were strenuously trained in the magical arts. Moses' feats of magic at Pharaoh's court would tend to support this teaching.

The Bible is, of course, our greatest source of Hebrew magical lore. Among the different types of Hebrew amulets it mentions are the following:

1. *The Saharon.* This amulet was made of metal in the form of a crescent. It was worn by women and by kings and also by camels, and it was believed to protect its owner from the evil eye. This moon symbol was a favorite amulet of the goddess Isis. The Hebrews, who were deeply influenced by the Babylonians' magic, probably took it over from them (Isa. 3:18; Judges 8:21, 26).

2. *The Teraphim.* These amulets were shaped in the form of men or gods and were mostly used for divination purposes. They were made generally of clay, but those that were worn on the body were probably made of semiprecious stones. In Genesis 31:19,30 we are told that Rachel stole her father's "gods," as she fled his house with her husband, Jacob. Her father, Laban, was "sore displeased" with this action and reproved Jacob bitterly for having taken the gods. These gods were known in Hebrew as teraphim. Although all forms of idols were an abomination in the eyes of Jehovah, many of the Hebrew elect possessed them, notably King David and Micah, who had "a house of gods," and made an ephod and teraphim (Judges 17:5). The Hebrews probably inherited their use of teraphim from the Babylonians, who sold their houses together with the vast quantities of these protective figures that were believed to be part of the house property.

3. *The Lehashim.* This is a plural word that means "amulets." It was used to describe any object or ornament that was used for protective, divinatory, or any other magical purpose. Practically every article of apparel was amuletic in nature, as worn by women. Isaiah condemned the use of all the ornaments worn by the daughters of Israel. Among the objects he bitterly criticized were earrings, girdles, finger rings, bracelets, armlets, scent tubes, and mirrors. All of these objects were originally created to protect their owners from evil spirits and to bring good luck (Isa. 3:20 ff.).

4. *Bells.* The vestments of Aaron and the high priests had bells and pomegranates around their hems. The bells were to protect them from evil spirits; the pomegranates were an ancient symbol of love and fertility. The high priest's garments were made according to strict specifications given by God himself to Moses (Exod. 28:33).

5. *Figures of Gods.* Although the first commandment sternly forbids the worship of any other god but Jehovah, or the engraving of any images, some of the Hebrews still clung to the worship of heathen deities. The worship of Baal and Ishtar was frequently reviled by the prophets, and the Apocrypha tells how Judas Maccabaeus found idols of the Jamnites hidden among the clothes of the felled Hebrew soldiers (2 Macc. 12:39, 40). Judas and his companions realized that "this was the cause wherefore they were slain."

The Hebrew High Priest attired with the robe, the ephod, the girdle, the mitre and the breastplate, according to the Mosaic tradition. (*From Johann Braun's "Vestitus Sacerdotum Hebraeorum," Amsterdam, 1680.*)

6.   *Phylacteries or Tefillin.* These were frontlets that were worn on the arm and between the eyes. They were probably made of some form of leather. Inside they carried strips of parchment inscribed with the Shema Ysrael: "Hear, O Israel: The Lord our God is One Lord . . . " (Deut.6:4–8).* Phylacteries are still worn today by devout Jews during their morning prayers.

---

*   The translation is that found in the King James version of the Bible. Most Modern Jews translate the Shema Ysrael as "Hear, O Ysrael: The Lord our God, the Lord is One."

MARBODAEI
GALLI CAENOMANENSIS DE
gemmarum lapidumǧ pretioforum formis, natu
ris, atǥuiribus eruditū cū primis opufculū, fane ǥuǎle, cum
ad rei medicæ, tū fcriptūræ facræ cognitionē:nūc primū nō
mō cětū ferme uerfib. locupletatū pariter & accuratius emē-
datū, fed & fcholijs ǧǥ illuftratū ꝑ Alardū AEmftelredamū

Cuius ftudio
additǥ funt & præci
puæ gemmæ lapi
dūǥ ꝑtiofoꝛæ expli-
catiōes, ex ueruftifl.
ꝗbusǥ autoribꝰ co-
aǧtæ. Cū fcholijs Pi
ǎtorñ Villingēñ

Ερ´ μάϟϧάριτοϻ .τ̄
μιοϻ... Αποδ´ουǥ
άϟαντǥ λόμβανǥ.
En margariū no-
bile, E me fi cupis
ditefcere.
Rationale Exodi.
28. & 39. Lxui.8.

Doctrina — & Veritas

3 Smaragdus Leui	4 Carbūcul̨. Iuda	5 Saphirus Zabulon
2 Topazius̨ Simeon	9 Amethyftus Afer	6 Iafpis Ifachar
1 Sardius Ruben	10 chryfolitus Nepthalim	7 Lincurius J'an
Beryllus Beniamin	11 Onychinus Iofeph	8 Achates Gad

The High Priest with the names and the tribal attributions of the twelve stones of the breastplate. (*From the title page of the edition of Marbodus on Precious Stones, Cologne, 1539.*)

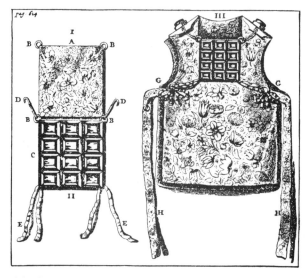

The first part of the figure shows the breastplate unfolded. The second part shows the ephod with the breastplate folded and attached. (*From Johann Braun's "Vestitus Sacerdotum Hebraeorum," Amsterdam, 1680.*)

7. *Mezuzah.* This word means "doorpost" and is used to describe the small cylinder that is usually found at the entrance of every devout Jew's home. Within the mezuzah there is a small strip of parchment or paper with the Shema Ysrael described above (Deut. 6:9).

8. *The Tzitzith.* This was a tassel or fringe that was commended by God to be worn on the borders of all Jewish garments "throughout their generations." A band of blue also was to be placed "on the fringe of the borders" (Num. 15:38). The use of the fringe and the blue band persists today in the tallith, or praying shawl of the Jews.

The making of the ephod, the robe, the girdle, the miter, and the breastplate of Aaron was conducted according to divine command. The magical power implicit in these vestments exudes from the Biblical narrative. In fact, all the ritualistic ceremonies that encompassed the worship of Jehovah were of an extraordinary magical nature. The preparation of the ark; the taboos concerning it; the mixtures of the holy oil and of the incense; the special measurements of the altar, with its horns of gold; the cherubim that were placed at the entrance of the Holy of Holies—all of these things, and many more, speak of the tremendous power, effected in total secrecy, that permeated the worship of Jehovah.

But perhaps the most powerful amulets of the ancient Hebrews were the letters of the Hebrew alphabet. Each of these are believed to be varying stages of cosmic energies. The ancient Hebrews believed that God created the universe by means of the letters of their alphabet and that the language he "spoke" at the moment of creation was Hebrew. Each letter is believed to have special magical powers that reach their ultimate potency in the four divine letters of the Tetragrammaton, or four-letter name of God (IHVH). This name, commonly known as Jehovah or Yaweh, was believed by the Hebrews to have the power to create and to destroy whole worlds. It was also believed to be a powerful deterrent of evil.

A variant of the Tetragrammaton is AHIH, pronounced usually as *Eheieh.* This was the name that God revealed to Moses from the burning bush, "Eheieh Asher Eheieh," meaning "I am that I am." In the ancient Hebrew work The Book of Raziel, (*Sepher Ratziel*)*

---

* The Hebrew section of the New York Public Library has a copy of this book, as does the British Museum.

The Tetragrammaton or four-letter name of God, commonly mispronounced as Jehovah. The name is read from right to left, as all Hebrew words.

an amulet based on AHIH is given to women for protection during childbirth. This amulet had a dual purpose. Its first intention was to protect both the mother and her child and to ensure a safe birth. The second intention was to ward off the evil machinations of the night-devil, Lilith, against both mother and child. This type of amulet was written in parchment, and sometimes on the door and the walls of the room where the mother-to-be lay waiting to give birth. In order for the amulet to be really effective, the ink used to write the text had

Amulet for protection against the she-demon Lilith.

to be mixed with holy incense and the words used had to be inscribed by a man who had been ceremonially purified.

The amulet itself is very unusual. It is composed of two parts, enclosed in their respective squares. The first section shows three figures representing Adam, Eve, and Lilith, who was Adam's spiritual wife before God gave him Eve as his physical mate. Above the three figures are the names of the angels Senoi, Sansenoi, and Samangeloph, who were believed to protect Adam, Eve, and Lilith, respectively. In the second section, the amulet gives the seals of the three angels. The text below the figures and seals states that the woman will be protected by the holy name of God, AHIH, from all forms of evil. The text above the drawings contains the names of the Seventy Great Angels whose protection is secured through the use of this amulet.

Another amulet from The Book of Raziel uses the Tetragrammaton, IHVH, and four permutations of the Hebrew word SLH, meaning "to prosper." The amulet was intended to give its wearer success in all business transactions. The book also gives many examples of amulets used to secure love, friendship, the favor of God, money, luck in business, and protection from enemies and lethal weapons. Most of the amulets given in The Book of Raziel are in ancient Hebrew, but many are inscribed with the Angelic Alphabet, the language believed to be used by the heavenly host. The examples cited here have been transliterated so that they will be easier to understand.

The Star of David, also known magically as the Seal of Solomon, is a powerful symbol that was very popular in the preparation of amulets. It is a hexagram formed of two equilateral triangles superimposed upon each other. The upward-pointing triangle represents the element of fire, while the downward-pointing triangle represents the element of water. Its mystical and magical qualities are many; in the Middle Ages it was used to guard its

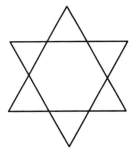

The six-pointed star or Star of David.

owner against fire, lethal weapons, and the onslaught of enemies. It has become the most prominent symbol of the Jewish faith, and to many Jews it represents the union of matter and spirit. In the times of David it symbolized his ability to unite the tribe of Judah

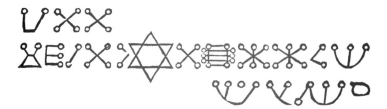

Amulet to give the wearer favor with both God and Man.

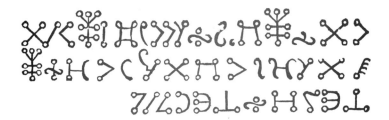

Amulet to procure love and friendship.

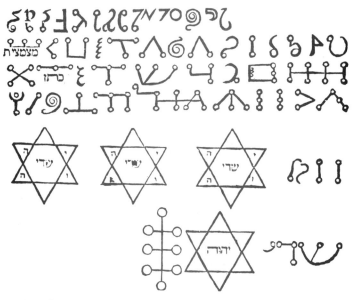

Amulet against the attacks of enemies and injuries from deadly weapons.

Hebrew terra-cotta Devil Trap with a magical inscription containing a spell against the evil eye.

Devil Trap, this time containing a curse on all devils and magicians.

with the rest of the Israeli tribes, thus uniting the twelve tribes into one single, mighty kingdom.

Another star, the pentagram, was also very commonly used in the preparation of amulets. Magically, the pentagram represents a man with legs and arms outspread. When the single point, or head, points upward it is a symbol of light and peace. When two points are uppermost, the pentagram represents Satan and the powers of evil. But although the Star of David and the pentagram were used profusely by the Jews in the preparation of their amulets, and in most of their magical rituals, both of these symbols predate the Jews. No one knows the true origins of the two stars, but they were popular also among the Egyptians, the Assyrians, and the Babylonians. These ancient symbols have also been found in the ruins of India, China, Peru, and Mexico.

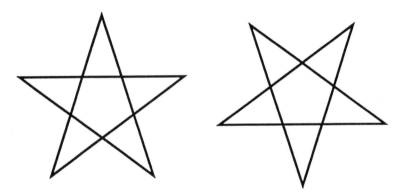

When the pentagram is shown with one point uppermost, it symbolizes a man with outspread arms and legs, surrendering himself to the will of Heaven; with the two points uppermost, the pentagram represents black magic.

The greatest of all the amulets used by the Hebrews was undoubtedly the Book of the Law, also known as the *Torah* or Pentateuch, the first five books of the Old Testament. It was often reproduced in miniature form and carried on a chain around the neck. It was supposed to deliver a woman safely at childbirth and to heal a sick child if placed near his crib. The practice of carrying a miniature Torah around the neck is still observed in modern times by many devout Jews. The tiny roll is placed within a white metal case, with a small ring to hang it around the neck. A small magnifying glass accompanies the case so that the wearer will be able to read the Scriptures whenever he wishes. This amulet is supposed to repel all forms of evil and to protect its owner from harm.

The Psalms were also part of the Hebrew magical tradition. The Book of Raziel gives an example of an amulet where the entire Psalm 104 was inscribed on parchment with a copper pen, and with ink made of lilies and crocuses. The purpose of the amulet was to draw love and friendship to its wearer. The use of the Psalms for magical purposes is still very much in vogue, and there is a small book available that explains in detail how each Psalm may be used and for which purpose.

As I mentioned earlier, the eighth letter of the Hebrew alphabet is a very popular amulet. It is known as Chai and is a symbol of life, believed to promote good health, good luck, and longevity. It is not to be confused with one of God's holy names, El Chai, meaning "The Lord," which is believed by Kabbalists to rule the moon in all its spiritual and magical aspects.

In the Middle Ages, many Jews inscribed special sections of the Bible on a fresh apple and ate the fruit. This was believed to transfer to a person the magical power of the Biblical words and the healthy vibrations of the apple. As apples are Venusian symbols, these spells were probably done for love or friendship. It was also common to dip chosen passages of the Bible in water and then drink the water to obtain health and protection from evil.

Other aspects of the Hebrews' use of magic will be discussed later on in this book, particularly in the section on talismans.

PHOENICIAN AMULETS

The Phoenicians were not a cultured people like the Egyptians, and it is dubious that they were the inventors of the alphabet as Pliny would have us believe, since they left no literature or written history of their own. Many modern scholars feel that the Phoenicians "had no feeling for the written word" and that "they were nothing but clever philistines and crass capitalists."* The char-

---

* See G. Herm, *The Phoenicians,* (New York, 1975).

Cylinder-seal inscribed with three human figures, which was dedicated to the god Hadad.

Cylinder-seal engraved with a bearded figure of a king with two pairs of wings, who is grasping in each hand a foreleg of a beast.

Cylinder-seal inscribed with a figure of a man who is standing in worship of lightning. Priests wearing winged garments stand on each side.

acters they used were the same as those of the Moabites and other ancient peoples. But it is true that the alphabet they used was the basis of Greek and Latin, from which most of the European languages evolved.

If the Phoenicians had a native religion, very little is known about it and their theology. Many of their legends and religious myths are similar to those of the Babylonians, the Egyptians, and the Greeks. The names of Babylonian and Egyptian gods such as Ishtar, Tammuz, Bel, Isis, Osiris, and Thoth have often been found in Phoenician inscriptions, lending credence to the belief that their religion was not of their own creation. They also originated very little literature or in arts and crafts. Instead, they devoted their strength and talent to refining and polishing the original conceptions of other races with whom they came in contact. Their work, however, was carefully undertaken and finely polished, as we can see in the embossed copper bowls from Nimrud found in museums throughout the world.

The Phoenicians shared the same views about the survival of the soul as the ancient Hebrews, but their customs were more barbaric. They would, for example, sacrifice their first-born children to their gods in times of trouble, without any remorse. This custom brings to mind Abraham's willingness to sacrifice his first-born, Isaac, to God before He stopped him. Since Abraham came originally from Chaldee, a region of Babylonia, it is possible that the Babylonians, as well as the Phoenicians, practiced this type of human sacrifice.

Human victims were often sacrificed to the gods of the Phoenicians. Their prisoners of war were the most common victims. Holy prostitution (what the Greeks would later call the *hieros gamos*) was also popular, and young women willingly sacrificed their virginity on the altars of Astarte.*

The amulets of the Phoenicians also show the influence of other races. For example, they adopted the cylinder-seals of the Babylonians and the Assyrians, and the scarab of the Egyptians. But although the figures inscribed upon these amulets are Assyrian and Egyptian in origin, the manner of engraving has the typically delicate and careful execution of all Phoenician art.

The Phoenicians believed that they could have contact and in-

---

* See E. M. Harding, *Women's Mysteries.* (New York, 1971).

tercourse with the dead by dropping small metal rolls (made of thin sheets of lead and inscribed with magical signs) into their tombs. It is unknown whether they used these rolls as amulets for protective purposes.

The belief in mythical beasts with magical powers was popular among the Phoenicians, and all their cylinder-seals show at least the figure of an animal as part of some magical ceremony. Lions, goats, scorpions, gazelles, and sphinxes were commonly used for amuletic purposes. Likewise the power of wings seems to have been very present in the Phoenicians' minds. And many of the figures on their amulets show one or two pairs of wings, though their meaning and purpose is not clear.

GREEK AND ROMAN AMULETS

The magical practices and beliefs of the Greeks were deeply influenced by those of the Babylonians, Assyrians, Egyptians, Hebrews, and Phoenicians. The Romans were so influenced by the Greeks that practically all the beliefs, the customs, and the gods of Greece could be found in Rome, albeit with Roman names. Like their predecessors, the Greeks and the Romans practiced human sacrifice. They also believed in the use of animal amulets to avert evil.

For protection against the evil eye, the Greeks used an amulet shaped like a phallus that they called alternately *baskanion, probaskanion,* and *fascinum.* Because children were believed to be particularly susceptible to the dangers of the evil eye, this particular amulet was often hung around their necks on a chain or string. But houses were also protected by it, and models of the amulet were placed in gardens, in front of blacksmiths' forges, and sometimes under chariot wheels. The Romans knew the same amulet as *Satyrica sigma.*

The Udjat, or Eye of Horus, was also adopted by the Greeks for their own magical customs. It was used to protect against the evil eye and against thieves. There was a spell that could help one discover a thief by means of the Udjat and two herbs called *khelkbei* and *bugloss.*

The worship of many gods was a custom that coincided with

using carved figures of those gods as powerful amulets. Hera, the goddess who protected marriage and the hearth, was worshipped by women who invoked her to protect their homes. Small statues of the goddess where kept within the house walls to protect it from evil. Statues of Aphrodite would attract love; those of Athena, wisdom, and so on.

Six of the twelve Olympians. From left to right, Hestia, Hephaestus, Aphrodite, Ares, Demeter and Hermes. The other six, not shown here, were Poseidon, Athena, Zeus, Artemis and Apollo. (*From a relief in Tarentum.*)

Plants, herbs, and flowers were believed to possess magical powers and were carried on the body for protective purposes and to attract good luck. To effect cures of afflicted limbs and organs, the ancient Greeks made images of the organ and carried it about.

The Romans, on the other hand, practiced very much the same type of magic as the Greeks, with the difference that they were later on influenced by the early Christians and the Gnostics. One of the most popular of the Roman and Christian amulets was called a *bulla.* this was an inflated or round object, such as a bubble, a metal stud, a door knob, or the head of a pin. This amulet was made of wood or metal, and was worn by both the living and the dead. The metal bullas were inscribed with magical characters. This amulet was hollow and was filled with many different types of substances, all of which were known as *praebia.* The bulla and the praebia were used to drive away evil spirits and to protect the wearer from all sorts of dangers.*

---

* See E. A. Wallis Budge, *Amulets and Superstitions* (New York, 1978).

One of the most famous of the known Greek amulets dates from the fourth or fifth century and is a mixture of Greek letters and Kabbalistic symbols. On the upper part of the border is inscribed the well-known *Ablanathanalba*, while on the center is *Akkrammachamarei*, the word of power. Some of the magical symbols on the amulet are representations of the heavens, the sun, the moon, and the stars. This amulet was probably used for protection as well as to overcome others.

But perhaps one of the most famous amulets in the history of mankind has been traced directly to the Romans' doorstop. It is the amulet based on the word *Abracadabra*. This was a formula believed to have been invented by Serenus Sammonicus, the physician of the Roman emperor Caracalla, to cure fever. The letters of the word were to be written on parchment in the following order:

ABRACADABRA
ABRACADABR
ABRACADAB
ABRACADA
ABRACAD
ABRACA
ABRAC
ABRA
ABR
AB
A

The patient, or someone on his behalf, recited the formula as has been described. As the formula diminished, his fever lessened. The amulet was to be carried on the body of the sick person until he was cured.

The word *Abracadabra* was probably derived from the Chaldean *Abbada Ke Dabra*, which meant, approximately, "perish like the word." And it is possible that the good doctor Sammonicus borrowed at least some of his medical know-how from the healing magic of the ancient Babylonians.

I must mention in this context that the ancient Hebrews possessed a similar formula, at least one that worked in the same diminishing fashion. The magical name used was Shebriri, but its use was intended to protect against the evil eye or to effect the cure of any disease of the eye. The repetition (nine times) of the first letter of the

Hebrew alphabet, aleph, was also believed to have healing properties.

It is obvious from what has been discussed thus far that the magical practices of ancient peoples seemed to blend together in many of their aspects. This was caused by the constant traffic that took place among them. The Babylonians, the Assyrians, the Egyptians, and the Phoenicians all traded with each other. The Phoenicians, especially, because of their extensive traveling to other lands, were probably largely responsible for this fusion of magical beliefs.

GNOSTIC AMULETS

The Gnostics were the members of a group of religious sects that flourished between 250 B.C. and A.D. 400. They believed that matter was evil and that emancipation could come to man only through *gnosis*, or knowledge. According to their tenets of belief,

A disc with ancient Near Eastern pictographs.

this "knowledge" was obtained through a series of revelations that were made directly by God to worthy persons who had prepared themselves to receive them. Preparation entailed self-abnegation, fasting, and prayer. These beliefs were derived primarily from India, from where they traveled through Persia to Syria, Palestine, Egypt, and Greece. Modern research has shown that the pictographs of the ancient Indians and Sumerians were practically identical in character. From this source we may assume that the Indians, and later on the Gnostics, gained their interest in astrology from the Sumerians, who invented it.

It is obvious from the study of their literature and their religious objects that the Gnostics were very influenced by many types of religious and magical beliefs. They seem to have been particularly influenced by the teachings of the Zend-Avesta, the cult of Mithras, Manichaeism, and Hebrew and Christian literature.*

The Gnostic amulets were made of several kinds of semiprecious stones such as bloodstone, green jasper, carnelian, onyx, lapis lazuli, obsidian, and sard. Some of these stones were believed to be under the influence of the various planets and thus were able to confer upon their owner wisdom, wealth, love, strength, and knowledge. They varied in size and shape, some being triangular, square, oval, or round. Their length varied from half an inch to three inches.

The inscriptions on almost all Gnostic amulets were in Greek uncials, but some were engraved in a form of pictographic script.

The Gnostics used the names of God and of the archangels in many of their amulets, transliterated from Hebrew into Greek. The most popular names of God for amuletic uses were the Tetragrammaton, Adonai, Jah, and Tzabaoth. The names of the archangels Michael, Gabriel, Paniel, Raguiel, Uriel, Suriel, and Raphael also accompanied some of the amulets.

Although all of the Gnostic amulets we know are post Christian in origin, the symbols engraved upon them are Egyptian. These symbols were believed to give the wearer good health, love, strength, wealth, and protection from evil. As such, they were closer to magic than to religion. By adopting them, the Gnostics gave these magical symbols religious meaning.

---

* Manichaeism, a clear Gnostic sect founded by Manes, influenced traditional Gnosticism so deeply that it later merged with Manichaeism, adopting many of its ideas.

Venus, the goddess of love, surrounded by her attendants. Flowers and turtle doves are some of the symbols around her. The turtle dove was her sacred bird and the rose was her flower. This silver medallion was probably a mirror cover. From the first century of our era. (*British Museum.*)

One of the most important god figures that were used by the Gnostics in their amulets was the Agatho-demon, a type of sun god. He was shown in the shape of a huge serpent with the head of a lion upon which rested a crown with seven or twelve rays. He was called Chnoubis, Chnouphis, or Chnoumis. One of his names was also Semes Eilam, which means "sun of the universe." His crown of seven stars represented the seven heavens. To each star was connected one of the seven vowels of the Greek alphabet. The name of the god and his image were used on amulets for healing purposes and for longevity. The magical sign of Chnoubis, which is found at the back of his amulets, is probably a variation of the serpent and staff carried by Aesculapius, the god of medicine. It later was refined into the *caduceus,* which is the symbol of medicine.

Another popular group of Gnostic amulets is known as "Abraxaster" and comprises a group of figures of gods, goddesses, and symbols, also derived from Egypt although not as old as Chnoubis. The principal god among these figures is the jackal-headed Anubis, who, according to the ancient Egyptians, led the souls of the dead to the kingdom of Osiris. To the Gnostics, however, he was supposed to lead the dead along the paths of the planets to a place called Pleroman, or heaven. The Gnostics identified him with Christ.

According to the late Egyptologist Sir E. A. Wallis Budge, the Egyptian Her-pa-Khart or Harpokrates, also known as Horus the Child, was very popular among the Gnostics and often appeared in their amulets. He was represented as a child with a flail in his left hand and a finger of his right hand in his mouth.* He was usually shown seated on a lotus in a boat, one whose ends terminated in an ass' head and the other in a falcon's head. He was given the holy name of IAO, one of God's names among the Gnostics.

The Menat, an Egyptian symbol popular among the Gnostics. It was a symbol of the goddess Hathor and was said to protect the home and to increase virility.

Isis, Hathor, Osiris, and Thoth were also popular figures in Gnostic amulets. *Ablanathanalba* was usually written on the back of these figures.† The meaning of this word is obscure, though it is often translated as "Thou art our father."

The central god in these groups of figures is Abraxas or Abrasax, whose amulets date from the first and second century of our era. Some scholars believe that this name originated from the Hebrew word *Habberakah*, meaning "the blessing," but it is more probable that it is the corrupted form of the name of some Egyptian god. The total numerical value of Abraxas, according to the Gnostic numerical system, is 365, the number of days in a year. This is also the numerical value of the name Mithras, a Persian god of light popular among the Romans, and later among the Celts. It is believed that Abraxas and Mithras were the same god.

Abraxas represented the 365 eons or emanations from the Primordial Cause, and was believed to be the "All God." He was represented on his amulets with the head of a cock or a lion, the body of a

---

* See E. A. Wallis Budge *Amulets and Superstitions* (New York, 1978).

† *Ablanathanalba* is considered to be a palindrome by most occultists, since it reads the same way backwards and forwards, the middle *h* being silent.

Amulets 1–4 are Gnostic gems engraved with the likeness of the god Abraxas. The letters IAW appear in all the figures. They represent one of the mystic names of God among the Gnostics. The fifth gem is a jasper inscribed with a figure of the Agathodaemon serpent.

man, and legs of serpents, which terminated in scorpions. In his right hand he held a flail or club, and in his left, a round or oval shield. He was called by all the names of the Hebrew god Jehovah, namely Jah, Adonai, and Tzabaoth. In later centuries, his barbarous name and his terrifying appearance made him lose much of his popularity, and in 1852 he was listed as a demon in De Plancy's *Dictionnaire Infernal*. But the Gnostic writer Basilides, who is said to have invented Abraxas, claimed that the god acted as a mediator between mankind and the Godhead.

The Gnostic amulets that have been discovered did not really have the total influence of the Gnostics' spiritual beliefs, and were probably simple charms used to protect the wearer from evil and to procure good health and general success in his affairs.

Many of the symbols used as amulets by the Babylonians, the Egyptians, the Phoenicians, the Hebrews and the Gnostics were also used for the same purposes by the Incas, the Mayas, and the Aztecs. They were also in common usage in Carthage, India, and China, although the materials used to make the amulets varied between cultures. The answer to this apparent riddle is dual. On one hand, we can say that the magical beliefs of the world must have intermingled by way of trade and by still-unexplained migrations. On the other hand, we can say that the use of amulets as protective devices was an instinctive and unconscious response of primitive people to the dangers and the challenges of everyday life—a response that continues to find echoes in our modern times.

3 Astrology and Amulets

ASTROLOGY HAS BEEN TRACED BACK TO THE ANCIENT SUMERIANS and the Chaldeans, but it is suspected by many scholars that it may have existed before that time. Nevertheless, it is generally accepted that the Babylonians, or Chaldeans, were the first people to have made a meticulous study of astrology, which formed an important part of their religion. The oldest astrological work attributed to the Babylonians was *The Day of Bel,* dating from 3000B.C. Bel, a Babylonian god, was believed to be the foundation of astrology.

| Venus | Mercury | Mars | Saturn | Jupiter |

The Egyptian symbols of five of the seven planets. The symbols for the sun and the moon are not included.

From Babylonia, astrology spread to Egypt, to Greece and eventually to Rome, where it flourished and developed further. *The Astronomican* is an astrological thesis written during Roman times about the first century of our era by the poet Marcus Manilius. In the second century, the great astronomer Claudius Ptolemy wrote a treatise that is still considered quite valuable by astrologers. The name of this work is *Tetrabiblos,* or "Four Books on the Influence of the Stars."

Astrology has always been a subject of study for educated people. During the Middle Ages it was necessary to know Latin, Greek, and sometimes Hebrew or Arabic in order to be an astrologer. The

1. Aries. 2. Taurus. 3. Gemini.
4. Cancer. 5. Leo.
6. Virgo. 7. Libra. 8. Scorpio.
9. Sagittarius. 10. Capricorn.
11. Aquarius. 12. Pisces.

The Egyptian symbols of the twelve signs of the zodiac.

Both astrology and astronomy use ancient symbols to depict planets, stars and constellations. These are three versions of the astronomical symbol of the asteroid Ceres, named after the Greek goddess of the harvest.

Various versions of the symbol for the asteroid Pallas, named after Pallas Athena, the Greek goddess of Wisdom.

Two versions of the symbol for the asteroid Juno, named after the Roman goddess who rules marriage and is married to Jupiter.

Two versions of the symbol for the asteroid Vesta, named after the Roman goddess of the hearth.

reason for this need was that most of the astrological treatises of those times were written in the classical languages. In addition, it was important to be familiar with mathematics, as astrology requires complicated mathematical computations to determine the position of the planets at specific times.

During the Middle Ages astrology became extremely popular. Kings usually had a personal astrologer at their courts. The famous Nostradamus served as astrologer and physician to three French kings. During this period astronomy and astrology walked hand in hand. Johann Kepler, Tycho Brahe, and Galileo Galilei were all firm believers and practitioners of astrology. Two of Galileo's books contain horoscopes made by him. By this time astrology had been developed into three distinct branches—judicial, horary, and mundane. Judicial was the branch that determined a person's destiny according to the horoscope cast for his moment of birth. Horary astrology answered questions by means of a horoscope prepared the moment the question was asked. Mundane astrology was concerned with the forecast of events of national or international importance. These three astrological branches are still in use in modern times.

Dante seemed to be familiar with the three branches of astrology, for he mentioned them in the "Purgatorio" and the "Paradiso" of his *Divine Comedy*. Chaucer, Shakespeare, and Milton also spoke about astrology in their works. Chaucer went so far as to cast horoscopes for some of the characters of *The Canterbury Tales*. And Goethe, in a letter to Schiller, said:

> Astrology has its origin on our dim sense of some vast cosmic unity. Experience tells us that the heavenly bodies which are nearest us have a decisive influence on weather and plant life. We need only move higher, stage by stage, and who can say where their influence ceases?...Such fanciful ideas and others of the same kind, I cannot even call superstitions; they come naturally to us and are as tolerable and as questionable as any other faith.*

As a divination system, astrology uses the hour, the time, and the place of birth of an individual to determine (through some rather complex computations) in which sign of the zodiac the sun was posited at the time of birth. This reveals what zodiac sign rules that person's destiny. The birth sign also determines personal char-

---

* See Johann C. von Schiller, *Philosophical Letters*, (London, 1929).

acteristics and tendencies in each individual.

There are twelve zodiac signs. They are listed here in their traditional order: Aries, Taurus, Gemini, Cancer, Leo, Virgo, Libra, Scorpio, Sagittarius, Capricorn, Aquarius, and Pisces. Each of these signs is ruled by a planet. During Babylonian times, there were only five planets known to man. These were Nebo (Mercury), Ishtar (Venus), Nergal (Mars), Marduk (Jupiter), and Ninib (Saturn). The Moon and the Sun are known now as luminaries, and with the five planets, make the fabled seven planets of ancient times. In the past two hundred years three more planets were discovered by astronomers. These are Neptune, Uranus, and Pluto. They are now taken into consideration by astrologers during the preparation of a chart or horoscope.

Almost all the signs are ruled by their own individual planet. The exceptions are Taurus and Libra, who share Venus, and Virgo and Gemini, who share Mercury. The other signs are ruled as follows: Aries by Mars, Cancer by the Moon, Leo by the Sun, Scorpio by Pluto, Sagittarius by Jupiter, Capricorn by Saturn, Aquarius by Uranus, and Pisces by Neptune.

Aries	♈	Libra	♎
Taurus	♉	Scorpio	♏
Gemini	♊	Sagittarius	♐
Cancer	♋	Capricorn	♑
Leo	♌	Aquarius	♒
Virgo	♍	Pisces	♓

The Signs of the Zodiac.

Sun	☉	Jupiter	♃
Moon	☽	Saturn	♄
Venus	♀	Uranus	♅
Mars	♂	Neptune	♆
Mercury	☿	Pluto	♇

The Signs of the Planets.

The twelve signs and the ten planets, including the Sun and the Moon, are each distinguished by a special symbol. These symbols have become increasingly popular in our modern times, and practically everyone is familiar with his own zodiac sign. They are often worn on chains around the neck or in rings, key holders, scarves, and other clothing articles. Just as our ancestors considered the zodiac signs important, so they are important amulets for us. Whether they are worn as good-luck pieces or as symbols of self-assertion, the zodiac signs serve well their amuletic purpose by strengthening personal identity and self-assurance in the individuals who wear them.

The planetary symbols are not as well known as the signs of the zodiac, but they are of greater importance in the preparation of amulets, and indeed in the performance of all kinds of magic. But for these purposes, only the seven original planets can be used. This is not because the newer three planets lack magical power, but because they were unknown to the ancient magicians, who were the architects of most of the magic that we practice today.

According to an old magical treatise known as *The Arbatel of Magic*, greatly revered by magicians, the heavens were divided into 196 provinces or districts that were ruled by seven planetary angels. Each angel had a seal that the ancient magicians inscribed on amulets and used in working their magic. The names and seals of the angels were as follows:

ARATRON—The angel of Saturn, ruled 49 provinces, could change beasts or vegetables into stone, turn lead into gold, and possessed infinite knowledge.

Seal of Aratron

BETHOR—The angel of Jupiter, ruled 42 provinces, could give wealth and the friendship of kings and important people.

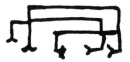

Seal of Bethor

PHALEG—The angel of Mars, ruled 35 provinces, could give dominion over others and victory in war.

Seal of Phaleg

OCH—The angel of the Sun, ruled 28 provinces, was able to heal the sick and change anything into gold and precious stones.

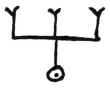

Seal of Och

HAGITH—The angel of Venus, ruled 21 provinces, could transmute gold into copper and copper into gold, and confer love and friendship unto the magician.

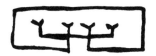

Seal of Hagith

OPHIEL—The angel of Mercury, ruled 14 provinces, could transmute quicksilver into a white stone and give speed and great knowledge.

Seal of Ophiel

PHUL—The angel of the Moon, ruled 7 provinces, could change anything into silver, cure dropsy, and destroy the evil spirits of the water, the element it ruled.

Seal of Phul

The planets were ascribed many different symbols by the ancients. One was the astrological symbol, another was its seal, which was used only for magical purposes, especially in the preparation of amulets and talismans. In addition to the two symbols and the seals of the angels, the planets were also ascribed a spirit and an intelligence, or demon. Both these two entities were also identified by means of the proper seals.

Left to right: The alchemical symbols for spirits of silver, mercury, copper, and tin.

MOON

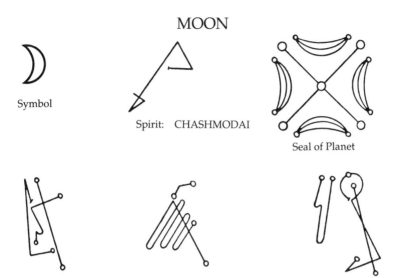

Symbol

Spirit: CHASHMODAI

Seal of Planet

Intelligence of the Intelligences of the Moon: MALCAH
BETARSHISIM VE-AD RUACHOTH HA-SCHECHALIM

Spirit of the Spirits of the Moon:
SHAD BARSCHEMOTH
HASCHARTATHAN

Symbol and Seals of the Moon

MERCURY

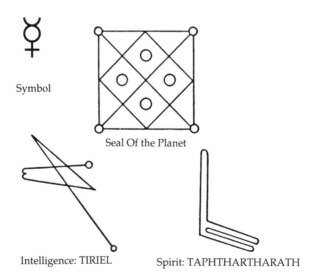

Symbol

Seal Of the Planet

Intelligence: TIRIEL

Spirit: TAPHTHARTHARATH

Symbol and Seals of Mercury

VENUS

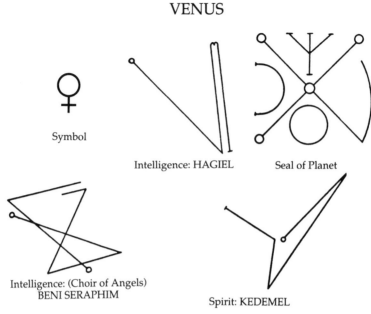

Symbol

Intelligence: HAGIEL

Seal of Planet

Intelligence: (Choir of Angels)
BENI SERAPHIM

Spirit: KEDEMEL

Symbol and Seals of Venus

MARS

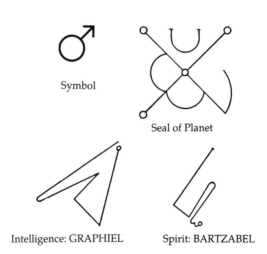

Symbol

Seal of Planet

Intelligence: GRAPHIEL

Spirit: BARTZABEL

Symbol and Seals of Mars

SATURN

Symbol

Seal of the Planet

Spirit: ZAZEL

Intelligence: AGIEL

Symbol and Seals of Saturn

JUPITER

2

Symbol

Seal of the Planet

Spirit: HISMAEL

Intelligence: YOPHIEL

Symbol and Seals of Jupiter

SUN

Symbol

Intelligence: NAKHIEL

Seal of Planet

Spirit: SORATH

Symbol and Seals of the Sun

Each planet was believed to rule over a metal and a color as follows:

Saturn — lead; black
Jupiter — tin; blue
Mars — iron; red
Sun — gold; yellow
Venus — copper; green
Mercury — quicksilver; orange
Moon — silver; violet

Three alchemical symbols for silver, which was associated with the Moon.

The planets were also believed to rule over certain stones, herbs, flowers, animals, trees, fruits, and perfumes. The following is a list of the stones ruled by the planets:

Sun — amber, hyacinth, topaz, chrysolite
Moon — diamond, crystal, opal, beryl, mother-of-pearl
Mars — ruby, hematite, jasper, bloodstone
Mercury — agate, carnelian, chalcedony, sardonyx
Jupiter — amethyst, turquoise, sapphire, aquamarine, blue
    diamond
Venus — emerald, jade
Saturn — jet, onyx, obsidian

These stones are not to be confused with those ascribed to the zodiac signs. The zodiac stones should be worn according to the birth sign one is born under, as good-luck amulets. The planetary stones are used, with the appropriate planetary metal, for special purposes, mostly to acquire the particular benefits conferred by each planet.

Here is a list of the stones and colors ascribed to the signs of the zodiac:

Aries — diamond; red
Taurus — emerald; pink, turquoise
Gemini — agate; silver
Cancer — ruby; silver, violet
Leo — sardonyx; gold, orange
Virgo — sapphire; navy, grey
Libra — opal; blue-green
Scorpio — topaz; blood red
Sagittarius — turquoise; purple, green
Capricorn — garnet; black, brown
Aquarius — amethyst; pale blue or white in patterns of checks or stripes
Pisces — bloodstone; lavender, sea green

These attributions are subject to much controversy among magicians and astrologers, with some contending, for example, that the stone ruled by Leo is the ruby, and not the sardonyx, while still others claim that the proper stone is the peridot or the topaz. But the following series of verses, of very old and unknown origin, tend to agree with the stones I have ascribed to the zodiac signs.

JANUARY — Capricorn
By her who in this month was born
No gem save Garnets should be worn—
They will insure her constancy,
True friendship, and fidelity.

FEBRUARY — Aquarius
The February born shall find
Sincerity and peace of mind,
Freedom from passion and from care
If they the Amethyst will wear.

MARCH — Pisces
Who on this world of ours their eyes
In March first open shall be wise,
In days of peril, firm and brave,
And wear a Bloodstone to their grave.

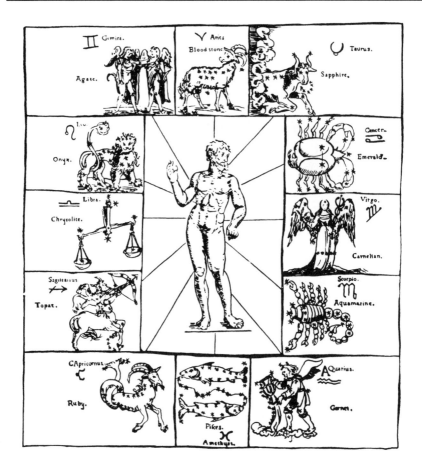

The symbols of the zodiac with an ancient version of the stones ruled by them. Each sign is supposed to affect a certain part of the human body, indicated by the lines going from the figure to the various signs. Precious stones were often used in remedies for special ailments by physicians before the 17th century.

APRIL — Aries
        She who from April dates her years—
        Diamonds should wear lest bitter tears
        For vain repentance flow; this stone
        Emblem of innocence is known.

MAY — Taurus
        Who first beholds the light of day
        In spring's sweet, flowery month of May,
        And wears an Emerald all her life
        Shall be a loved and happy wife.

JUNE — Gemini
> Who comes with summer to this earth,
> And owes to June her hour of birth,
> With ring of Agate on her hand
> Can health, wealth, and long life command.

JULY — Cancer
> The glowing Ruby shall adorn
> Those who in warm July are born,
> Then will they be exempt and free
> From love's doubt and anxiety.

AUGUST — Leo
> Wear a Sardonyx or for thee
> No conjugal felicity—
> The August born without this stone,
> 'Tis said, must live unloved and lone.

SEPTEMBER — Virgo
> A maiden born when autumn leaves
> Are rustling in the September breeze,
> A Sapphire on her brow should bind,
> 'Twill cure diseases of the mind.

OCTOBER — Libra
> October child is born for woe,
> And life's vicissitudes must know;
> But lay an Opal on her breast
> And hope will lull those woes to rest.

NOVEMBER — Scorpio
> Who first comes to this world below
> With dread November's fog and snow
> Should prize the Topaz's amber hue,
> Emblem of friends and lovers true.

DECEMBER — Sagittarius
> If cold December gave you birth,
> The month of snow and ice and mirth,
> Place on your hand a Turquoise blue,
> success will bless whate'er you do.

THE RING AMULET

The Mars (male) symbol, a circle with an arrow; and the Venus (female) symbol, a circle with a cross; represent physical union between a man and a woman when they appear intertwined. This is a very popular love amulet that is also said to ensure fertility and marital bliss.

Whenever a person desires to benefit from the special attributes of a given planet, he or she may prepare a ring made of that planet's ascribed stone and metal. It is advisable also to have the seals of the planet, its angel, and its spirit engraved on the ring as well, in order to gather their powerful influence. For example, the planet Jupiter is believed to patronize honors and riches, as well as friendships and the protection of important persons. Therefore, a ring made of tin (Jupiter's metal) in which an amethyst (one of Jupiter's stones) was set would be sure to bring to the wearer all the things patronized by Jupiter. The seals of Jupiter, its spirit, and its angel should be engraved on the tin.

Following are the various types of endeavor ruled by the planets:

Saturn — wills and legacies, servants, old age, the dead, land, property, mines, lead.

Jupiter — honors, riches, the friendship of rulers and employers, finances, speculation, law, judges, bankers, shipping business, foreign affairs.

Mars — war, military success, valor, destruction, justice, strength, raw sex, surgery, chemistry, police officers, fire fighters, power over enemies.

Sun — money, hope, health, prosperity, high office, publicity, success, fame, positions of rank and title.

Venus — love, friendship, the arts, culture, kindness, pleasure.

Mercury — messages, teaching, writing, publishing, literature, traveling, speaking, bookkeeping, secretaries.

Moon — sailing, intuition, women's affairs, maternity, visions, deliveries, public contact.

The use of rings as amulets is ancient. In fact, all rings were worn for protective purposes in the beginning. Primitive people probably associated the ring with the solar disk and therefore attributed to it the strength and the power of the sun. The sun-god Shamash of the Babylonians is holding a ring and a staff in the famous "sun-god tablet." In another well-known relief, the god Marduk is armed as a warrior, also holding a ring and a staff.

The Greeks had a myth that attributed the creation of the first ring to their god Zeus. It seems that when Zeus freed the titan Prometheus from the rock to which he had been chained as a punishment for having given fire to men, the god forced Prometheus to wear forever on his finger a link of the chain, upon which had been set a piece of the rock of his torture.*

People began to engrave their names upon their rings from very early times. In order to do this, the front part of the ring had to be widened and thickened. This provided a large space where any names, initials, or seals could be engraved. This was the beginning of signet rings, which were well known as far back as the archaic period in ancient Egyptian history. During this time, the gods and the goddesses were shown holding signet rings symbolizing the sphere of the earth ruled by the sun.

Many rings made of red jasper, red faience, and red glass have been found in Egyptian tombs; all of these are uninscribed and with a small opening on one side. It is unknown why or how these were worn, but many scholars believe their purpose was to stop the flow of blood. They were probably worn by soldiers as amulets to prevent them from being wounded in battle, and by women in childbirth to prevent hemorrhaging.

Archaeological findings have shown that the ancients made rings of different types of material, such as gold, silver, iron, bronze, crystal, alabaster, carnelian, chalcedony, agate, ivory, amber, jet, and innumerable other stones. Sometimes both gold and silver were

* See "The Marriage of Peleus and Tetis," in *The Poems of Catullus,* Ed. William Aiken, (New York, 1950).

used, probably to increase the magical power of the ring.

The very popular fertility amulets were rings with the image of a frog or a phallus inscribed on them. Silver rings studded with gold bits were used as protection against the evil eye. Rings set with pieces of horn were supposed to preserve the wearer from epilepsy attacks, while gold and silver rings wet with a "toadstone" were believed to be effective against kidney disease and to safeguard infants. The toadstone is not a stone but the tooth of small fish called the *Lepidotus.*

Engagement rings are of Roman origin, and in the beginning they were engraved with two hands clasping each other to show unity and love. Wedding bands were also intended as symbols of the sun's life-generating powers, and when a husband and wife exchanged them during the wedding ceremony, they were also believed to be exchanging lives.

From the very early rings of primitive man were developed royal rings, papal rings, episcopal rings, poison rings, perfume rings, mortuary rings, zodiac rings, and an infinite variety of signet rings, engagement rings, and wedding bands.

Today rings are worn mostly for ornamental purposes, but there are many rings inscribed with magical or astrological symbols such as the zodiac and planetary signs, the ankh, the love and peace symbols, and the star and crescent, which are the typical symbols of witchcraft.

The Crescent and the Star

These ring amulets are as popular now as they were in the times of the Egyptians. The last tzar of Russia, Nicholas II, always wore a ring that was said to contain a piece of the wood of the true cross. The ring had belonged to Nicholas' grandfather and was believed to have great protective powers. The day that Nicholas forgot to wear it, he was assassinated.

Ring amulets that are bought ready-made in a jewelry store, such as ankh rings and zodiac rings, can be effective good-luck amulets because their intrinsic magical power lies in their symbolism. But the the most powerful ring amulets by far are those specially made by or for an individual. Admittedly it is a rather complicated and technical process to make a ring of a particular metal and have it set with the proper stone. This should be done by a jeweler or an artisan who is experienced in the making of rings. But any competent jeweler can make a ring according to specifications, of any metal or stone desired. The inscriptions of the planetary seals and those of the spirits and angels, however, should be made by the ring's owner. This is easily done by means of any engraver's tool. But it should only be undertaken during the waxing period of the mood and during the hour of the planet in question.

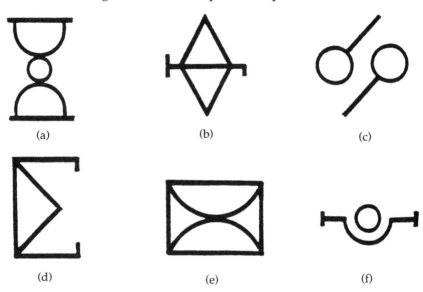

(a)   (b)   (c)

(d)   (e)   (f)

Ancient astrologers divided time carefully and found symbols for each division. Here are the symbols for (a) the hour; (b) the day; (c) day and night; (d) the week; (e) the month; and (f) the year.

According to the ancient magicians each of the seven planets ruled one of the days of the week and several hours of each day. Every magical work had to be conducted on the day and on the hour ruled by the planet whose influence was desired. The days of the week were ruled as follows:

Saturday — Saturn   Wednesday — Mercury
Sunday — Sun   Thursday — Jupiter
Monday — Moon   Friday — Venus
Tuesday — Mars

The planetary hours are indicated in Table 1. (They are computed from midnight to midnight.) Ring amulets based on the zodiac sign of an individual should also be made according to the planetary days and hours. The planet used should be the one that rules the zodiac sign concerned.

TABLE 1
THE PLANETARY HOURS*
Planetary Hours Computed from Midnight to Midnight

HOURS OF THE DAY

	Sunday	Monday	Tuesday	Wednesday	Thursday	Friday	Saturday
1.	Sun	Moon	Mars	Mercury	Jupiter	Venus	Saturn
2.	Venus	Saturn	Sun	Moon	Mars	Mercury	Jupiter
3.	Mercury	Jupiter	Venus	Saturn	Sun	Moon	Mars
4.	Moon	Mars	Mercury	Jupiter	Venus	Saturn	Sun
5.	Saturn	Sun	Moon	Mars	Mercury	Jupiter	Venus
6.	Jupiter	Venus	Saturn	Sun	Moon	Mars	Mercury
7.	Mars	Mercury	Jupiter	Venus	Saturn	Sun	Moon
8.	Sun	Moon	Mars	Mercury	Jupiter	Venus	Saturn
9.	Venus	Saturn	Sun	Moon	Mars	Mercury	Jupiter
10.	Mercury	Jupiter	Venus	Saturn	Sun	Moon	Mars
11.	Moon	Mars	Mercury	Jupiter	Venus	Saturn	Sun
12.	Saturn	Sun	Moon	Mars	Mercury	Jupiter	Venus

HOURS OF THE NIGHT

	Sunday	Monday	Tuesday	Wednesday	Thursday	Friday	Saturday
1.	Jupiter	Venus	Saturn	Sun	Moon	Mars	Mercury
2.	Mars	Mercury	Jupiter	Venus	Saturn	Sun	Moon
3.	Sun	Moon	Mars	Mercury	Jupiter	Venus	Saturn
4.	Venus	Saturn	Sun	Moon	Mars	Mercury	Jupiter
5.	Mercury	Jupiter	Venus	Saturn	Sun	Moon	Mars
6.	Moon	Mars	Mercury	Jupiter	Venus	Saturn	Sun
7.	Saturn	Sun	Moon	Mars	Mercury	Jupiter	Venus
8.	Jupiter	Venus	Saturn	Sun	Moon	Mars	Mercury
9.	Mars	Mercury	Jupiter	Venus	Saturn	Sun	Moon
10.	Sun	Moon	Mars	Mercury	Jupiter	Venus	Saturn
11.	Venus	Saturn	Sun	Moon	Mars	Mercury	Jupiter
12.	Mercury	Jupiter	Venus	Saturn	Sun	Moon	Mars

The seals of the planets, the spirits, the angels, and the intelligences are also inscribed on metal plaques and on parchment paper with magic ink. The intelligences are considered to be the demons of the planets, and for that reason are not used in the making of amulets. They are engraved on metal plaques and pentacles, and are used for invoking purposes, but this is the concern of talismanic magic and will be discussed in the second part of this book.

---

* According to *The Key of Solomon* and *Magical Elements*, by Peter de Albano.

4 Colors, Numbers, and Letters

EVERYTHING THAT EXISTS IS BASICALLY ELECTRICAL IN NATURE. THAT IS, everything we know is composed of atoms that interact with each other by means of electrical impulses. Even our thoughts are electrical discharges emitted by the brain. The interaction of electricity and magnetism results in the radiant energy we know as light. Matter and light are fundamentally inseparable. When matter is reduced to its primordial essence it is converted into a radiation identical with light.

Like electricity, light manifests itself in the form of waves. These waves are of definitely limited length, shorter than the invisible infrared and radio waves and longer than the ultraviolet and x-rays.

Color is the property of light which depends upon wave length. When light falls upon an object some of it is absorbed by the object's atoms. That portion which is not absorbed is reflected. The apparent color of an object depends upon the wave length of the light that is reflected. For example, a red object observed in sunlight appears red because it reflects only the long light waves producing red light. An opaque object that reflects all wave lengths appears white, while one that absorbs all wave lengths appears black. White and black are not considered true colors. White is said to result from the presence of all colors mixed together, while black is the result of the absence of any color.

When white light passes through a prism, its colors are separated and appear as a continuous, seven-color band called a spectrum. These colors are arranged in the following order: red, orange, yellow, green, blue, indigo, and violet. Red has the longest wave length and violet the shortest.

The blaze of colors that is the spectrum can only be perceived by us through the ingenious mechanism of the human eye. Light energy flows through the eye retina in varying wave lengths, leaving behind color impressions. But even the eye, with its complicated machinery of nerve fibers, chemical reactions, and metabolic processes, could not perceive the splendor of light if it were not for the brain. It is there that the impression produced by the light waves upon the sensitive eye retina first becomes light and color.

It has been scientifically proven that brain tissues emit visible color radiations, as well as infrared radiations, radiations of ultraviolet rays and radiations beyond the ultraviolet range.* The visible color radiations emitted by the brain form the faint color shroud that envelopes the human body, and which is known as the human "aura." Not everyone can see the aura but its existence has been tested and proven in laboratories. The Russians, who are very active in this type of research, call the aura our "bioplasmic body."

The human aura is believed to be made of the thoughts and emotions of an individual. We have already said that the brain emits colors; these colors are therefore the visible manifestations of human thought and feeling.

The seven colors of the spectrum are also known as the Seven Rays, and have been known to magicians for thousands of years. They compose one of the Kabbalistic color scales and are the visual representations of the seven planets of the ancients.

Occult scholars believe that the spectrum is an epitome of the evolution of the universe. Each of the Seven Rays is a manifestation of seven cosmic periods. The first three periods, corresponding to the red, orange and yellow rays, have already passed. We are now in the fourth or green-ray period, midway between the first periods of struggle and primitive development and the higher periods of soul growth and spiritual attainment.

The colors of a person's aura reveal his talents, habits and general character. Each color or ray has a special characteristic which it imparts to everything connected with it. These characteristics are as follows:

>   *Violet* — Spirituality
>   *Indigo* — Intuition
>   *Blue* — Religious inspiration
>   *Green* — Harmony and Sympathy
>   *Yellow* — Intellect

---

* See S. G. J. Ousely, *Colour Meditations*, (London, 1949).

Orange — Energy
Red — Life

According to British occultist S. G. J. Ousely, the color rays are divided into many hues. Violet, for example, is subdivided into heliotrope, amethyst, orchid, royal purple, wisteria and lavender. Each of these hues is known as a minor ray. The following are the meanings of the various colors or rays, according to Ousely:*

RED — The symbol of life, strength and vitality; the physical nature. Clear, bright red shows generosity and ambition, as well as affection. An excess of red in an aura means strong physical propensities.

> *Dark Red,* deep passion, e.g., love, courage, hatred, and anger.
> *Reddish-brown,* sensuality, voluptuousness.
> *Very dark, rich tones,* selfishness.
> *Cloudy red,* greed and cruelty.
> *Crimson,* lower passions and desire.
> *Scarlet,* lust.
> *Deep crimson shot with black,* gross materialism.

In contrast to these dark, earthy reds, there is the beautiful *rosy pink,* the symbol of unselfish love.

ORANGE — The symbol of energy, the etheric-astral nature. Excess of orange in the aura indicates vital dynamic force.

> *Bright, clear orange,* health and vitality.
> *Deep orange,* pride.
> *Muddy, cloudy orange,* low intellect.

YELLOW — The symbol of mind and intellect, the mental plane. An excess of yellow in the aura shows an abundance of mental power.

> *Golden yellow,* high soul qualities.
> *Pale primrose yellow,* great intellectual power.
> *Dark, dingy yellow,* jealousy and suspicion.
> *Dull, lifeless yellow,* false optimism, visionary mentality.
> Gold present in the aura is a good sign.

---

* See S. G. J. Ousely, *Colour Meditations,* (London, 1949).

GREEN — The symbol of harmony and sympathy, the higher mental plane. An excess of green in the aura denotes individualism, supply, independence.

> *Bright clear greens* bespeak good qualities.
> *Light green,* prosperity, success.
> *Mint green,* adaptability, versatility.
> *Clear green,* sympathy.
> *Dark green,* deceit.
> *Olive green,* treachery, double-nature. The darker shades have more "sinister" implications.

BLUE — The symbol of inspiration and devotion, the spiritual nature. An excess of blue in the aura signifies an artistic, harmonious nature and spiritual understanding.

> *Deep clear blue,* pure religious feelings.
> *Pale ethereal blue,* devotion to a noble ideal.
> *Bright blue,* loyalty and sincerity.

INDIGO — Symbol of the mystic borderland.

> *Indigo* symbolizes spiritual attainment and self-mastery, wisdom and holiness.

VIOLET — The symbol of spirituality.

> *Deep purple,* high spiritual attainment and holy love—the divine radiance.
> *Pale lilac and wisteria tints,* cosmic consciousness and love for humanity.
> *Bluish-purple,* transcendent idealism.

MINOR COLOR MEANINGS:

> *Light grey,* fear.
> *Dark grey,* conventionalism, formality.
> *Heavy, leaden grey,* meanness, lack of imagination.
> *Greyish-green,* deceit, duplicity.
> *Brownish-grey,* depression.
> *Black,* malice, vice, depravity.
> *Pink,* modesty, gentleness, unselfishness.
> *Silver,* versatility, vivacity, movement. An excess of silver in the aura is a sign of inconstancy and of a fickle nature.
> *Light brown,* practical mind.

Dull, grey-brown, selfishness.
Clear brown, avarice.

When a person shows a particular predilection for a color, the characteristics of that color usually affect his or her personality very deeply. Likewise, when one desires to influence someone magically, colors are a very important part of the magic used. Colored candles of the shade representing the zodiac sign of the person are often burned. Sometimes the candles chosen represent the kind of feeling one desires to evoke in that person, such as red for passion or green for harmony and friendship.

Colors have been associated with the making of amulets for thousands of years. The Egyptians, for example, were very careful with the color of the inks they used on their amulets or written spells. The instructions given on the Book of the Dead are all inscribed in red ink. Since red is the color of life and the instructions concerned the rites of the dead, it is obvious that this color was used to ensure eternal life. But in the "Book of Overthrowing Apep," it is ordered that Apep's name, who is a fiend, should be written in green ink. Some of the darker shades of green symbolize treachery and deceit.

In our modern times, the color blue is believed to bring harmony and joy. And many brides wear on their wedding day,

Something old, something new

Something borrowed, something blue . . .

The "something blue" is a good luck amulet for the bride. Of course, a white wedding gown is a symbol of purity and virginity. Traditionally, it should only be worn by a virgin, or at least by someone who has never been married before. If white cannot be worn by the bride, then blue is the second choice for good luck in the marriage. Yellow and pink are not good luck colors for wedding gowns, according to some superstitions. Some ancient cultures, like the Chinese, wear red wedding gowns, while the North American Indians prefer yellow.

Colors by themselves can be used as good luck amulets. Green is the color of the "lucky Irish," while purple is a symbol of power and glory. Yellow is branded by many as a "coward's color," but in reality it conveys great intellectual power to those who wear it often.

Healing by means of colors is becoming increasingly popular.

Green and yellow are favored by hospitals for the colors of their walls. Some color healers suggest that colored lamps be used to soothe the mind and replenish the aura. The lamp should reflect that color which is believed to be mostly lacking in an individual.

Colors are intimately connected with numbers. Each color is given a number in the magical tradition.

NUMBERS AND LETTERS

A number is a symbol used to convey an idea, an abstraction. Many scientists agree that all possible knowledge is present in the mind in an abstract form. In the abstract world of the mind there is no time or space, for nothing in it ever changes. To the mind, knowledge is absolute, and past, present and future blend together into eternity.

The study of the abstract comes under the jurisdiction of mathematics, especially number theory, which teaches that numbers have characteristics and that no two numbers have exactly the same ones. On the other hand, numbers are also a kind of language, a means of communication. We communicate our thoughts by using languages based on numerical symbolism.

Carl Jung said that numbers were pre-existent to consciousness, and that they were not invented, but rather discovered by man. According to Jung, numbers are probably the most primitive element of order in the human mind, and are used by the unconscious as an ordering factor. Pythagoras believed that all things are numbers, and that the elements of numbers are the elements of all things.

The Sumerians were skilled mathematicians, and are in fact believed to be the founders of mathematics. The Greeks and other peoples probably borrowed many of their beliefs about the sacred and mystical properties of numbers.

The Babylonians reserved the numbers 1–60 for their gods. For instance, Anu was ascribed the number 60, Bel was 50, Ea was 40, Sin was 30, Marduk was 25, Shamash was 20, Ishtar was 15, and

The Oracle of Zoroaster was composed of five separate symbols. The first was Sisamora—the Good Principle, represented by an O inside a triangle, Omega Manifested.

The second symbol of Zoroaster was Senemira—the Bad Principle, represented by an A-Alpha—inside a circle surrounded by a pentagram stressed by lightning bolts.

The central symbol of Zoroaster was Sum-—I am—a representation of the ego as well as of the Sun.

The fourth symbol of Zoroaster was Sallak, the Lucky Genius.

The fifth and last of the Zoroaster symbols was Sokak, the Unlucky Genius. Each symbol was surrounded by a hexagram, a six-sided figure which was of great magical importance among the ancients.

The ancients believed that human intelligence was ruled by nine spirits, each ruled by one of the seven planets. Their symbols were used in talismans and, like the Oracle of Zoroaster, were enclosed within a hexagram. Each planet was centered on a square, a symbol of the four elements and the planet earth. The first spirit of intelligence was ruled by the sun and its symbol was Genhelia, representing Birth and Growth.

The second spirit of intelligence was ruled by the waxing moon and its symbol was Celeno, representing Slowness and Dullness.

The third spirit of intelligence was ruled by Venus and its symbol was Erosia, representing Love and Enjoyment.

The fourth spirit of intelligence was ruled by Mercury and its symbol was Panurgio, representing vitality and wit.

The fifth spirit of intelligence was ruled by Saturn and its symbol was Letophoro, representing Malady and Death.

The sixth symbol of intelligence was ruled by Jupiter and its symbol was Aglae, representing Recovery and Health.

The seventh spirit of intelligence was ruled by Mars and its symbol was Adamasto, representing Conflict and Violence.

The eighth spirit of intelligence was ruled by the waning moon and its symbol was Psykomena, representing Folly and Ridicule.

The ninth spirit of intelligence was ruled by a sun within a sun and its symbol was Psykelia, representing Luck and Fortune.

Ramman was 10. Their greatest holy number is 12,960,000 which has been shown to be the *number of Plato*. This number is of great importance astrologically because it is believed to rule the universe and man. Every number that is a divisor of 12,960,000 is a luck number. The numerals 7, 11, and 13 were considered unlucky by the Babylonians because they were not divisors of the sacred number.

The numbers 3, 4, 5, 7, 10, 12, 40, 70 and 100 were sacred to many ancient people, and of these 3 was the most mystical in nature. This could be because most of the world's greatest religions are based on a holy trinity. Brahma, Vishnu and Shiva among the Hindus, exemplified by the mantra AUM, is an instance of this practice. The Father, Son, and Holy Spirit of Christianity is another.

In the Hindu Vedas the numbers 3, 7, 21, 55, 77 and 99 are considered magical numbers. Number 99 is very sacred to the Arabs as they believe God to possess 99 names. The Persians revered numbers 3 and 7. The Greeks and the Romans believed that 3, 9 and 12 had magical properties. The Celts favored 3 and 9, and the Slavs, the numbers 3, 9 and 7. From these assorted beliefs of various peoples throughout the world we can see that the number 3 is the most popular of all numbers. The triangle, which is one of the world's most important symbols, magically and mathematically, is the visual representation of number 3. This symbol appears in all religions and magical systems. In the Hebrew religion, it is exemplified by the Star of David, which is composed of two interlaced triangles. In alchemy, the four elements of the ancients, namely water, earth, fire, and air are all expressed within the form of the triangle. The Egyptians also believed in the magical power of 3. The eye of God sometimes appears within a pyramid to show that it is a symbol of the Almighty and that He knows and sees all. This ancient magical symbol is prominantly displayed on the back of the American one dollar bill.

The following is a list of the meanings ascribed to the first ten numbers by the ancient magicians:

ONE — This number represented God. The Egyptians declared in their Hymns to Ra or Amen that he was the "one ONE" or the "only ONE." Moses said to the Hebrews, "Hear O Israel, the Lord our God is ONE." (Deut. 6:4). To the Pythagoreans the number ONE represented the Godhead, indivisible and embracing all things. The Koran also says that "God is One God." Astrologically, number one is represented by the Sun.

TWO — This is the perfect number, the symbol of duality, of man and woman. To some, it is the sign of matter and the origin of evil. But it was often considered a protective symbol by the ancients. The Egyptians had a good luck amulet in the form of two fingers, and the Christian priests raise two fingers to confer their blessings on their congregations. Number two corresponds to the Moon astrologically.

THREE — This number symbolized life, birth and also death. It was the number of God manifested, as in the Holy Trinity. Like in our modern religions, the ancients had triads of gods. In Babylonia they had Anu, Ea and Bel. In Egypt, they had Isis, Horus and Osiris. In classical mythology there were many instances of number 3, such as the 3 Fates, the 3 Graces, the 3 Harpies, the 3 Gorgons, and the 3 Furies. There were 3 Magi adoring Jesus, and 3 parts in humans: body, mind, and soul. Number 3 corresponds to Jupiter astrologically.

FOUR — In Egypt, number 4 stood for the 4 quarters of the earth, the 4 sons of Horus, and the 4 cardinal points. In the Bible we find the 4 evangelists, the 4 beasts and Ezekiel, the 4 anchors, and 4 horns. There are 4 elements. The Tetragrammaton or holy name of God has 4 letters. Number 4 corresponds to Uranus astrologically.

FIVE — This number was considered very lucky and extremely sacred by the ancient magicians. In the Bible we find that God's altar had to be 5 cubits long and 5 cubits wide. The peace offering was to be 5 rams, 5 goats and 5 lambs. Five of the virgins were foolish and 5 were wise. The pentacle of Solomon, also known as the pentagram, has 5 points, representing a man with outspread arms and legs. We have 5 physical senses and our skulls are formed of 5 bones. We have 5 fingers in each hand and 5 toes in each foot. Number 5 is considered very lucky in games of chance. It corresponds to Mercury astrologically.

SIX — This is considered to be one of the perfect numbers because creation took place in 6 days. The Star of David has 6 points, each point representing one of the days of creation. The number of the Great Beast of Revelation is 666, which has been ascribed to many individuals and groups of people in the past. Because of its peaceful, and yet often conflicting policies, the United Nations is seen by many occultists as a modern version of the Beast 666. Number 6 is ruled by the planet Venus. The turtle dove, one of the symbols of the United Nations, is also ruled by Venus.

SEVEN — Number 7 is one of the most mystical of all the numbers. There are so many instances of this number in both magic and religion, I could not enumerate them all here. To wit, it is indivisible and it represents the 7 heavens, the 7 planets, the 7 pillars of wisdom, the 7 ears of corn, the 7 days of the week, the 7 branches of the candlestick, the 7 sacraments, the 7 deadly sins, the 7 wonders of the world, the 7 hills of Rome, the 7 colors of the spectrum, the 7 archangels, the 7 notes of music, the 7 ages of man. It is represented by Neptune astrologically.

EIGHT — This number represents two worlds, the material and the spiritual. It is a number of sorrow and restriction. Among the ancients it was believed to represent death and fate. It is also a symbol of justice, and it is often represented by the figure of a woman, blindfolded, with a sword pointing upwards and a balance in her left hand. The Jews practiced the rite of circumcision 8 days after birth. There were 8 sects of Pharisees. Noah was the 8th in direct descent from Adam. The number 888 has been often attributed to Jesus by occult scholars, as the champion of justice and the redeemer of the world. This number is in direct opposition with 666, the number of the Great Beast of Revelations. Astrologically, 8 is represented by Saturn.

NINE — This is another highly mystical number. Perhaps its most interesting characteristic is that it can be multiplied by any number, and the result, when added together, will always add up to nine. It has been called the number of attainment, and of spiritual perfection. Perhaps the reason for this perfection of 9 is that it is made of 3 multiples of 3, the most mystic of all numbers. It is essentially a number representing life and all its struggles, but with success invariably as the outcome. This is symbolized by the fact that the period of human gestation is 9 months. The hidden meaning of this number is one of the greatest secrets of occultism, and one which has been concealed in myriad ways. It represents matter that cannot be destroyed, and in this sense it is a symbol of the universal first cause. Its astrological ruler is the planet Mars.

TEN — This is a number of change, of being and non-being. This latter symbolism results from the fact that 10 is composed of one and zero. One is a symbol of God, of total being. Zero is matter unmanifested, non-being. It was revered by the Hebrews as one of the hidden numbers of God (1+0). It is represented in the 10 commandments and the 10 spheres of the Kabbalistic Tree of Life. It is a number basically associated with the planet Earth.

The number 13 is considered lucky by some, and unlucky by others. Actually, it is a combination of 1 and 3 adding to 4 so it is a number of conflict, requiring both wisdom and self-sacrifice from those it rules. But it is also a number of potential victory, for those who have the courage to try to achieve it. Perhaps one of the reasons why this number is so feared by some people is that there were 13 present during the Last Supper. This number is also associated with the price of the hangman in old England. He was always paid 13 1/2 pence for each hanging, but the half pence was the price of the rope. Today the superstition surrounding number 13 has extended to all Fridays that fall on the 13th day of the month.

The powers of the numbers are intimately associated with letters. In the ancient alphabets letters and numbers were interchangeable and were identified with each other. This was particularly true of both the Arab and the Hebrew alphabets. The Hebrews believed that the 22 letters of their alphabet were the essence of all things, and that God used them to create the universe. The Romans, the Vikings, the Celts, and all the ancient races shared this belief in the power of letters and their identification with numbers. The runes of the Scandinavians were believed to possess great magical qualities, and they were used commonly in the preparation of spells. They were also used to evoke admiration for the wearer. The Fehe was the runic charter used generally for love, although there was a composite rune called Aegishjalmur, which was popularly used for irresistibility. Some of the runic letters and signs are so powerful, tradition warns the uninitiated against trying to perform any feat of magic with them.

The Aegishjalmur, an old Icelandic rune that is said to render the wearer irresistible to others.

The Tyre, a rune for fidelity.

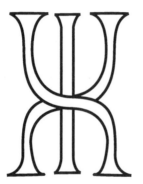

The Gilch, a rune to attract wealth and prosperity.

The Fehe, a rune to attract love.

The Minna, a rune used commonly to awaken admiration for the wearer.

The Feon, a Scandinavian rune for good luck.

The 22 letters of the Hebrew alphabet are the foundation of the Hebrew Kabbalah, and therefore extremely important in the preparation of amulets and talismans in our modern times. Kabbalah is the most powerful element in today's occultism. Many of the various mystery schools, like The Hermetic Order of the Golden Dawn, the Aurum Solis, the Rosicrucians, the Free Masons and the O.T.O. (Ordo Templi Orientalis), use Kabbalistic rites in their practices. Modern witchcraft also borrows quite freely from Kabbalistic magic.

The preparation of amulets according to the Kabbalistic system is based on a series of correspondences between the 22 letters of the Hebrew alphabet and the rest of the universe. Thus every letter is at the same time a number, to which is ascribed a color, a planet or a zodiac sign, a musical note, and various birds, animals, flowers, trees and herbs. The array of correspondences is so large, it has been compared to an infinite filing system, in which everything ever created down to the last atom and the last human thought, can be filed away. The magician uses his knowledge of the correspondences to prepare his amulets. His filing system tells him which day is best for a particular kind of magic, which angel rules that day and which type of symbol should be used to acquire what he wants. One of the best attempts that has been made by any occultist to set down some of the extraordinary correspondences in the Kabbalistic system was made by Aleister Crowley, the late English magician. The result of his painstaking scholarship was a book he entitled 777, which is perhaps one of the most valuable magical treatises ever written.*

According to the Kabbalists, each of the 22 letters of the Hebrew alphabet are also linked with the 22 Major Arcana of the Tarot cards. Each Tarot Arcana is a cosmic principle that embodies the same symbolism as its attributed Hebrew letter. The Tarot cards are believed to have evolved from Egypt, and they could very well be the strongest surviving link between Hebrew and Egyptian magic.

Each Tarot deck consists of 78 cards. These are divided into two groups, the Minor Arcana and the Major Arcana. The Minor Arcana are formed of 40 numbered and 16 court cards, from which our ordinary playing cards evolved. The Major Arcana are a group of 22 cards, each of which represents a cosmic principle, a human emotion, and a material endeavor. Each card encompasses a vast array of symbols. The symbols act as keys to the human unconscious. The

---

* See A. Crowley, *777*, (New York, 1970).

TABLE 2
The Hebrew Alphabet

א	ב	ג	ד	ה	ו	ז	ח	ט
ALEPH (A) Ox	BETH (B) House	GIMEL (G) Camel	DALETH (D) Door	HE (H) Window	VAU (V) Peg, Nail	ZAYIN (Z) Weapon	CHETH (CH) Enclosure	TETH (T) Serpent
1	2	3	4	5	6	7	8	9

י	כ	ל	מ	נ	ס	ע	פ	צ
YOD (I) Hand	CAPH (K) Palm of the hand	LAMED (L) Ox-Goad	MEM (M) Water	NUN (N) Fish	SAMEKH (S) Support	AYIN (O) Eye	PE (P) Mouth	TZADDI (TZ) Fishing Hook
10	20	30	40	50	60	70	80	90

ק	ר	ש	ת	ך	ם	ן	ף	ץ
QOPH (Q) Back of Head	RESH (R) Head	SHIN (SH) Tooth	TAV (TH) Sign of Cross	Final Caph	Final Mem	Final Nun	Final Pe	Final Tzaddi
100	200	300	400	500	600	700	800	900

Hebrew alphabet, from which all this symbolism has been derived, is given in Table 2.

According to the famed astrologer and occultist Sepharial, the Hebrew letters (and the corresponding letters in our Latin alphabet) can be identified with numbers 1 to 22. Each number has a divine, an intellectual, an emotional and a material attribute.* The following analysis of the first 22 numbers and their Tarot correspondences is that given by Sepharial, but with some variations.

THE NUMBER 1

The Kabbalistic letter is A.

The divine principle is over-all dominion.

The intellectual attribute is austerity.

The emotional attribute is selfishness.

The material factor is bureaucracy.

The planetary association is the planet Mercury.

The appropriate metal is quicksilver.

The divinatory or Tarot signification (Arcanum I, The Magician) denotes WILL—DEXTERITY.

---

* See Sepharial, *The Book of Charms and Talismans*, (New York, 1969).

Illustrations from the Robin Wood Tarot Deck. (Llewellyn Publications).

THE NUMBER 2

The Kabbalistic letter is B.

The divine principle is the manifestation in material form of spiritual conceptions.

The intellectual attribute is the analyzing of thought processes.

The emotional attribute is calmness.

The material factor is ambition.

The zodiacal association is the sign Virgo.

The appropriate stones are pink jasper, hyacinth.

The vibratory color is dark blue striped with white.

The divinatory or Tarot signification (Arcanum II, High Priestess) denotes SCIENCE.

THE NUMBER 3

The Kabbalistic letter is G.

The divine principle is forgiveness.

The intellectual attribute is understanding.

The emotional attribute is tenderness.

The material factor is enjoyment or luxury.

The zodiacal association is the sign Libra.

The appropriate stones are the diamond and opal.

The vibratory color is dark blue or ultramarine.

The divinatory or Tarot signification (Arcanum III, the Empress) denotes MARRIAGE or ACTION.

THE NUMBER 4

The Kabbalistic letter is D.

The divine principle is wisdom.

The intellectual attribute is absorption of knowledge.

The emotional attribute is pride.

The material factor is continuity of effort.

The zodiacal association is the sign Scorpio.

The appropriate stones are the carbuncle and turquoise.

The vibratory color is yellow tinged with red.

The divinatory or Tarot signification (Arcanum IV, the Emperor) denotes REALIZATION.

Illustrations from The Robin Wood Tarot. (Llewellyn Publications).

THE NUMBER 5

The Kabbalistic letter is E.
The divine principle is reflection.
The intellectual attribute is reverie.
The emotional attribute is repose.
The material factor is idleness.
The planetary association is the planet Jupiter.
The appropriate metal is tin.
The divinatory or Tarot signification (Arcanum V, the
    Hierophant) denotes RELIGION-LAW.

THE NUMBER 6

The Kabbalistic letters are U.V.W.
The divine principle is intuition.
The intellectual attribute is aspiration.
The emotional attribute is self-indulgence.
The material factor is independence.
The planetary association is the planet Venus.
The appropriate metal is copper.
The vibratory color is blue.
The divinatory or Tarot signification (Arcanum VI, the
    Lovers) denotes TEMPTATION.

THE NUMBER 7

The Kabbalistic letter is Z.
The divine principle is the triumph of good over evil.
The intellectual attribute is applied knowledge.
The emotional attribute is righteous anger.
The material factor is conquest.
The zodiacal association is the sign Sagittarius.
The appropriate stones are jasper and malachite.
The vibratory color is crimson or blood red.
The divinatory or Tarot signification (Arcanum VII, the
    Chariot) denotes VICTORY.

THE NUMBER 8

The Kabbalistic letter is H.
The divine principle is justice.
The intellectual attribute is calculation.
The emotional attribute is equilibrium.
The material factor is the balance between greed and
    improvidence.
The zodiacal association is the sign Capricorn.

The appropriate stones are the white onyx and the moon-stone.
The vibratory color is dark brown streaked with white.
The divinatory or Tarot signification (Arcanum VIII, Justice)
  denotes JUSTICE and EQUILIBRIUM.*

THE NUMBER 9
The Kabbalistic letter is Th.
The divine principle is prudence.
The intellectual attribute is analysis.
The emotional attribute is fear.
The material factor is caution.
The zodiacal association is the sign Aquarius.
The appropriate stone is the sapphire.
The vibratory color is blue with white.
The divinatory or Tarot signification (Arcanum IX, the
  Hermit) denoted WISDOM or PRUDENCE.

THE NUMBER 10
The Kabbalistic letters are I.J.Y.
The divine principle is faith.
The intellectual attribute is learning.
The emotional attribute is self-confidence.
The material factor is self-preservation.
The planetary association is the planet Uranus.
The appropriate metal is Uranium.
The vibratory color is black or brown with white checks.
The divinatory or Tarot signification (Arcanum X, the Wheel)
  denotes CHANGES of FORTUNE.

THE NUMBER 11
The Kabbalistic letters are C.K.
The divine principle is fortitude.
The intellectual attribute is continuity.
The emotional attribute is sympathy.
The material factor is persistence.
The planetary association is the planet Neptune.
The appropriate metal is helium.
The vibratory color is mauve.
The divinatory or Tarot signification (Arcanum XI, Strength)
  denotes SPIRITUAL POWER or FORTITUDE.

---

* Some Tarot packs ascribe Number 11 to the Arcanum Justice and Number 8 to the
Arcanum Strength.

Illustrations from The Robin Wood Tarot. (Llewellyn Publications).

THE NUMBER 12

The Kabbalistic letter is L.
The divine principle is compassion.
The intellectual attribute is investigation.
The emotional attribute is patience.
The material factor is indifference to the vicissitudes of fate.
The zodiacal association is the sign Pisces.
The appropriate stones are the white chrysolite and
    moonstone.
The vibratory color is dazzling white.
The divinatory or Tarot signification (Arcanum XII, the
    Hanged Man) denotes SACRIFICE or EXPIATION.

THE NUMBER 13

The Kabbalistic letter is M.
The divine principle is hope.
The intellectual attribute is inspiration.
The emotional attribute is devotion.
The material factor is reconstruction.
The zodiacal association is the sign Aries.
The appropriate stones are the amethyst and the diamond.
The vibratory colors are red and white.
The divinatory or Tarot signification (Arcanum XIII, Death)
    denotes DEATH or TRANSFORMATION.

THE NUMBER 14

The Kabbalistic letter is N.
The divine principle is toleration.
The intellectual attribute is moderation.
The emotional attribute is temperance.
The material factor is vacillation.
The zodiacal association is the sign Taurus.
The appropriate stones are the moss agate and the emerald.
The vibratory color is greenish yellow or russet.
The divinatory or Tarot signification (Arcanum XIV,
    Temperance) denotes REGENERATION or
    TEMPERANCE.

THE NUMBER 15

The Kabbalistic letter is X.
The divine principle is predestination.
The intellectual attribute is eloquence.

The emotional attribute is sadness.
The material factor is fatality.
The planetary association is the planet Saturn.
The appropriate metal is lead.
The vibratory color is black.
The divinatory or Tarot signification (Arcanum XV, the
Devil) denotes FATALITY or BLACK MAGIC.

THE NUMBER 16

The Kabbalistic letter is O.
The divine principle is godly fear.
The intellectual attribute is study.
The emotional attribute is belief.
The material factor is hard work.
The planetary association is the planet Mars.
The appropriate metal is iron.
The divinatory or Tarot signification (Arcanum XVI, the
Tower) denotes ACCIDENT or CATASTROPHE.

THE NUMBER 17

The Kabbalistic letters are F.P.
The divine principle is immortality.
The intellectual attribute is expression of ideas.
The emotional attribute is expression of beauty in form.
The material factor is artistic creation.
The zodiacal association is the sign Gemini.
The appropriate stones are the beryl and aquamarine.
The vibratory color is pink.
The divinatory or Tarot signification (Arcanum XVII, The
Star) denotes TRUTH, HOPE, FAITH.

THE NUMBER 18

The Kabbalistic letter is Ts or Tz.
The divine principle is universal understanding.
The intellectual attribute is mental reflection.
The emotional attribute is reaction.
The material factor is a danger of wrong action.
The zodiacal association is the sign Cancer.
The appropriate stones are the emerald and the black onyx.
The vibratory color is bright green.
The divinatory or Tarot signification (Arcanum XVIII, the
Moon) denotes DECEPTION, FALSE FRIENDS,
SECRET FOES.

Illustrations from The Robin Wood Tarot. (Llewellyn Publications).

THE NUMBER 19

The Kabbalistic letter is Q.

The divine principle is universal religion.

The intellectual attribute is reason.

The emotional attribute is vanity.

The material factor is progress through effort.

The zodiacal association is the sign Leo.

The appropriate stones are the ruby and diamond.

The vibratory color is fiery red and vermilion.

The divinatory or Tarot signification (Arcanum XIX, the Sun) denotes HAPPINESS or JOY.

THE NUMBER 20

The Kabbalistic letter is R.

The divine principle is eternal life.

The intellectual attribute is study of philosophy.

The emotional attribute is impulse.

The material factor is responsibility.

The planetary association is the Moon.

The appropriate metal is silver.

The vibratory color is sea green.

The divinatory or Tarot signification (Arcanum XX, Reawakening) denotes AWAKENING or RESURRECTION.

Illustrations from The Robin Wood Tarot (Llewellyn Publications).

THE NUMBER 21

The Kabbalistic letters are S, SH.

The divine principle is continuity of life.

The intellectual attribute is dramatic expression.

The emotional attribute is sensation.

The material factor is being in command.

The planetary association is the Sun.

The appropriate metal is gold.

The vibratory color is orange.

The divinatory or Tarot signification (Arcanum XXI, The World) denotes SUCCESS or ATTAINMENT.

THE NUMBER 22

The Kabbalistic letter is T.

The divine principle is infinity.

The intellectual attribute is doubt.

The emotional attribute is uncertainty.

The material factor is lack of progress.

The planetary association is the Earth.

The appropriate metal is—none—as the Earth contains all metals.

The vibratory color is green.

The divinatory or Tarot signification (Arcanum 0, the Fool) denotes FAILURE, FOLLY, MISTAKE.*

Largely based upon the Hebrew alphabet was the "Celestial Script" used on some ancient amulets and talismans of definite Kabbalistic origin. This alphabet was probably derived from the old, "square" Hebrew characters with which the Torah or Mosaic Law was written. Cornelius Agrippa believed these were the letters used by Moses and the Prophets, but this is doubtful. It is more probable that Phoenician characters were in use at this time. A similar script, known as the *Malachim* or *Angelic alphabet,* was believed to be used in angelic writings and all communications between heavenly beings and man. They were very popular in the preparation of amulets and talismans.

---

* Some Tarot decks place Number 0, The Fool, at the beginning of the Major Arcana. Others allot Number 22 to this Arcanum and place it at the end of the Major Arcana. The system given here is the one most commonly accepted among modern occultists.

The so-called Theban alphabet was of runic origin and was also very common in the practice of magic. It is said to have been invented by a Theban called Honorius, and to have been handed down by the well-known medieval magician Peter de Abano. The Theban alphabet is used by modern witches for the inscriptions of the ceremonial knives and swords. The Runic alphabet is used by witches as an alternative script. Another magical script very popular in the making of amulets is known as "Passing the River," but its origin, apart from its slight similarity with ancient Hebrew is not clear.*

Other magical scripts, such as the Masonic/Rosicrucian alphabet, the Enochian alphabet, and the "Writing of the Magi," have been used at one time or another to prepare amulets or talismans. Perhaps the most mysterious of these amulets is the Ogham alphabet, which the magical tradition ascribed to the mythical Atlantis. The Etruscan alphabet is of interest also because of its obvious similarities to the Latin alphabet, of which it was probably the forerunner.

Sanskrit was and is very popular for the preparation of magical formulas and amulets. Perhaps the most famous of these is the mantra AUM, which is used as an amulet by many Hindus. The three letters A, U, and M, stand for the divine trinity of Hindu religion, Brahma, Vishnu and Shiva. A stands for Brahma, the Creator; U, for Vishnu, the Preserver, and M, for Shiva, the Destroyer. The amulet is said to prevent its possessor from being reincarnated and to let him

The AUM symbol, a protective amulet of great efficacy.

pass directly from this life into a state of Buddahood, or divinity. The sign symbolizing AUM, which resembles a rather ornamental tree, is used as a wall hanging, together with five other words. The words are Ma, Ni, Pad, Me, and Hun. The first prevents its owner from being reincarnated as a Titan, the second prevents his return as a human being, the third, prevents rebirth as an animal, the fourth,

---

* See Johannes Abbot Trithemius, *Polygraphia,* (Frankfurt, 1600). English versions of this work are available in various editions.
See also Simon Magus, *Runes and Magickal Alphabets* (New York, 1973) which is based on the *Polygraphia.*

as a "Tantalus," and the fifth saves him from the fires of hell.* Each of these words is written on a different color square underneath the symbol of AUM. The entire amulet reads AUM–MANI–PADME–HUN, and is a very well-known mantra or formula for meditation purposes.

The Chinese also used their characters for the making of amulets and talismans. These were made for those who lacked "true power," and thus had to acquire it second hand from the magical properties of the characters inscribed on the amulets. The characters were believed to embody some of the magical powers of the gods and the spirits they represented. The Chinese, especially the Buddhists, believed that a man of perfect spiritual development did not need amulets or any other type of charm. He already had the power he needed within himself. This power was developed through concentration and meditation. The Japanese also shared this belief.

The Shou—a Chinese amulet for longevity.

Japanese Mitsu Domo amulet, a triple protection against fire, flood and theft.

We have seen in this chapter that colors, numbers and letters are all expressions of the same cosmic principles, and that even different alphabets share a common link between them. This link is what makes communication between peoples of different lan-

---

* The Tantalus referred to here is not the character of mythology punished by Zeus to remain forever hungry and thirsty in the presence of food and drink. It is in all probablility a mythical Hindu monster, based loosely on the Greek character.

Arabic amulet in silver inscribed with versicles from the Koran.

guages and backgrounds possible. This link is the human mind, whose language is entirely based on symbolism. We really do not need language or speech to communicate with each other. Symbols can serve just as well, and in some instances, even better.

Nevertheless, the spoken word can be of great power, especially for magical purposes. A man or a woman of power can bring about the most extraordinary changes around them by the simple assertion of their wills in carefully worded sentences. These same words are just as effective written down because they are simply expressions of cosmic will.

In the beginning of this chapter we said that everything that exists is electrical in nature, and that even our thoughts are electrical discharges emitted by the brain. These electrical discharges are manifested in the form of light, which is then broken down into various colors. The colors in turn depend upon the motions of each individual. Those persons dominated by certain characteristics are constantly emitting the color represented by that characteristic. This color is diffused throughout the body and surrounds it like a halo, which is known as the aura.

Spirits, angels, archangels, elementals and demons are likewise electrical impulses that populate the cosmos. They are in a sense thought concentrations, mind entities that exist without the benefit, or should we say, without the hindrance, of a human body. These are the cosmic forces that control the workings of the universe, and to whom we have recourse in times of need. Because they lack a body, and are essentially mental in nature, they must be contacted through the symbolic language of the mind, a language which is universal in all its aspects. Numbers, letters, colors, are some of the symbology used to establish a mental link with these forces. These are then grouped in certain patterns, with the aid of other natural symbols, and the result is an object that communicates "magically" with spiritual entities. The object then serves as a channel through which these entities can help us with our spiritual needs. This object is what we commonly know as an amulet.

5 Natural Amulets

TO PRIMITIVE PEOPLES, ALL NATURAL THINGS POSSESSED AN INNATE POWER which became known as *Mana*. This word, which was coined by the natives of Polynesia, can also be found in the Biblical narrative spelled somewhat differently as *Manna*. This was the bread substitute that God sent daily to the Jews during their wandering in the desert. Manna rained down every morning and had to be consumed the same day it was gathered—otherwise it would lose its substance and deteriorate rapidly. It was like the coriander seed, and the taste of it "like wafers made with honey." (Ex. 15:14, 31). "The people went about and gathered it, and ground it in mills, or beat it in a mortar, and baked it in pans and made cakes of it: and the taste of it was as the taste of fresh oil." (Num. 11:8). The Jews ate Manna during the 40 years of their wandering, until they came unto the borders of the land of Canaan. "And the Manna ceased on the morrow after they had eaten of the old corn of the land; neither did the children of Israel eat Manna any more; but they did eat of the fruit of the land of Canaan that year." (Josh. 5:12). Today, many people believe that carob, also known as St. John's bread, is the Biblical Manna.

The Yogis have a slightly different name for this substance, although they do not conceive of it as having physical properties. They call it *Prana*, the essence of life which proceeds from the sun, and which can be absorbed by living beings through breathing. Special breathing exercises, designed to extract the maximum possible benefits from the life essence, are known as *Pranayama*, and are, according to the Yogis, sufficient in themselves to maintain life. In other words, we could subsist without food consumption, if we could only train ourselves to gather from the air we breathe the life-sustaining essence of Prana.

The Manna of the Jews was the materialization of Prana, with all its life-giving properties. This materialization took place, according to the Pentateuch, through God's Divine intervention, to ensure the survival of the Jews in the desert.

The creative force which has been called alternately Mana, Manna and Prana, and which is the source of life and all magical acts, is present in all living things to a lesser or greater extent. The extent to which Mana is present in something depends on that something's ability to gather Mana unto itself. Thus it is said that some substances have special magical properties and are great repositories of power and good luck. These are the substances known as natural amulets.

VEGETABLE AMULETS

All amulets that represent herbs, leaves, fruits, trees, roots, and flowers are vegetable amulets. Sometimes the actual vegetable substance is used as an amulet. Typical among these are "magic" roots like High John the Conqueror and Adam and Eve, which are used to attract love. These roots are usually carried in red flannel bags together with other natural amulets such as dried corn (for money), peony (for good luck), and ebony (against the evil eye).

The following is a list of the most common vegetable amulets:

Acorn. Used as a symbol of immortality.

Adam and Eve. These are two roots that are worn together to attract love. Sometimes the two roots are divided between husband and wife or between two lovers to ensure mutual fidelity.

African Mojo Wishing Beans. To make a secret wish come true, two wishing beans are carried around for three days. On the fourth day, the beans are thrown into moving water such as a river or the sea, and the wish comes true within seven days.

Alfalfa. It is often kept in the home to protect against poverty.

Anise Seed. This seed is carried in a small red flannel bag to attract love and to facilitate marriage.

Apple. One of the symbols of Venus, it is very popular in love spells.

Asafoetida. This is worn on a small bag around the neck to safeguard against cold and to repel evil. The highly aromatic herb is also known as the "devil's incense," and is burned during magic rituals to dispel evil.

Ash Tree Leaves. They have many uses, both to bless and to curse. They are believed to prevent death by drowning, to protect against the evil eye and to attract the love of the opposite sex.

Baba Corn Dolls. These dolls are made of corn husks and kept in the house to ensure good crops and good luck. They are very popular with European farmers and the American Indians.

Bay Leaf. Carried in a purse or pocket, this leaf is believed to protect against witchcraft. A leaf is also placed on each corner of a house to protect it from evil.

Buckeye. A dollar is often wrapped around a buckeye and carried in a pocket or purse to attract money. It is also said to prevent rheumatism.

Buckthorn. A tea brewed with this herb and sprinkled in a circle on the floor surrounding a person, is supposed to make that person's wish come true. The same tea is believed to be very efficacious in removing warts.

Caraway Seed. This seed is believed to protect a child from illness if placed under his crib or bed.

Cascara Sagrada. A tea made with this bark and sprinkled around the bed the night before appearing in front of a judge will ensure his ruling will benefit the person who used the tea. This bark is also used to protect against evil.

Chamomile. Used by gamblers to attract good luck.

Clover. A very magical plant with many uses. It is carried in a red flannel bag to bring good luck. To dispel evil spirits, clover can be soaked in vinegar for three days and then the vinegar is sprinkled in each corner of the house. The *four-leaf clover* is used for good luck. Each leaf has a special meaning. The first leaf to the left of the stem brings fame, the second brings wealth, the third brings a lover, and the fourth brings good health. This is one of the few plants which is worn both in its natural state and in symbolic form. This amulet is of Irish origin and can be made of tin or alloy, enameled in green. It is associated with the zodiac signs of Cancer and Pisces.

Cloves. If a handful of cloves are held tightly in one's hand while thinking of a lover, he or she will feel compelled to do one's bidding.

Comfrey Root. This root is placed at the bottom of all luggage before a trip to ensure safety during traveling.

Coriander. The seeds are carried in a small bag to prevent all kinds of illnesses. It is also used in love potions.

Corn. Hard corn is carried in a red flannel bag to attract money.

Corn Flower. This flower is sprinkled inside a house to bring peace and harmony to its inhabitants.

Damiana. When this herb is soaked in a glass of wine for three hours and then sprinkled outside the front and back doors, it will ensure the return of a wandering lover.The sprinkling has to be faithfully done during 21 days. Damiana is also popular for love potions.

Dandelion. It is buried at the northwest corner of a house to bring favorable winds.

Dill Seed. A few grains added to the bath water before meeting a lover is said to make a person irresistible.

Dragon's Blood. This reed is said to bring good luck when carried around in a purse or pocket. It is sometimes placed under a mattress to cure impotency. A very powerful magic ink is made of this reed which is also a very popular ingredient in love spells.

Ebony. The black wood of the ebony tree is very popular in the preparation of amulets against the evil eye.

Eryngo. Also known as sea holly, this flower was worn by Greek brides to ensure the fidelity of their husbands. Legend says that eryngo was the magic ingredient used by Sapho to win the love of Phaon.

Eyebright. It is used as an amulet against all types of eye diseases.

Eucalyptus. It is said to be an excellent protection against cold if stuffed in one's pillow.

Fennel. The fennel seed is said to cure the fits caused by black magic and demonic possession if tied around the neck or carried in the pockets in a small bag.

Fleur-de-Lis. A symbol of fertility associated with the goddess Isis.

Garlic. If hung from windows and door sills it will avert the evil eye and all sorts of evil spirits. Sailors used it in ancient times to protect their ships from sinking.

Heartsease. If a bit of this herb is placed in the sole of a lover's shoe without his or her knowledge, it will soften his or her heart, and fill it with tender feeling for the person who used the herb.

John the Conqueror Root. One of the most popular of magic roots, John the Conqueror is used for good luck and prosperity and to bring to its owner the love and good will of others. It is also used by gamblers who carry it around for good luck.

Lavender. This fragrant plant is very popular in love spells, and also to help a dream come true. Some lavender is placed under one's pillow before retiring. A wish is strongly formulated. If one dreams of anything connected to the wish, the wish will come true.

Licorice Stick. If one wishes to make a person change his or her mind, one should write his or her name in a piece of parchment nine times with Dove's Blood Ink, an ingredient easily obtainable at any occult supply store. The paper is then wrapped around a piece of licorice stick and tied with a red ribbon. It is buried near the home of the person one wishes to influence. The change in his or her attitude should be noticeable in three days.

Lotus. This flower is very popular in the East, particularly in India where it is associated with the highest consciousness. It is commonly worn, either in natural form or effigy, to attract good luck and success and to protect from the evil eye.

Lovage Root. If worn near the heart it is said to attract a lover.

Low John Root. It is said that money wrapped around this root will bring money and good luck to its owner.

Lucky Hand Root. If this root is carried in a purse or pocket it will revert all evil spells back to the sender.

Magnolia Leaves. Spread beneath a mattress, they are said to arouse passion in the most indifferent person.

Mandrake Root. This legendary root is very difficult to find, and according to tradition it should be uprooted by the person who wants to use it. The ancients believed that the plant emits a piercing scream when it is uprooted so the person who wants it should stuff his ears with cotton and use a dog to pull the plant out of the ground. The dog is to be tied to the plant and then offered some food. As the dog jumps for the food, the mandrake is pulled out by the roots, killing the dog with its scream. The uses of the mandrake are many. It is a powerful aphrodisiac, and if placed under one's pillow it will make an indifferent lover become tender and passionate. It is also reputed to give its owner great sexual potency. It should be soaked in white wine every Friday and then kept carefully wrapped in a red, silken cloth. If carefully cared for, it is said to cause money left near it to double overnight. Mandrake roots can be bought in some herbal shops, but often at exorbitant prices.

Male and female mandrakes.

Marjoram. This herb is attributed to Venus and is sprinkled in all the corners of the house by a woman who wants to attract a husband. It should be renewed every month.

Mistletoe. This herb was called the *all healer* by the ancient Druids. It must be gathered on the first day of the New Moon and must not be cut with knives, scissors or any implement made of iron or steel. The Druids used a short scythe made of solid gold to cut mistletoe. The plant should be placed on a white cloth immediately after being gathered and should never be allowed to touch the ground. It is said to protect against evil spells, epilepsy and evil spirits. It is also used to promote fertility.

Mugwort. This herb is said to help in astral projection if placed by the bedside.

Myrtle. This is believed to be the favorite herb of Venus. The Greeks and the Romans used it in garlands to preserve youth and to promote love.

Nutmeg of India. This is a favorite with gamblers, as it gives good luck in games of chance. To increase the powers of the nutmeg, a hole is made in one end of it, which is then filled with quicksilver. The hole is sealed with wax and the nutmeg is then placed in a red flannel bag.

Oak. The oak tree is an attribute of Jupiter and as such it is a symbol of good luck. The leaves and the bark of the oak are very powerful in all magic works, especially for love spells. They bring good luck and strength to those who carry them in a pocket or purse.

Orange Blossoms. Traditionally associated with weddings, orange blossoms are said to bring love and to promote marriage if carried in a red flannel bag together with aniseed, orris root and orange hips.

Orange Pomander. The orange has always been considered a symbol of fertility and love because of its many seeds and sweet taste. A clove is also a love symbol, as we have already seen. An orange studded with cloves and then rolled in a mixture of spices for added fragrance is believed to be a powerful amulet for love and marriage. The pomander is tied with a red ribbon and hung in a closet to work its magic in secret.

Orris Root. This is carried around to promote love and is used in many magic spells for the same purpose.

Peony. Carried in a purse or pocket, peonies are said to bring good luck.

Pine Cone. A symbol of life and fertility, the pine cone is used for good health, longevity and fertility purposes. When one is very tired, pressing the fingers against the rough surface of the pine cone is said to revitalize the body.

Primrose. If sewn into a child's pillow it will ensure his respect and loyalty.

Rice. A symbol of fertility, it is well known for its use in weddings. A few grains of rice carried in a pocket or purse will also ensure there will always be good food on one's table.

Rose. The rose is one of the symbols of Venus, and it is a common ingredient in love spells. Rose buds and petals tossed in a fire are said to bring good luck. Rose hips carried around in a red flannel bag are said to bring love and to promote marriage. Rose buds placed around a sprained ankle will heal it quicker.

Rose of Jerico. This is a dried green flower that closes up when it is removed from water and opens up when it is placed in it. It is usually placed in a shallow dish of water with a small piece of paper in its center where a wish has been written down. The rose is kept in the water during nine days. At the end of this time it is removed from the water with the paper still in place. Within a few hours it will close up, with the wish tightly held within it. The wish should come true nine days later.

Rosemary. This herb is carried around to bring good luck, improve the mind and the memory, and to promote love and friendship. It is a very popular ingredient in love spells.

Rue. A sprig of rue tied with a red ribbon and placed over the front door of a house will prevent evil from entering. It is used in baths for protective purposes and to dispel the evil eye.

Sandalwood. A popular ingredient in love spells, it is also burned as an incense to make a wish come true. As one burns the incense, one should say, "Adonai, Elohim, Elohim, Adonai."

Spearmint. This aromatic herb is said to attract customers to a store if crushed and burned as incense.

Spikenard. If brewed into a tea and then sprinkled over the photo of a recalcitrant lover he or she will return and never leave again.

Sweet Bugle. Crushed and sprinkled around a bedroom, it will attract new lovers and promote marriage.

Thyme. This herb is burned in the home to attract good health for all its inhabitants.

Tonka Bean. It is carried in red flannel bags to attracted good luck and wealth.

Valerian. Placed under one's pillow it is said to soothe the nerves and promote peaceful sleep. It is also burned to dispel evil.

Vervain. One of the herbs of Venus, it is used in many love spells, and carried around for love and marriage. But it is also a powerful protection against fevers and poisoning.

Violet. If one desires to attract the blessings of good spirits, one should sprinkle violets around the corners of the house. Violets are believed to give off healing vibrations and are also helpful in protecting against all types of diseases.

MINERAL AMULETS

Metals (precious and semi-precious), lodestones, ordinary stones, chemicals and resins, soils, sand, rock—all of these fall under the heading of mineral amulets.

The most valuable of the stone amulets is not a diamond, an emerald or a ruby, but a natural stone which has become perforated by means of natural processes such as wind and rain. This type of stone is believed to possess great magical powers and is highly prized in primitive societies. Hollow stones which can be filled with a smaller stone are also very valuable as fertility symbols. This type of stone is known as *Even Tekumah.*

Some types of rock are also considered very efficacious for amuletic purposes, and in the Southwest of the United States the Navajo Indians prepare an amulet called "talking rock medicine" out of rock scrapings from caves that have echoes. This amulet is believed to be a powerful protection against black magic.

Also very powerful are the igneous stones believed by the Yorubas to be the result of lightning and thunder. These vary in size and shape and are believed to be the property of Chango, the god of thunder. They dispel evil and attract good health and good luck. The Yorubas called these stones *odduaras* and used them in a variety of amulets and magic spells. They are still popular in Africa and in Latin America.

Flint, one of many forms of silica, was probably one of the first stones valued by man for amuletic purposes. Because flint originated from the earth it was equated with the child of the earth mother. To the Egyptians, flint was one of the attributes of Horus, the son of Isis in Egyptian mythology.

In some parts of Africa, where fetishism is still practiced, some stones are believed to be inhabited by spirits which are worshipped by individual members of a tribe. The stones are carried around as protective amulets. The fetish priest is believed to have the power to imprison a spirit within a stone or other kinds of natural objects.

The Australian aborigines prepare certain stones when children are born which they call *churingas*. The churinga is usually a flat stone or piece of wood that is inscribed with magical symbols and kept in the sacred cave shared by each community. The stone is believed to protect its owner from harm and to bring good luck throughout his or her life. Some of these inscribed stones have been preserved from the Stone Age.

The use of precious and semiprecious stones as amulets extends throughout the world. Certain amulets called *magatama*, or crooked jewels, have been found in Japanese graves dating from the

This Matabeli witch doctor is literally covered with amulets and charms. Roots, dried animal skins, claws, fangs, horns, feathers and furs, as well as colored beads, are among his protective devices. In reality the term "witch doctor" is misleading because the approximate translation of his African title is more that of a "ritual specialist." (*Courtesy of the American Museum of Natural History.*)

Iron Age. They were made of various materials, such as jasper, carnelian, agate, rock crystal and jade. They are generally perforated at the wider end and worn on a string around the neck with other magic symbols. These ornaments were used to adorn the statues of the gods and were also used as symbols of high rank. At present, the magatama are one of the three emblems of sovereignty in Japan.Both the Koreans and the Chinese used two magatama symbols to represent the union of the masculine and the feminine principles known as the *yin* and *yang*. Some authorities believe the swastika belongs to the same type of symbol as the magatama.

One of the oldest amulets made of precious and semiprecious stones is the Hindu *naoratna* or *nararatna*, also known as the nine-gem jewel. It is mentioned in the old Hindu "ratnascastras," or treatises on gems, where its design and composition is carefully explained. The naoratna is set either as a pendant or as a ring. It is composed of a ruby, a diamond, a pearl, a coral, a jacinth, a sapphire, a topaz, a cat's eye, and an emerald. Each stone represents one of the planets or either the north or the south node. According to the Hindus the "Maharatnani," or great gems, are the diamond, the pearl, the ruby, the sapphire and the emerald. The virtue of every gem depended upon its perfection, and defective or poor stones were regarded as the source of unhappiness and misfortune. The naoratna was a most powerful amulet, as it combined within itself all the magical properties and virtues of the planets.

Also of legendary fame is the mythical vessel known as the *Holy Grail*. According to an ancient legend, when Satan rebelled against God, he was wearing on his crest an enormous stone, which is alternately identified as an emerald or a ruby. When the archangel Michael struck down Satan, this jewel fell to earth and was found by some unidentified sea-faring people who shaped it into a magnificent chalice. This was somehow acquired by King Solomon, and from him it descended to Jesus, who used it at the Last Supper to institute the Sacrament of Communion. This same chalice was used by Joseph of Arimathea to gather the blood of Jesus while He was still nailed to the cross. After the resurrection, Joseph of Arimathea was jailed but he was able to flee to Britain with some of his followers. He took the Grail with him and had it enshrined for some time at Glastonbury. From there it was taken to various places, such as the castle of Monsalvat in Spain, the kingdom of Keriat in Northeast Asia and lastly, to Antioch, where it has reputedly been seen by many people.

The quest for the Holy Grail was one of the most important pursuits of King Arthur and his Knights of the Round Table.* Although this beautiful legend is founded mostly on mythical facts, several stones answering to the description of the Holy Grail have been uncovered.

The Breastplate of Aaron is another legendary amulet made with precious stones. The instructions for the preparation of the Breastplate are given in the Bible:

> And thou shalt make the breastplate of judgment with cunning work; after the work of the ephod thou shall make it of gold, of blue, and of purple, and of scarlet, and of fine twined linen shalt thou make it.
>
> Foursquare it shall be, being doubled; a span shall be the length thereof, and a span shall be the breadth thereof.
>
> And thou shalt set in it settings of stones, even four rows of stones: the first row shall be a sardius, a topaz, and a carbuncle: this shall be the first row.
>
> And the second row shall be an emerald, a sapphire, and a diamond.
>
> And the third row a ligure, an agate, and an amethyst.
>
> And the fourth row a beryl, and an onyx, and a jasper; they shall be set in gold in their enclosings.
>
> And the stones shall be with the names of the children of Israel, twelve, according to their names, like the engravings of a signet; every one with his name shall they be according to the twelve tribes.
>
> And thou shalt make upon the breastplate chains at the ends of wreathen work of pure gold.
>
> And thou shalt make upon the breastplate two rings of gold, and shalt put the two rings on the two ends of the breastplate.
>
> And thou shalt put the two wreathen chains of gold

---

* The Grail is sometimes described as a chalice within which a bloodied spear has been thrust; sometimes as a dish bearing food; and sometimes as a precious stone. But it is always associated with a king, known as the Fisher, who is either dead or dying. See M. Esther Harding, *Women's Mysteries,* (New York, 1971).

in the two rings which are on the ends of the breastplate. And the other two ends of the two wreathen chains thou shalt fasten in the two settings of filigree, and put them on the shoulder pieces of the ephod before it.

And thou shalt make two rings of gold, and thou shalt put them upon the two ends of the breastplate in the border thereof, which is in the side of the ephod inward.

And two other rings of gold thou shalt make, and shalt put them on the two sides of the ephod underneath, toward the forepart thereof, over against the other coupling thereof, above the curious girdle of the ephod.

And they shall bind the breastplate by the rings thereof unto the rings of the ephod with a lace of blue, that it may be above the curious girdle of the ephod, and that the breastplate be not loosed from the ephod.

And Aaron shall bear the names of the children of Israel in the breastplate of judgment upon his heart, when he goeth in unto the holy place, for a memorial before the Lord continually.

And thou shalt put in the breastplate of judgment the Urim and the Thummin; and they shall be upon Aaron's heart, when he goeth in before the Lord: and Aaron shall bear the judgment of the children of Israel upon his heart before the Lord continually. (Exod. 28:15–30.)

The Jewish historian Josephus (A.D. 37–95)* had this to say about the miraculous properties of the stones of the Breastplate:

From the stones which the high-priest wore (these were sardonyxes, and I hold it superfluous to describe their nature, since it is known to all), there emanated a light, as often as God was present at the sacrifices; that which was worn on the right shoulder instead of a clasp emitting a radiance sufficient to give light even to those far away, although the stone previously lacked this

---

* See Flavius Josephus, *De Antiq. Jud.*, (Paris, 1845).

splendor. And certainly this in itself merits the wonder of all those who do not, out of contempt for religion, allow themselves to be led away by a pretense of wisdom. However, I am about to relate something still more wonderful, namely, that God announced victory in battle by means of the twelve stones worn by the high-priest on his breast, set in the pectoral. For such a splendor shone from them when the army was not yet in motion, that all the people knew that God himself was present to aid them. For this reason, the Greeks, who reverence our solemnities, since they could not deny this, called the pectoral our oracle. However, the pectoral and the onyxes ceased to emit this radiance two hundred years before the time when I write this, because God was displeased at the transgressions of the Law.

The twelve stones represented alternately the twelve tribes of Israel, the twelve months of the year and the twelve signs of the zodiac. After the capture of Jerusalem by Titus in A.D. 70, the treasures of the Temple were taken to Rome, and the Breastplate, according to Josephus, was deposited in the Temple of Concord,which had been constructed by Vespasian. From there it disappeared and no one has been able to discover with any degree of certainty what became of it, although some scholars believe it may be buried in one of the treasure chambers of one of the old Persian capitals.

The story of the breastplate illuminates the important role gemstones have played throughout history. Their value and importance was often enhanced by engravings.

The idea that special designs should be engraved on the surface of gems dates from ancient times. The emerald, for example, was to be engraved with a scarab, underneath which stood the figure of Isis. The jewel was to be worn as a brooch and was believed to bring good luck not only to the wearer, but to his or her entire family.

The Book of Wings, a magical treatise dating from the thirteenth century, gives a list of the most common designs to be engraved on gems. This book was believed to have been written by a magician known as Raziel, who was obviously deeply influenced by both the Hebrew and the Greco-Roman tradition. Although the Book of Wings was largely inspired by the Book of Raziel, it bears little resemblance to that work.

This sculptured jade mountain is probably the largest mass of sculptured jade in existence. It weighs about 640 pounds and used to be part of the collection of the Summer Palace near Peking.

Here is a partial list of the gem designs described in the Book of Wings:

The beautiful and terrible figure of a dragon. If this is found on a ruby or any other stone of similar nature and virtue, it has the power to augment the goods of this world and makes the wearer joyous and healthy.

The figure of a falcon, if on a topaz, helps to acquire the good-will of kings, princes, and magnates. The image of an astrolabe, if on a sapphire, has power to increase wealth and enables the wearer to predict the future.

The well-formed image of a lion, if engraved on a garnet, will protect and preserve honors and health, cures the wearer of all diseases, brings him honors, and guards him from all perils in traveling.

An ass, if represented on a chrysolite, will give power to prognosticate and predict the future. The figure of a ram, or of a bearded man, on a sapphire, has the power to cure and preserve from many infirmities as well as to free from poison and from all demons. This is a royal image; it confers dignities and honors and exalts the wearer.

A frog, engraved on a beryl, will have the power to reconcile enemies and produce friendship where there was discord.

A camel's head or two goats among myrtles, if on an onyx, has the power to convene, assemble, and constrain demons; if any one wears it, he will see terrible visions in sleep.

A vulture, if on a chrysolite, has the power to constrain demons and the winds. It controls demons and prevents them from coming together in the place where the gem may be; it also guards against their importunities. The demons obey the wearer.

A bat, represented on a heliotrope or bloodstone, gives the wearer power over demons and helps incantations.

A griffin, imaged on a crystal, produces abundance of milk.

A man richly dressed and with a beautiful object in his hand, engraved on a carnelian, checks the flow of blood and confers honors.

A lion or an archer, on a jasper, gives help against poison and cures from fever.

A man in armor, with bow and arrow, on an iris stone, protects from evil both the wearer and the place where he may be.

A man with a sword in his hand, on a carnelian, preserves the place where it may be from lightning and tempest, and guards the wearer from vices and enchantments.

A bull engraved on a prase is said to give aid against evil spells and to procure the favor of magistrates.*

---

* See G. F. Kunz, *The Curious Lore of Precious Stones,* (New York, 1971).

PRECIOUS AND SEMI-PRECIOUS STONES

Whether they are engraved or not, stones have always been very popular amulets, particularly those stones which are believed to be attributes of the planets or the signs of the zodiac. The following is a list of the most common stone amulets:

Aquamarine. This is believed to be one of the sacred stones. It is a symbol of youth, hope and health. If worn in the form of earrings it is said to gain love and affection for the wearer.

Agate. The stone is said to make its wearer agreeable and persuasive, and also gives one the favor of God. The agate is also said to confer victory and strength on its owner and to avert tempests and lightning. In the eighteenth century a Brazilian priest is said to have designed an airplane which was to be operated

An engraved agate amulet. Arabic inscriptions from the Koran.

Bagdhad, ca. 1113

by means of a battery of agates drawing their energy from the sun. The agate comes in a variety of colors, but the brown and black types with a white ring in the center are the most popular for amuletic purposes.

Alabaster. Not really a stone, but a type of gypsum, alabaster is worn (especially in Italy) to increase the milk of nursing mothers.

Alexandrite. This stone is a variety of chrysoberyl from the Ural region of Russia. The stone is characterized by a polychromatic range from a spectacular shade of bright green to a shimmering scarlet red. The stone is said to be a powerful good luck omen, highly valued by the Russians.

Amethyst. The most famous property of this stone is its reputed ability to cure drunkenness. But it is also said to control evil thoughts and to strengthen the intellect.

Beryl. This stone renders its owner unconquerable and quickens his intellect. It is also said to be a cure for laziness.

Bloodstone. This stone was believed to have the power to cause thunder, lightning and tempest. It was said to give prophetic powers to the wearer and to preserve him or her from deception and all bodily harm. In the Leyden papyrus the bloodstone is praised extravagantly and is said to "assuage the wrath of kings and despots, and whatever the wearer says will be believed. Whoever bears the stone . . . and pronounces the name engraved upon it, will find all doors open, while bonds and stone walls will be rent asunder."

Carbuncle. This stone was worn as a heart stimulant. Its blood-red tones also suggested its use as a symbol of the Passion of Christ. It was used for wealth and power.

Carnelian. It is said to give courage, to protect against envy and the evil eye. Like all red stones, it was worn to prevent wounds or to heal them. The ancient races favored this stone highly. the Arabs engrave the carnelian with magical characters to avert the evil eye. The prophet Mohamed was supposed to have worn a carnelian mounted on silver on the little finger of his right hand. Both Napoleon I and Napoleon III wore a Carnelian seal inscribed with Arabic characters for amuletic purposes.

Cat's Eye. A variety of the chrysoberyl, the cat's eye is used mostly to protect against the evil eye. The stone is either greenish yellow or brownish yellow shot with blue. The Arabs believe this stone makes its wearer invisible in battle. It is also used to test husbands and wives and their fidelity.

This carnelian seal was worn by Napoleon I and Napoleon III. The characters engraved on it mean, "The slave Abraham relying upon the Merciful (God)."

An ornate silver cross with a cat's eye in the middle, a protective amulet from 16th-century Russia.

Chalcedony. This stone was said to cure fever and to give a man an amiable and kind disposition.

Chrysoberyl. This stone is used by the natives of Ceylon against evil spirits. It is greenish yellow in color and comes from Borneo, Burma, Ceylon, India, Madagascar and the United States.

Chrysolite. This stone, highly valued among the Egyptians, must be set in gold in order to exert its full powers. There are two varieties, the peridot and the olivine, both of which are associated with the sun and sometimes with the zodiac sign of Leo. Chrysolite is believed to dispel the "terrors of the night" and to protect against the evil spirits.

Diamond. This stone is the symbol of purity and as such, it is said to bring victory, strength, fortitude and courage to the wearer. According to St. Hildegarde, the powers of the diamond were recognized by Satan who claimed the stone resisted his evil influence by day and by night. The diamond should be set in gold and worn on the left arm or hand for amuletic purposes. Many authorities associate the diamond with lightning, claiming it owes its origin to the thunderbolt. In the Talmud we read of a stone (believed by some to be the diamond) which was worn by the high priest to determine innocence or guilt. If a person brought to the high priest for judgment were guilty, the diamond would grow cloudy and dim, but if the person were innocent, the diamond would shine more brilliant then ever. Some occult scholars attribute to the diamond the ability to make its owner invincible in all human struggles, but its virtues only exist when the diamond has been received as a gift. That is the reason why diamond rings are given to commemorate an engagement and why they are worn on the left hand. When a diamond is purchased it should not be worn by its purchaser, as it is believed it would bring him or her bad luck. Diamonds which have been the subject of such strife or greed are believed to be the depositors of evil and bad luck. The most notorious of these carriers of disaster is the famed Hope Diamond, whose owner is said to die shortly after its acquisition.

Emerald. This stone was believed to foretell the future and to destroy all evil spells. It was also said to strengthen the memory and to make its wearer an eloquent speaker. Moreover it revealed the truth or falsity of a lover's promise, but was an enemy of raw sex or violent passion. In this regard, Albertus Magnus tells a story recounted to him by King Bela of Hungary. It seems the King tried to embrace his wife while wearing an emerald ring on his finger, and at the moment of the embrace the stone broke into three parts. Tradition tells another story, according to which the emerald was one of four precious stones God gave to Solomon to ensure his dominion over all creation. One of the emerald's virtues is its power to foretell the future. For this purpose, its owner must place it under his tongue. The emerald was used as an amulet by the Egyptians, the Hindus, the Greeks, the Romans and the Incas. The Moslems frequently engraved verses from the Koran on this stone and wore it for protective purposes.

Garnet. An amulet made with this stone is said to protect a person from evil and from bad dreams. It is also believed to prevent skin diseases and wounds. It assures its wearer love and faithfulness.

Jacinth or Hyacinth. Amulets of jacinth were worn in antiquity around the neck or as rings. They are still used to protect women during childbirth, to restore the appetite, to fortify the heart and to promote sleep. Jacinth is also believed to dispel evil and to strengthen the mind.

Jade. Another stone used to help women during childbirth. It is also believed to aid in healing stomach and intestine troubles. It cures thirst and dropsy, protects from lightning and heart ailments, and gives victory in battle. Its use as an amulet in Western Asia dates from 4,000 B.C., and it is still commonly in use among the Arabs, Turks and Armenians. The ancient Egyptians and the Aztecs also used jade for amuletic purposes. In

The Mayas prized jade very highly. This jade plaque shows a cross-legged figure with the typically deformed forehead so admired by the Mayas that they applied pressure on it during childhood to acquire it. The figure holds a circle with a cross within it. This cross has no relation to the Christian cross and is rather a representation of the four cardinal points and the four seasons dominating the earth, symbolized by the circle.

China, a jade butterfly is a love amulet of great efficacy. It is also a favorite among people in business. They carry a piece of jade around with them for good luck before any important business transactions. Jade is actually divided into two different types of minerals, nephrite and jadeite. A variety of jadeite with a rich, emerald-green color is known by the Chinese as *feits'ui,* or Kingfisher Plumes. Another term the Chinese have for this stone is "Imperial Jade." The Maoris use the nephrite variety of jade to carve figurines of their ancestral gods which they wear for protective purposes.

Jasper or Jaspis. The green variety of jasper is almost indistinguishable from nephrite. When there are red flecks in the stone, it is known as bloodstone. Red jasper is the most popular variety used in amulets. The Egyptians associated the stone with the blood of Isis, and used it to protect against wounds and to prevent hemorrhages. It is still used for this purpose in modern times, as well as to protect against the evil eye and to help women in childbirth.

Lapis Lazuli. One of the most highly valued stones of the ancients, lapis lazuli was said to cure gallstones, melancholy, sleeplessness, and to prevent miscarriages and all sorts of calamities. Many of the cylinder-seals of the Babylonians were made of this beautiful stone, and the Sumerians believed that the wearer of the stone carried with him the veritable presence of a god. The Egyptians used it to make figures of the sacred scarab and of the gods. The lapis stone known as *stamatopetra* is still used at present in parts of Greece to prevent miscarriages. The name means "stop stone."

Magnetite or lodestone. Not a precious or semi-precious stone, it is perhaps one of the most powerful amulets to attract good luck, love and general success. It is particularly popular in Mexico and Latin America. It is carried around in pairs, a male and a female stone, in a red-flannel bag, with iron filings which serve as its "food." It is placed in white wine on Fridays so it may replenish its strength. The female stone is believed to give birth to other stones, and indeed after some time, the stone is seen to grow and split into several pieces, which are known as its "sons."

Malachite. This stone is said to protect against the evil eye and is especially recommended for small children.

Moonstone. This stone is said to protect its wearer against epilepsy, and to promote large fruit crops. In India the moonstone is regarded as a sacred stone that brings good luck. It is favored by lovers who believe that the stone awakens passion and tenderness in a loved one, and gives them the power to read the future. In order to foretell the future, the stone must be placed in the mouth while the moon is full.

Onyx. In India this stone is used to cool the ardors of love. This belief originated from the idea that the onyx provokes discord and separates lovers. Generally regarded as an unlucky stone, it is said to provoke miscarriages and nightmares, and dissension between friends. But some people consider it a powerful amulet against the evil eye, especially in India and Persia.

Opal. This is another stone with a dubious reputation. Most occult scholars believe that the only people who can wear the opal with impunity are those born under the sign of Libra. To these people the stone is very lucky and fulfills their every wish. But to all others it is a symbol of evil and discord. Nevertheless there is one variety of opal known as the *black opal,* which is believed to be one of the luckiest stones in existence regardless of the sign one was born under.

Peridot. Traditionally associated with the sun and the sign of Leo, the peridot is a symbol of good health and a deterrent of the evil eye, especially when worn on the left arm.

Pink Quartz. A symbol of Venus and of the moon, it is said to be a powerful love amulet and a strong promoter of marriage and fertility.

Rock Crystal. A symbol of the moon and light, the rock crystal is used to promote well-being and to attract the protection of beneficent spirits. This stone was very popular among the Aztecs, who used it to carve human skulls. The skull is a symbol of the spirit of death among the Mexicans, who worship Death as a beneficent spirit.

Ruby. The ruby is the most valued stone among the Hindus who call it *ratnaraj* or "king of precious stones." It is said to aid in love matters, to preserve mental health, and to dispel arguments. The qualities of the ruby are so many that entire treatises have been written on the subject. Some people believe the ruby will help its owner attain his every desire, while at the same time protecting him from all evil. In Burma, it is not sufficient to own a ruby to enjoy its supernatural powers. It is necessary to insert the stone in the skin so it becomes part of the body of its owner. Those who wear a ruby in this fashion live in the complete certainty that no evil can ever befall them.

Sapphire. In India and Arabia this stone is worn as a good health amulet and as a protection against the evil eye. Its fame partly originates from the legend that says that the Law given by God to Moses on Mount Sinai was engraved in sapphire tablets.* According to some legends, the sapphire gives its owner the power to divine the future and protects him or her against poisons, envy, and evil spirits. It is reputed to be one of the stones most favored by witches and necromancers because of its many supernatural powers. The well-known writer Sir Richard Francis Burton possessed a large star sapphire or asteria, as the stone is also known. Sir Richard took it with him wherever he went. He liked to think of it as his "guiding star." This type of stone was known as a *siegstein*, or victory stone, among the Germans. So potent is the power of the star sapphire that it is said to continue to exercise its beneficent influence over a person long after he or she no longer owns it.

Sard. This stone was believed to be a protection against incantations and sorcery and to render its owner fearless and victorious in all battles. It was also believed to assist women in childbirth.

Sardonyx. One of the stones assigned by tradition to the zodiac sign of Leo, the sardonyx is said to bring love, success and felicity to the natives of that sign. To all others it protects against evil spells. It is also believed to prevent miscarriages.

Staurolite. This unusual mineral, also known as fairy stone or cross stone, is shaped naturally in the form of a cross. It is used to protect children from black magic, and is usually worn in little bags around the neck or carried around in a pocket. This is a very popular amulet, around which many beautiful legends have been interwoven. One of the legends claims the cross is formed of fairy tears shed by these spirits upon hearing of Christ's suffering on the cross. President Teddy Roosevelt is said to have carried one of these natural crosses mounted on his watch as a good-luck charm.

Topaz. Another stone attributed to the sun, and very valued as a guardian against all forms of evil. It was commonly worn strung on the hair of an ass and worn on the left arm.

Turquoise. Also known as the "Turkish" stone, the turquoise is highly valued in Asia and Africa for its alleged therapeutic properties. The Arabs know it as *Fayruz* or "lucky stone." It is

---

* See George F. Kunz, *The Curious Lore of Precious Stones,* (New York, 1971).

mounted on rings, necklaces, earrings and head ornaments, and it is said to protect its owner from poison, eye disease, and snake bites. Some people use it as a protection against the evil eye. The Aztecs also used the turquoise as a powerful amulet against evil. It is still popularly used in Mexico as a good-luck amulet.

Staurolite crystals are naturally shaped like crosses. They are also known as fairy stones because according to tradition they are the tears shed by fairies upon hearing of Jesus' suffering on the cross.

ORGANIC SUBSTANCES AS AMULETS

There are some substances in nature which are neither of a vegetable or of an animal nature, but which are the result of a complicated natural process of elimination. For example, sometimes wood becomes fossilized and is transformed into *wood-opal*, which very much resembles the precious stone that bears that name. Extinct vegetation is often transformed into coal, but under certain circumstances it produces a very valuable substance we know as *Jet,* which is formed from the wood of cone-bearing plants. The following is a list of some of nature's refuse which is happily scavenged by people to use both as ornaments and as amulets.

Jet. It is used for healing purposes, especially against epilepsy, headaches and tumors. It is also said to be a powerful protection against the evil eye. Beads of jet with bits of coral set on tiny gold bracelets are worn by many Latin American children to protect them against the evil eye. Rosaries and crucifixes are also made of jet for protection purposes. One of the most precious heirlooms in my family is a cross carved out of a single piece of jet, which is supposed to be over 300 years old. There are innumerable legends attached to it, and it is believed to possess great healing powers.

Amber ornaments. (1) Perforated amulet from an Assyrian grave. (2) Ring from Pompeii. (3) Large amber bead with a hole in its center from the Aztec ruins in Mexico. (4) Amber wedding necklace from the Baltic provinces, 18th century. (5) and (6) amber beads worn by African natives for amuletic purposes.

Amber. A fossilized resin that ranks as a semi-precious stone, amber is one of the most magical of all amulets. It is one of the stones

Witchcraft. The other stone used is jet. Amber is used both internally and externally for healing purposes. Externally it is used in amuletic form to bring good luck and to protect against evil spirits. It is one of the stones attributed to the sun and it is believed to have electrical properties. The Greeks and the Romans favored it so much that Pliny used to complain that an amber figurine cost more than a slave.

Coral. This precious substance is in fact the skeletal matter of certain sea creatures distantly related to jelly-fish and sea anemones. Coral is highly valued for its alleged magical properties. It is said to protect against the evil eye and to prevent almost any disease. It also protects against sterility.

Ambergris. A very valuable substance in the perfume industry, ambergris is thrown up by the intestines of the sperm whale. It is light grey in color and has a very strong odor. It has the unusual quality of bringing out other scents when it is mixed in with several fragrances. For this reason it is very important in the making of perfumes. It is also very popular in love spells and is often used as a fertility amulet and to ensure the duration of a marriage.

Bezoar. Many animals and even some birds develop stones in all parts of the body, particularly in hollow organs. These stones are somewhat similar to human calculi, are known as *bezoars*. They are particularly common in goats and horses, and are believed to protect against poisons. Pope Innocent XI is said to have collected a large number of rings, both in gold and in silver, which had been set with bezoar stones.

Ivory. This is the material of which teeth are made and is obtained in large quantities from the remains of huge mammals with tusks, such as the elephant, the walrus, the hippopotamus and the mammoth. Ivory is considered precious in many countries, particularly in India and China. It is said to prolong life.

Pearl. This very precious stone is formed by introducing an irritant, such as a grain of sand, into a mollusk. The mollusk (usually a pearl oyster or pearl mussel) starts to secrete a calcareous substance that envelops the grain of sand in a concentric fashion until a pearl has been formed. Because it is formed through an

Amulets of mother of pearl. The first shows the baptism of Jesus by John the Baptist. The second is worn by single girls to preserve their virginity until they marry, and to attract a husband quickly.

organic defect of the mollusk's body, the pearl is considered a symbol of tears and sorrow. Brides are warned against wearing pearls on their wedding day, although some of its defenders claim the pearl is the best symbol of purity, and as such, of good luck to a bride. Another tradition claims the pearl is a symbol of Jesus and of salvation. The archangel Gabriel is said to protect all those who wear or carry a pearl. The Virgin Mary is said to be represented by *mother of pearl*. This substance is also believed to have magical properties and has always been ascribed to moon goddesses. It is said to have great healing properties and to guard against evil.

Tortoise Shell. Cups made out of this shell are believed to prevent poisoning, and combs and brushes made of it are said to make hair grow strong and abundant.

Certain salts and chemical substances such as rock salt, saltpeter, and sulphur are sometimes used for amuletic purposes, but always in conjunction with other substances. Their purpose is mostly to cleanse and purify during rituals. Table salt (contrary to popular belief) is a powerful deterrent of evil and is always used in purification rituals, such as the main ceremony of witchcraft. Saltpeter is used with incenses to provide some sparkle to magic rituals. Sulphur (or brimstone as it is sometimes called) is used with asafoetida to dispel evil.

ANIMAL AMULETS

Animal symbols have long been used as amulets. Parts of animals (such as horns, claws, and fangs) are sometimes highly prized for their magical properties. The following is a list of the best known animal amulets.

Cat. Although superstition has branded the black cat as a forerunner of disaster, it is considered to be the possessor of great magical powers. In fact, all cats are believed to be lucky omens, but the black cat in particular. To the ancient Egyptians the cat was associated with the goddess Baster, who ruled over the beneficent powers of the sun. The black cat is said to dispel evil and to make wishes come true. If salt is rubbed on the back of a black cat at midnight, riches will soon be forthcoming, according to an old tradition. Images of black cats worn as brooches are said to bring

This Egyptian statue of a cat has pierced ears and wears earrings to symbolize its status as a deity. Egyptians worshipped cats, who were said to be powerful deterrents of evil.

From the tomb of Tutankhamen,
The Egyptian Museum, Cairo.

good luck. The cat is an attribute of the signs of Capricorn and Pisces.

Crab Claws. This amulet is worn as a love amulet and to promote fertility. It is an attribute of the sign of Cancer.

Dove. The traditional symbol of peace, it is a powerful religious sign, symbolizing the Holy Spirit.

Bulldog. A traditional symbol of strength, the bulldog is a very popular mascot in baseball, football, or any other type of team sport. Team players are notoriously superstitious and most of them boast of an object that they carry around for good-luck purposes. Baseball players, for instance, have been known to carry wads of chewing gum attached to their caps to help their hitting averages. Many baseball players wear chains around their necks with several religious or good-luck symbols to help them during the game.

Bear. Traditionally attributed to Diana, (the Roman goddess of the moon) using the bear image or its claws is said to help a woman during childbirth.

Bee. This is another symbol of Diana, which is said to bring plenty and fertility.

The bee was used as a symbol of royalty by Charlemagne and some scholars believe that the fleur-de-lys, the French symbol of royalty, was derived from a bee instead of a flower. The bee is a feminine symbol sacred to Venus. It represents wisdom, happiness and prosperity.

Butterfly. It is a symbol of the soul and is worn as an amulet to ensure longevity and eternal life.

Deer. The horns of deer are fertility symbols and are also used as love amulets. The hooves of deer are popular symbols of success and business acumen. They are sometimes used as sex amulets. Powdered deer horn is considered by some to be an aphrodisiac and is very popular in love spells.

Dolphin. This amulet was first adopted by Ulysses, hero of the Odyssey, as a symbol of love, devotion and hard work. It is also a symbol of the sea and is said to avert shipwrecks.

Dragon. To the Chinese it is a symbol of the powers of waters. It is also a symbol of life and is worn to ensure a happy life, love, and fertility.

Feather. The feather was a very popular symbol with the Egyptians. A gold feather was often worn to bring prosperity in business. Feathers were believed to represent the gods Ra and Thoth, one of which was a symbol of wealth, and the other a symbol of the mind.

Egg. This has always been a traditional symbol of love and fertility. The custom of giving painted eggs during Easter commemorates the resurrection of Jesus. From here stems the egg's life-giving symbolism. Many farmers deposit eggs among their crops to see a plentiful harvest.

Elk's Tooth. Commonly used as a good-luck amulet for swiftness and virility.

Fish. Worn as an amulet, it is said to give its wearer fertility and prosperity. It is usually made of gold or mother of pearl. It is especially favorable for people born under the sign of Pisces.

Fox Tail. Best known as an ornament for boy's bicycles, fox tails are symbols of cunning, swiftness, and general prosperity.

Grasshopper. Usually made of tin or alloy, and enameled in green, the grasshopper is said to bring riches to its wearer. It is also believed to be of good luck to farmers and to bring them plentiful harvests.

Horn. Very popular in Italy as a powerful protection against the evil eye. The horn is usually worn on a chain around the neck by men as a symbol of virility and sexual magnetism.

Horn of Plenty. Also known as cornucopia, this is a traditional symbol of riches and prosperity.

Horseshoe. One of the most famous symbols of good-luck, the horseshoe must be nailed, horns uppermost, over door sills to ensure protection from evil and general success. Miniature horseshoes are also used as gold charms in women's bracelets, in key chains, and in red flannel bags for protection against evil.

Lamb. A symbol of peace and of fertility. It is of great religious significance among the Christians, for whom it is a representation of the body of Jesus.

Lion. An attribute of the sun, the lion as an amulet is worn to attract good health, riches and success. It is also a symbol of strength and valor. Engraved on a garnet, it is said to bring honors and wealth to the wearer, and to protect him or her while traveling. It is an attribute of the sign of Leo.

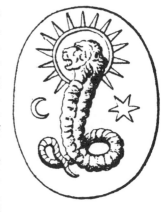

The Lion Faced Light Power, a Gnostic symbol representing the exaltation of the sun in the constellation of Leo.

Owl. As an amulet it should be made of gold, silver or copper and worn by those who are interested in learning and education. It is an attribute of the goddess Minerva and is particularly lucky for those born under the signs of Virgo, Taurus and Capricorn.

Ladybird. A symbol of good luck, it is supposed to bring wealth and success to its wearer. Particularly good for those born under the signs of Taurus and Leo.

Rabbit's Foot. A traditional symbol of fertility, it is also said to bring general good luck and happiness to its wearer.

Rattlesnake. All snakes are symbols of wisdom and sexuality. One of the first American flags showed a rattlesnake coiled around itself with the legend underneath reading, "Don't Tread on Me." This warning implied that although the snake would strike when treaded upon, it would not strike first if left unmolested. This left potential enemies with the impression of a dangerous yet noble opponent, the exact impression the flag was intended to give. The snake is one of the most ancient of occult symbols. With its tail in its mouth, it is a symbol of eternity.

Scarab. The most famous of all Egyptian amulets, the scarab is still worn today as a symbol of eternal life and as protection against evil.

Scorpion. Mostly worn by people born under the sign of Scorpio, the symbol of the scorpion is said to protect against enemies and against all forms of evil.

Spider. This symbol is supposed to bring general good-luck and wealth and to protect against enemies. Some people feel it is a lucky omen to find a small spider inside a house, and to let it walk over their hands. Spiders are generally associated with the planet Mercury.

Swallow. This amulet is said to be very lucky, especially if made of silver. Some people encourage swallows to build nests on the roofs of their houses in order to profit from their alleged magical powers.

Unicorn. A traditional symbol of fertility and sexuality, the unicorn is worn by those who desire to increase their sexual magnetism. It is commonly made of silver or white enamel.

Wishbone. One of the most famous amulets, wishbones are said to make their wearers' dreams come true. They are most lucky when made of gold.

Heart. A symbol of love and friendship, hearts are worn to bring love to their owners. They are particularly lucky when made of precious or semi-precious red stones, such as rubies, garnets or carnelians. They are sometimes made of gold and enameled in red.

Caduceus. One of Mercury's sacred symbols, its twin snakes are said to bring good luck to business persons and writers. Physicians are also traditionally associated with this symbol.

Phallus. Most powerful against the evil eye, it is also often worn to increase a man's virility.

Peacock. One of the symbols of the goddess Isis, it is said to give immortality to its wearer. Peacock feathers however, are believed to bring bad luck to unmarried women.

Ram. Another mascot of football teams, the ram as an amulet is said to promote fertility.

6 The Human Touch

HUMAN AMULETS, LIKE THOSE MADE OF FOSSILIZED MATERIALS OR natural wastes, are mostly made of refuse matter or expendable parts of the human body. Hair, teeth, and nails are examples of human substances which have been used as amulets throughout the centuries.

Locks of hair have been carried around in lockets by people all over the world. The hair belongs sometimes to a son, daughter, or parent; and sometimes to a wife, husband, or lover. The locket is often worn for purely sentimental reasons, but sometimes the intention is to ensure the perpetuation of the love bonds between the former owner of the hair and the one carrying the lock of hair in the locket.

The laws of sympathetic magic are very important in the preparation of amulets. One of these laws, the law of contagious magic, says that a substance that has been in contact with a person will remain in contact with that person, long after their separation. According to this law, when we own a lock of somebody's hair and keep it with us constantly, we are maintaining a vicarious contact with that person across time and distance. It is even possible to influence people through their hair, and force them to do our will. This, of course, depends on who possesses the strongest will and the greatest magical know-how. Teeth, nail clippings, and articles of clothing can be used for the same purposes.

In many primitive societies, the nail clippings and the hair of highly admired people are carried by pregnant women in the hope that the child to be born will inherit these admirable traits. The nail clippings or the hair of children are also attached to the tools of skilled craftsmen to ensure that the children will develop special skills. These practices and similar ones are common among many cultures, such as that of the African, the Australian, the European, and the American Indian.

The belief that people's strength and will power is embodied in their hair is also a common belief among different cultures. The jailers of some African tribes used to cut off a lock of hair of a prisoner and then place him in an unguarded cell. The prisoner, fearing his life would be destroyed by means of his hair if he tried to escape, did not dare to run away.

So deeply ingrained is the belief in the power of hair that many people take the most painstaking care to ensure that their hair or that of their children does not fall into the hands of an enemy. This superstition is not confined only to primitive societies, but extends as well to well-educated individuals. People have hidden hair in churches, buried it in the ground, burned it, and set it on banana leaves to float down a river. All this is done in order to protect the owner of the hair from the powers of magic.

Perhaps the most famous instance of the destruction of someone by means of his hair is the well-known Biblical story of Samson and Delilah. According to the Book of Judges, God bestowed upon Samson the gift of being all-powerful and invincible in battle as long as he did not cut his hair. The moment he allowed a "razor to come upon his head," he would lose all his powers and become weak and helpless.

All went well for a long time, and Samson's fame grew as a mighty warrior, awesome and undefeatable. He fought primarily against the Philistines, whom he blamed for the loss of his wife. But although Samson hated the Philistine men, and destroyed them at every opportunity, he loved Philistine women. Like his wife, Delilah was also a Philistine. Commissioned by the lords of the Philistines to discover the source of Samson's strength, Delilah wove her charms around Samson until he revealed to her that his strength was in his hair. She immediately betrayed his secret to the Philistines, who waited until Samson was asleep in Delilah's arms and cut seven locks of his hair. This rendered Samson helpless and allowed the Philistines to take him prisoner, and later on, to gouge out his eyes.

The story of Samson and Delilah tells us that the belief in the power of hair dates from Biblical and maybe from pre-Biblical times. It also tells us that according to the Bible, the magical power of hair is God-given. The fact that the mystic number seven was used by the Philistines to reinforce the magical strength of the hair, exemplified by the seven locks, underlines the supernatural element in the story. This is one of the many examples of magical practices told in the Bible.

Like hair and nails, teeth are also popular as amulets and as ingredients in magic spells. The teeth of ancestors are often worn for protective purposes in some primitive cultures. In Australia, a tooth is commonly knocked out during puberty initiations. The tooth is carefully safeguarded by its owner, as it is believed that whatever happens to the tooth will happen to him also. This ancient custom finds a faint echo in the well-known belief in the "good tooth fairy." Even in our modern times, parents often exhort their young children to leave their discarded teeth under their pillows. The tooth fairy is said to come in the middle of the night and exchange the teeth for shiny silver coins. So popular is this belief that Avon (the well-known cosmetics firm) once designed a special container for these fairy teeth to be used by little girls. The fact that it is usually a parent who plays the part of the tooth fairy does not seem to detract from this charming traditional custom.

It is interesting to note that human substances (such as teeth or hair) which are used as amulets are mostly residues, no longer of any use to the body. These residues were never absolutely necessary for the survival of the organism. Like body excrements, they were rejected or marked obsolete by the biological computer which is the human body. Strangely enough, these human wastes are traditional symbols of power.

Feces and urine are used by some animals to indicate the boundaries of their territories and to act as deterrents to other animals, who recognize in the scent both a mark of authority and a warning against trespassers.

Human beings sometimes use their own excrements to develop symbols of power over others. In magic, not only the feces and the urine of a person are used to overcome others, but also saliva, sweat, and menstrual blood. In fact, anything that is rejected by the body or which the body does not need for survival is treated by the knowledgeable magician as surplus power fuel. For example, a well-known controlling spell calls for the name of the victim to be written on a piece of white paper and then is placed in a wide-necked bottle. Since the magician has already spat and urinated in that bottle, this is said to place the victim under the magician's control. In love magic, hamburger patties which have been mixed with sweat and menstrual blood before cooking are supposed to overcome the most reluctant lover.

Most commonly, these spells are made in total secrecy and without the victim ever suspecting what is going on, but sometimes a magician may chose to let a victim know he is the target of a spell. Naturally only a person with superb self-assurance and contempt for consequences will dare let a victim know of his intentions. Alistair Crowley, the famed English magician, was such a person. The "enfant terrible" of modern magic, Crowley conducted the most appalling rites with total aplomb and studied insolence. One of his favorite tricks was to invite himself to the house of an enemy or detractor and then defecate in the middle of the drawing room. This was both his way of showing his contempt for his host and his total control of the situation. The person thus treated, perhaps because of shock, seldom gave Crowley any further troubles.

Other bodily wastes, such as the human afterbirth and the umbilical cord, are very popular as amulets. Both of these are believed to be connected with the soul of the child to which they belong. The afterbirth, particularly, has always been considered a good luck amulet. Sailors have traditionally carried an afterbirth to sea to prevent shipwreck and all sorts of evil. In the late nineteenth century, English sailors were still practicing this ancient custom.

Both the afterbirth and the umbilical cord are said to influence the fate of a child. Whatever happens to one of these objects will also happen to their owners. In many primitive societies, the afterbirth or umbilical cord of a boy is sometimes buried in a battle field to ensure he will grow up to be a fierce warrior. Other times it is left inside a lion's den so that he grows up as courageous as a lion, or placed inside a bag with a few coins so that he will grow up to be rich. A girl's afterbirth or umbilical cord are placed in a kitchen so that she will become a good cook, or in a seamstress shop so she will be a good seamstress, or near an anthill so she will be as industrious as the ants. In Europe today, many women are careful to place their children's umbilical cords in locations directly connected with the profession or trade they would like their children to follow. For example, hospital grounds are favored by mothers who wish their children to become doctors or nurses. Schools are believed to engender new teachers, and the insides of books are said to encourage the development of young philosophers, writers and intellectuals. These same beliefs are practiced extensively in Latin America.

REPRESENTATIVE AMULETS

Amulets that imitate the form of a living thing or organ are *representative amulets*. Among these are human hearts, eyes, and hands. The eye and hand amulets are usually worn as protections against the evil eye. Amulets in the shape of a heart are used to attract love and friendship. The heart as a symbol of love is well-exemplified in the traditional custom of sending heart-shaped cards to loved ones on Saint Valentine's Day. These cards, known as "valentines" in the saint's honor, are probably a survival from a pagan love festival celebrated in ancient times around February fourteenth. Saint Valentine himself was a Roman martyr priest who died about A.D. 270. It is unknown how the love festival became associated with him, but it could be loosely connected with Candlemas, a fire festival observed by Witches and Pagans on February second as one of their sabbats. Fire is the element most closely associated with love in magic. The astrological sign of Leo, a fire sign, is traditionally associated with love and pleasure. All of this lends credence to the idea that St. Valentine's Day and Candlemas may be part of the same pagan festival.

Other representative amulets used for good luck and protection are skulls and skeletons. In countries like Mexico the day of the dead, celebrated on November first, is a big holiday. Skulls and skeletons are made of pastries and marzipan, and eaten for good luck and to ensure a long life. The Italians also make skeleton bones out of pastry around the same period. In Mexico, skeletons made of papier maché are often sculpted into musicians, each one playing a different musical instrument. The skeletons are given women's names and are highly valued as gifts. They are believed to represent the angel of death assigned to the person to whom the skeleton is presented. This allows the owner of the skeleton to pray to his "own death" and to call it by its proper name.

Death is believed to be a very powerful saint who will grant wishes if propitiated in the right manner. There is a very popular prayer directed to death where it is asked to awaken love between two people. This prayer is generally used in conjunction with another prayer to the angel of love. One of my friends, a well-known Cuban poet who also works with the United Nations in Vienna,

A marzipan skull from Mexico, where the spirit of Death is worshipped and prayed to like a saint. Thousands of these skulls and skeletons are sold in Mexico around Halloween.

brought back "her" death from Mexico during one of her trips to the Aztec capital. The name of this particular skeleton is Sylvia and she is standing saucily on a small pedestal, while strumming an oversized harp. Sylvia accompanies my friend wherever she goes and is said to be a great source of joy and inspiration.

Hunchbacks are also very popular representative amulets. They are commonly worn as gold and silver charms in womens' bracelets and are said to protect from evil and to bring general prosperity to the wearer.

Cameos can also be considered representative amulets. They are usually engraved in relief on a stone or gem. Coral and ivory are among the most popular materials used to engrave cameos. Jet, mother of pearl, and rock crystal are also commonly used for this purpose. Cameos made out of coral are considered to be particularly lucky amulets. The word cameo is said to originate from the term *Kame'a*, a magic square used for talismanic purposes.

Another type of representative amulet concerns itself with human endeavors. Keys, knots, and lucky pennies are all included in

An ivory net sinker inscribed with sympathetic magic symbols depicting a successful fishing expedition. The Alaskan Eskimos believe that the use of the net sinker will bring about this same fishing success depicted on the sinker's surface.

this group. Their shape is a clear indication of the influence they are believed to manifest. For example, a key is worn as an amulet so that it will open all the doors of opportunity to its wearer. Knots are worn to invite unions, usually between lovers. Lucky pennies are carried around for money and good luck. Sometimes bracelets made entirely of coins are worn for the same purpose. Bells and tassels are worn so that the sound and the movement they make will frighten away evil spirits. Anchors are associated with the sea and are said to bring stability to their owners. Arrowheads are worn as protections against enemies. Axes are used for the same purpose. Both these symbols are said to work best if worn on chains around the neck.

The four suits of the modern playing cards are also said to possess magical properties. Hearts are worn for love, diamonds for money, and clubs for business. Spades, which are symbols of sorrow and strife, are not commonly worn as amulets.

So popular are amulets in our modern society that even children's cereals have not been able to escape from their influence. One of the most popular breakfast cereals in the American market is made of bits of sugar and marshmallow in the shape of crescents, pentagrams, four-leaf clovers, hearts, diamonds, clubs, bells, crosses and wishbones. These tiny amulets in appropriate lucky colors are sponsored by a green-clad leprechaun.

7 Magical Designs

The houn'gan, or high priest of Voodoo, tracing the mystical veves around the central pole prior to a ceremony. The veves are the means used by the Voodoo priests and priestesses to invoke the loas or gods. Veves can be used as amulets by inscribing them on parchment with the Voodooist's blood. They can also be engraved on emeralds or rubies. This amulet must always be carried inside a red flannel bag. All the veves in this book are from Milo Rigaud's *Veve,* French & European Publications, 115 Fifth Ave., New York, New York, 1974.

MAGICAL SYMBOLS ARE SOMETIMES INSCRIBED ON WALLS AND FLOORS instead of being worn on the body. These are also amuletic in essence and are used, not only for protective purposes, but are also to invoke spiritual forces. Voodoo veves, sand painting and hex signs fall within this category.

VOODOO VEVES

A veve is a ritual diagram drawn on the floor around the center pole of the voodoo temple or *um'phor* with ashes, wheat flour, coffee grounds, brick dust or corn meal. Wheat flour is the basis of most veves because voodoo practitioners believe that wheat is the ideal food and the spiritual agent between worlds. On the other hand, corn is also considered a powerful basis for the veve because it symbolizes the pregnancy of the Virgin Mary, as well as Venus impregnated by Mars.

According to the voodoo tradition, a veve is a condenser of astral forces. It is used to attract planetary powers to which it is linked by a geometrical occult chain. This chain is said to be the source of writing and language.

A veve is one of the many geometrical attributes of the *loas* or spiritual forces invoked during the voodoo ceremony. When it is drawn on the floor of the um'phor, it is said to establish an immediate contact with the spirit or loa it represents, and to act as a bridge between the astral and the physical worlds. The loa is able to make the transition from the spiritual to the physical world by using the veve as its point of contact.

Only the high priest *(houn'gan)* or high priestess *(mambo)* of voodoo can construct a veve. Without the offices of the houn'gan or mambo the veve is powerless. The houn'gan or mambo are needed in the drawing of the veve because it is the power of their faith, strengthened by their ritualistic know-how, that creates the "soul" of the veve. In other words, the veve is concentrated power directed through a special channel, which is the loa symbolized by the diagram. This power is then earthed when the loa (using the veve as a bridge) takes possession of one of the followers present at the ritual. When the possession takes place, the houn'gan or the mambo is able to attain the material realization of his or her will through the astral channel of the veve.

Voodooists recognize in the veves cosmo-planetary patterns which agree in principle with Kabbalistic and Hindu cosmic ideologies. Each veve is seen as a sign which represents some of the

The veves of the loa Maraça, a representation of love, truth and justice, directed by reason.

The veve of the loa Milo-can (All the Saints). This veve is said to capture the influence of various planets on the corresponding Kabbalistic points. This veve can synthesize all of the loas.

The veve of the loa Erzulie, the Venus of the Voodoo pantheon.

The veve of Grand Erzulie. This powerful loa is often syncretized as the Holy Ghost of the Christian Trinity. She shares the dominion of the heart with the loa Legba.

Another aspect of Erzulie, this veve represents her as Erzulie Pethro.

The veve of Erzulie Phré-Da or Frèda. In this aspect Erzulie symbolizes a fish of the air or flying fish. Erzulie represents chastity, marriage, marital bond and purity. She is said to love jewels and perfumes and her favorite color is pink. Her attribute is marital union as a religious pact.

characteristics and attributes of one of the traditional planetary forces. In this sense, a veve can be compared to the Hindu mandala, which, like the veve, represents an astronomical synthesis of creation. It can also be compared to Kabbalistic planetary pentacles or seals, which are also representations of cosmic planetary forces. These planetary forces or spirits are known in voodoo as *loas of Mystéres* and are worshipped as the various gods or deities of the voodoo religion.

The veve, therefore, is said to exercise a planetary influence on the voodoo ceremony and on those present during the ritual. When energized by the high priest or priestess, the design is believed to possess a soul. The veve then becomes not only a geometric representation of a specific loa, but the loa itself. The soul of the veve is usually conferred on it ritualistically by pouring water over it. The water must be prepared by presenting it to the four cardinal points with a lighted candle. The water and the fire represent the loa known as Erzulie, which is the reflection of the sun as cosmic sex in the voodoo tradition.

The strength of the veve soul is inextricably bound to the sacrificial nourishment it receives during the ritual. This nourishment usually consists of the preferred foods, flavors, and drinks of the loa invoked by the veve. The food and drink act as materialization of cosmic energies, which are then used by the loa to effect its physical manifestation during the ritual.

The loas or planetary forces are said to respond to the summons of the houn'gan or mambo because of a pact or covenant that was made in the dim past between the priestly ancestors of voodoo and the same planetary forces. Since the ancestral souls are indestructible, they continue their spiritual evolution by associating with the planets and the ritual possessions that take place during the voodoo ceremonies.

The voodoo veve is the central point of the voodoo ceremony. Only through the veve can the loa be invoked and materialize during the ritual. Sometimes part of the material used to draw the veve is eaten by the initiated in order to gather some of the powers of the loa. Each loa has several aspects and several veves for each aspect. The veve used represents that aspect of the loa that is desired by the houn'gan or mambo to realize his particular needs (or those of a follower) at the time of the ritual.

Veves can be used for protective purposes, for simple love

The veve of Legba, representing God the Son. He is the African Osiris, King of Kings, and the guardian of roads, gates and doors. He walks on both the planetary points of the Sun and Mercury. In the Sun, he symbolizes the Sacred Heart of Jesus. In Mercury, he personifies medical science. Voodoo worshippers call him Papa Legba. In Santeria he is known as Eleggua.

The veve of Lega At-Bon. In this aspect the loa is syncretized as Saint Anthony of Padua. Legba is always honored in Voodoo ceremonies before the other loas. He has two wives, the loas Tsi-Lah Hwedo and Aida Hwédo, synthesized as Erzulie Freda.

The veve of Dambhalah and Aida Hwédo, the greatest of all the loas. Dambhalah is also known as Dambhalah Hwédo and is a representation of God the Father. He personifies simultaneous fire and water. Aida Hwédo is Dambhalah's wife and symbolizes God the Mother. She personifies the rainbow and all the waters. As Dambhalah is the biggest of all the fish, Aida Hwédo is the biggest of all *female* fish, often represented by the whale. Their combined symbol is two snakes, intertwined.

A veve symbolising various loas, including Dambhalah (the snake) and Erzulie (the heart).

rituals, and for complicated ceremonies. Voodoo priests claim that whole governments can be overthrown by the proper use of voodoo veves. Destinies can be reshaped and the most stubborn wills broken by means of a veve and its ascribed loa. Naturally, the power of the veve and of the loa depend on the faith and the concentration abilities of the houn'gan or mambo.

HEX SIGNS

Like voodoo veves, hex signs are combinations of cosmic symbols that have a distinct power parallel with Kabbalistic beliefs. Some hex signs, (such as the *Petschaft* or *Wunder-Siegle* design, which is used for curing sickness or for sexual stimulation) are based on planetary influences. The Petschaft design is in reality the Star of David surrounded by the traditional symbols of the seven planets of the ancients. Another hex sign,

This hex sign symbolizes the four elements and the four seasons. It represents the earth protected by the sun. It is also a prayer for plenty, fertility and balance in life's sorrows and joys.

the *Double Creator's Star*, is a geometrical design also centered on the Star of David.

Traditionally, hex signs are said to be the remnants of ancient Mesopotamian sun cults. They are most often found in the area known as the Pennsylvania Dutch Country in the Eastern part of the United States, but they are by no means restricted to this geographical location. Hex signs are found in other parts of the United States, as well as in many parts of Europe. Many of the colorful symbols found in furniture pieces and architectural designs of Scandinavia, the Austrian Tyrol, and Bavarian Germany are distinctly hex-like in

A hex sign commonly found on Pennsylvania Dutch barns. Circles, flowers, tulips, stars and suns are the most typical symbols used. This sign is composed of a circle divided into twelve sections with a sun at its center. The twelve sections represent the twelve months of the year and the hex sign is used to insure protection and good luck—symbolized by the sun—throughout the entire year.

The use of the star—whether with four, five, six, eight or more points—is very old and linked with the worship of the sun. It is also said to be a symbol of fertility and as such is much valued by Pennsylvania Dutch farmers who often use it on the barns where cattle are kept.

form. Some of these, such as hearts, tulips, and scalloped borders, are among the best known ingredients of the traditional hex signs. And indeed, the entire science of hexology or hexography is believed to have evolved largely in Germany and Northern Europe. The term *hex* itself is derived from the German word *Hexen* which means "to use witchcraft."

Hex signs are used for many reasons. They are used to protect a person or property from black magic and the evil eye. Hex designs are drawn on barn walls to protect the animals inside it against fire and the evil machinations of enemies. They are painted on furniture and utensils and are used as prayers, written in the symbolical language of the mind.

A very popular hex sign, where the entire annual cycle is enclosed by the dual protection of the circle and the eight-rayed star, symbols of life and balance.

Each design in a hex sign has a special meaning that is identical to the meanings ascribed to the same symbol by other traditions. This tends to underline the universal quality of

A sign for strength and courage. It uses the famous double-headed eagle motif to symbolize watchfulness. The tulips represent fertility.

of symbology and its direct link with the human unconscious. To a hex doctor or *hexenmeister* the heart symbolizes love, as it does to a Mexican witch or an African shaman. A tulip represents fertility; a circle, eternity; a snake symbolizes both wisdom and sexual powers; while pomegranates mean fertility and prosperity. All these symbols have the same meaning in many different cultures and reiterate the

One of the hex signs known as the Earth-Star Flower. It symbolizes life seen as beauty, with faith—represented by the flowers—sheltering each side of the eight-rayed star.

The Triple Star, a symbol of protection by heavenly powers and the giver of prosperity and longevity. It is a diagram of the internal lines of force which hold matter in form. As a sign, it seeks permanent enjoyment of abundance.

One of the versions of the hex sign known as the Great and Lesser Seals. It refers to the six steps of creation and protects all things.

One of the earliest versions of the swastika within the protective circle of life.

underlying spiritual connection between human beings. Because each symbol means the same thing to each human unconscious, a hex sign willwork just as powerfully for one person as it will work for another, regardless of their ethnic or socio-economic backgrounds.

Lee R. Gandee is a well-known American *hexenmeister*. His book, *A Strange Experience,* is required reading for anyone seriously interested in the ancient art of the hex sign.*

I would like to include here an excerpt from a letter I once received from Mr. Gandee, where he discourses at length on the subject of *Hexerei:*

> If one had the erudition, the research materials, the time, and the patience, he could write a treatise on *Hexerei* and *Braucherei*—I am really more of a *Braucher (herbalist)* than a Hexenmeister—showing that they are the surviving elements of the system of religious magic which was practiced in prehistoric times by whatever people gave rise to those groups which speak Indo-European languages, wherever they may be. It is the magic of the Caucasian race, just as Voodoo is of the Black race and Huna of the Polynesians. A Pennsylvania Dutch Hex Sign has its counterpart in the East Indian mandalas, and the Gundestrop Cauldron from a bog in Denmark, dating from a few hundred years B.C., has Hex signs in some panels, along with elephants in others. That late, there was some cultural contact between the Indo-Iranian and European descendants of the ancestral group. The Cauldron has a Pennsylvania Dutch design of tulips, considered to be of "Eastern Celtic" craftsmanship, probably made in the Black Sea area, and there is a hint that other groups besides Indo-Europeans were influenced, for there are Jewish Coffins with the same Hex sign, dating before the Christian era, and used to assure the protection of the dead from evil or from the molestation of their graves. I know two early 19th century tombstones here with this sign carved in them, over 2,000 years later, by Lutherans. Moreover, in Spain, the Celt-Iberians had the identical art traditions reflected by the Gundestrop Cauldron

---

* See L.R. Gandee, *A Strange Experience: The Secrets of a Hexenmeister,* Prentice-Hall, (N.J., 1976).

and Pennsylvania Dutch folk art, which in germany derived from the traditions of the Hallstadt culture, so Catelans, Austrians, Danes, Germans, Irish, Iranians and East Indians or whatever, the original "Old Religion" gave rise to the symbols and earth symbols. The Indians in America had a very similar religion, but they told of a White God, Quetzalcoatl, who taught them their religion. His symbol was the cross, but the cross was a key symbol in Hexerei long before the crucifixion, only ours is a Greek Cross symbolizing the four directions (among other things).

A *Braucher* is likely to be a herb doctor and use herbal magic (Where would I be without vervain!). It was one of the twelve herbs of the Sacred Cauldron, and is the love ingredient of any Hex portion. It was brought here from Switzerland, and grows for miles along the river.Welsh used its square stems for drawing lots, and I wonder what people in Puerto Rico use it for.

This is the end of the quotation from Lee Gandee's letter, but I would like to add here that the Puerto Rican herbalists use vervain in the same way the *Brauchers* do: that is, for love potions, for cleansing baths and for all sorts of curing remedies.

SAND PAINTING

The sand painting practiced by the Navaho Indians of the Southwestern part of the United States is also drawn on the floor like the voodoo veve. It is interesting to note that the earth-covered dwelling where the painting is made is called a *Hougan* which is similar to *houn'gan*, the name of the high priest of voodoo.

Sand painting is an important part of a magical ceremony usually performed for healing purposes. The medicine man places his patient directly upon the painting and/or rubs the patient with sand from the drawing.

Before starting to work on the sand painting, the Navaho medicine man undergoes a lengthy ritualistic cleansing. This renders him worthy of establishing contact with the cosmic forces of the universe which he then depicts from memory in his sand paintings. Each of these magical drawings is carefully destroyed after the ceremony because their power can only be used once.

The colored sands used in the paintings are made by the Indians. They grind stones from nearby cliffs. The main colors of the drawings are black and white. Black and white represent the dual nature of God, the male and the female, and the union of all

A Navaho sand painting of the "Male Shooting Way," which is a chant used during a five-day or nine-day healing ceremony. The black figure with the star designs represents "Father Sky." The blue deity on the right represents "Mother Earth." Several plants, such as corn, wheat and squash grow from her body.
Office of Anthropology, Smithsonian Institution.

opposites, thus providing a pictorial representation of sex on a cosmic level. Black and white are also the colors of the "Rainbow Guardian," who is believed to unite heaven and earth. Other popular colors in sand painting are red and yellow which are natural representations of the solar and life energies.

A common sand painting depicts Father Sky and Mother Earth, which according to Navaho mythology were the first beings created by the Great Spirit. Its intended symbology is that everything is conceived first in thought-forms (the sky) by the Great Spirit (God) and then brought into physical manifestation (the Earth). This highly sophisticated magical concept is the mainstream of all the esoteric schools, both ancient and modern. Its presence in the

A

A Navaho curing ceremony. (a) The shaman or priest makes the sand painting on the floor of the hougan. (b) He then proceeds to project some of his powers onto the painting by means of a magic chant accompanied by the shaking of his right hand. Waiting patiently on the side is his patient, a small baby held in his mother's arms. (c) After the chant is over, the mother sits within the protective circle surrounding the sand painting, and waits for the visual prayer symbolized by the diagram to heal her child. The ritual is repeated for several days. After the painting has been used it is always destroyed.

B

C

Navaho tradition again emphasizes the universality of mind symbology.

Sand painting is used by the Navahos, not just for healing purposes, but also to learn the structure of their own souls. A painting is often used as a meditation symbol, a form of mandala which reveals to the conscious mind many of the secrets of the cosmos or of the deep unconscious. The sand painting Father Sky and Mother Earth, for example, are sometimes used to educate children. Because the Navahos do not believe in the physical punishment of children, the painting is used to remind a child that his naughty behavior offends the Great Spirit. Left alone with the painting, the child endeavors to receive a message from the Great Sprit by concentrating on the colors and the designs.

THE HINDU KOLEM

Like voodoo veves and sand paintings, Hindu kolems are magical designs made on the floor. The symbols are made of rice flour and are drawn at the entrances of homes and inside shrines. They are treated as altars which attract the planetary influences embodied in the various Hindu deities.

The similarity between kolems and veves is quite marked. They are drawn in flour, they are essentially geometrical in form, and they are drawn on the floor to attract spiritual forces. There are 64 kolem motifs, and all of them have astrological significances. Each angle of each part of the kolem symbolizes one degree of the power of the planets and their influence on man.

The kolems are used by believers to distinguish between good and evil, and to tap the cosmic powers of the gods. They can be used for meditation purposes in order to discover the hidden links between God and humans. Each design acts as a key to the human unconscious. The kolem designs are as universal in their meanings as the magical designs used in veves, hex signs, and sand paintings. Thus a snake means sex or wisdom; fish, fertility and riches; and a cross symbolizes divinity and balance. When kolem designs include triangles, the triangles follow the symbology of the Star of David; a triangle pointing up represents masculinity; a triangle pointing down, femininity. Kolems may not be drawn when grieving for the dead.

TIBETAN AMULETS

In the preparation of Tibetan charms and amulets, magical designs alternate with sanskrit spells and incantations. These amulets are engraved directly on woodblocks which are then manually dipped in ink and then pressed on cloth or handmade paper to print the amulet. This kind of amulet has been made this way since the introduction of Buddhism in Tibet around the seventh century of our era. So complex and extensive is the art of amulet making in Tibet, that there are literally thousands of amulets made in monasteries for every possible endeavor known to human kind.

The Tibetan amulet is used in many different ways. It is inscribed on walls, ceilings and shrines for protective and invoking purposes. In this sense, it resembles the hex signs, the veves and the Hindu kolems. It is worn as an amulet on the body for protection against evil, rolled into prayer wheels, or eaten as "medicine." The very abstract designs, (combinations of figures and geometrical forms) are used to banish sickness and to create protection during rites. Among the most important are amulets representing wheels or mandalas. These mandalas are inscribed with many designs. The mandala is a *psychocosmogram*, or visual representation of cosmic forces. These forces can be invoked through the symbology of the design. Mandalas are worn as protective amulets and rolled and tied with colored threads. They are also used as base structures for altars, as meditation aids, and as protective inscriptions on the walls and ceilings of shrines.

Sometimes prayer flags are inscribed with magical designs and flown beside the house. Other times the same designs are printed on cloth and cast to the winds for good luck. These are considered to be simple amulets and any layman can prepare them.

The most complex of the amulets (and the most valuable) have to be empowered by a lama to be truly effective. The amulets are usually printed from the appropriate woodblocks and then additional information, such as the name of the person who will wear the amulet, are added by hand. The lama then reads the inscriptions aloud and charges them with his magical powers. Sometimes, the amulet is consecrated by throwing a few grains of barley, colored rice, or saffron water on its surface. It is then bound with colored threads in a mandala pattern and presented to its owner. Butter lamps and incense are often burned during the consecration ceremonies.

Magical diagrams (yantras) are intimately related to magical formulas (mantras), both in the structure of letters and in the vibratory rate used in their pronunciation. There is also a link between color, sound, and form. This interconnection between the forces and energies expressed in both mantras and yantras is known as tantra. The mantras used during the consecration of an amulet are actually the embodiment of the deity invoked. This establishes the importance of the spoken word in Tibetan magic. It is the manifestation of cosmic forces subjugated to the will of the magician.

Because the karma, or force of destiny, is affected and sometimes changed by the preparation of an amulet, only a person who knows how to change karma without unbalancing it should make an amulet. For this reason, lamas (who are considered to be highly evolved spiritually) are preferred for the preparation and empowerment of amulets. In spite of the power of the lama, an amulet will be powerless if the owner has no faith in it. The faith placed in the amulet and the lama's power both serve to activate the cosmic forces which are inherent in the design.

There are many examples of magical designs other than the ones discussed in this chapter. The Chinese and the Japanese use the symbology of their calligraphy to design protective amulets of great efficacy. In Poland, paper cuts are traditionally used to protect people and their homes from all sorts of evil. The shapes of the paper cuts vary, but they are mostly based on the Kabbalistic Tree of Life.

All over the world the symbolic language of the mind is used in myriad ways to tap the infinite source of cosmic power. The magical symbols used in amulets serve a dual purpose. They act as shields to repel evil and as magnets to attract the beneficent influence of spiritual forces. This polarity of amulets is another instance of the dual nature of all things, be they human or divine.

8 Amulets and the Evil Eye

THE BELIEF IN THE MALIGNANT POWERS OF THE EVIL EYE CROSSES many cultures and probably dates from prehistoric times. But the first written accounts of the evil eye are found in the cuneiform inscriptions of the Sumerians and the Babylonians which date from around 3000 B.C. The Sumerian words IG-HUL meant literally "eye evil." In one of the cuneiform tablets dating from this period, the text reads as follows:

> The roving Evil Eye hath looked on the neighbor-hood and hath vanished far away, hath looked on the vicinity and hath vanished far away, hath looked on the chamber of the land and hath vanished far away, it hath looked on the wanderer and like wood cut off for poles it hath bent his neck.*

This is a very common amulet against the evil eye.

The great Sumerian god Ea was constantly at war against the evil eye, which was often personified in the form of the she-demon Tiamat. But in most ancient writings, the most common way to depict the evil eye was in the shape of an eye. Many magical works dating from very early periods in our history also speak of a "little man in the eye," which is of course the reflection a person sees of himself when he looks into someone's eyes. This "little man" was believed

---

* See R. C. Thompson, *Devils & Evil Spirits of Babylonia*, (London, n.d.).

167

to be very powerful and to be, in many instances, the baleful force behind the evil eye. In the *Egyptian Liturgy of Funerary Offerings*, edited by E.A. Wallis Budge, the priest says to the dead upon the presentation of one of the many gifts offered to Osiris, "Osiris Unas, the child which is in the Eye of Horus hath been presented unto thee." The Arabs changed this term slightly to translate literally as the "daughter of the eye," and a similar phrase is used in Spanish today to describe the retina of the eye. The Spanish term is *la niña del ojo*.

The term *evil eye* is a literal description of the ability to harm living things with a glance of the eye. The evil eye is believed to be most injurious to small children and mothers-to-be, but anyone and anything can be injured by it, including animals and plants.

The evil eye is mostly an attribute of human beings; but certain beasts, reptiles, and even inanimate objects are said to possess the ability to cause harm by their proximity alone. Frogs, snakes, scorpions, spiders, and some stones, such as opals and pearls are all believed to be the carriers of evil vibrations.

As steeped in superstition as the belief in the evil eye is, many modern scholars think there may be more than the proverbial grain of truth in this belief. Anthropologists, and especially psychologists, are beginning to consider the possibility that under certain circumstances the human mind may be able to project psychic energies using the eyes as a focus point. These energies may be of either a positive or a negative nature but in either case are able to affect the recipient in a very marked way.

The famed *third eye* of the Hindus, which is believed to exist in the middle of the forehead between the physical eyes, is now believed to have a physical counterpart in the pineal gland. This tiny appendix of the human brain, though deeply buried within the brain folds, is located in direct line with the "third eye," and is believed to produce the chemical serotonin which is said to control the various psychic energies of the mind.* If the pineal gland is indeed the third eye, it is probably responsible for all the negative vibrations usually ascribed to the evil eye.

The Hindu belief in the evil eye probably originates in the terrible and all-powerful third eye of Shiva, the Destroyer, which is said to be able to destroy the whole universe with one single glance, and which on one occasion reduced the god Kama to ashes. Hindu

---

* See J.H. Gaddum and K.A. Hameed, *The British Journal of Pharmacology*, 9:240 (1959), and also J. Axelrod and H.Weissback, *Science*, 131.1312 (1960).

A small head of a Bodhisattva, with the third eye or urna clearly engraved in the metal.

caste marks are drawn in the middle of the forehead to mark the site of the third eye, as are the *tilaka* of married women. The Angami Nagas of Assam protect the spot with a small leaf, in the belief that other people's eyes can cause them harm if they look upon their third eye.

The most effective amulet against the evil eye has always been, according to tradition, an image of the eye itself. One of the most famous eye amulets known is the Egyptian Udjat or Eye of Horus. The use of the Udjat seems to have been universal among the Egyptians, perhaps because it symbolized the eye of the Sun-god and thus it was able to nullify the negative influence of the evil eye. Sometimes two eyes or Udjati were used instead of one. These were representations of the eyes of the Sun and the Moon. The Egyptian word for evil eye was *ir-t ban-t* and the hieroglyphics depicting it includes an eye and a knife.

Many cultures have adopted the image of an eye, believed to be the eye of God, as an amulet against the evil eye. In modern Mexico, the Huichol Indians prepare an eye amulet they call *Ojo de Dios* or the Eye of God, which is believed to protect people, homes and fields against the evil eye. The amulet is prepared of sticks and colored yarns, each color denoting a special type of protection. The same type of amulet is prepared by the American Indians of the Southwestern part of the United States.

Porcelain eyes are also worn in pins or in bracelets as deterrents of the evil eye.These are very popular in Latin America, and are often used to protect small children against the envy and jealousy of neighbors and ill-intentioned people.

The belief in the evil eye is also found in the Bible, and both the New and the Old Testaments warn against its dangers. Deuteronomy 15:9 warns, "Beware that there be not a thought in thy wicked heart . . . and thine eye be evil against thy poor brother . . ." While Proverbs 23:6 tells us to "eat not the bread of him that hath an evil eye, neither crave thou his dainty meats."

The ancient Hebrews, in spite of severe prohibitions against magical practices, still managed to employ some of them as protection. They endeavored to protect their children against the evil eye by surreptitiously passing them through the smoke of the blessed Sabbath candles. The Star of David was and still is believed to be a powerful shield against the evil eye. The fringes and the tassels on the prayer shawls and the bells attached to the priest's vestments were probably amuletic in essence. Fringes and bells have been used as amulets against evil since ancient times. The Egyptians, the Babylonians and the Assyrians, all used bells to drive away evil spirits. It is very possible that the Hebrews, who were deeply influenced by the magic of their neighbors, copied some of their magical beliefs.*

Hebrew amulets that were used for protection, such as the Mezuzah, were often encased in tiny cylinders and worn around the neck. Apparently the idea behind this practice was that since the amulet could not be seen it did not break the Mosaic law.

Contrary to the Hebrews, the early Christians did not feel guilty about protecting themselves against the evil eye. Their favorite amulet, the cross, was and is still worn as the most potent safeguard against all forms of evil. Salt, holy water, and a piece of the holy wafer are also commonly used for protective purposes. Relics of the saints and medals depicting their images are also popular

---

* See E. A. Wallis Budge, *Amulets and Superstitions,* (New York, 1977).

amulets among Christians.

In Mark 7:22, 23, Jesus says to his disciples, "Thefts, covetousness, wickedness, deceit, lasciviousness, an evil eye, blasphemy, pride, foolishness: All these evil things come from within, and defile the man." So it is clear that Jesus himself believed in the evil eye and condemned it.

According to a well-known Ethiopian legend, Jesus and his disciples went walking one day along the sea of Tiberias. After a while they came upon an old woman sitting on a filthy seat whose eyes shone like gold and whose hands and feet were like wheels. From her mouth spouted flames "sixty-eight cubits long." The disciples asked Jesus, "What is this thing, O Lord?" And Jesus answered, "This is the eye of earth, evil and accursed. When its glance falls upon a ship sailing on the sea, that ship sinks suddenly; when it pursues a horse, it casts down that horse and its rider; when it looks upon a cow that is being milked, it curdles the milk, which turns into blood; when it looks upon a woman with her child, it separates them and destroys them." He then pronounced the words, "Asparapses, Askoraskis," and with the power of those words destroyed the woman. Another version of the story says that the disciples destroyed "this eye of the earth, evil and accursed, and burnt her body in the fire, and scattered the ashes to the winds—east, west, south and north—so that the memorial of her might be blotted out from the earth."*

The ancient Greeks also believed in the existence of the evil eye which they knew as *Baskanos.* The most common Greek amulet against the evil eye was called *Probaskanion* and was and is still used by men, women and children alike. Among the Greek writers who have attempted to explain the evil eye was Heliodorus, who lived around A.D. 300. He said that "when one looks at what is excellent with an envious eye, he fills the surrounding atmosphere with a pernicious quality, and transmits his own envenomed exhalations into whatever is nearest to him."

The Romans, who were firm believers in legal processes, decided that attack is the best form of defense, and declared an injunction against the evil eye. Proper legislation was approved and vigorously enacted by the Roman senate to ensure that the illegal activities of the evil eye be properly punished and ultimately banished from the land. The intention was noble but, like many other Roman

---

* See E.A. Wallis Budge, *A History of Ethiopia,* (London, n.d.).

ventures, it proved a failure. In modern Rome, and indeed in all of Italy, the *mal d'occhio* or *iettatura*, most commonly known as the evil eye, is as insolently alive today as when it was declared illegal by the ancient Romans. Modern-day Italians, quite aware of the futility of declaring an injunction against the evil eye, have resorted to other methods of defense against its perils. Chief among these are small horns mounted in gold and worn in chains around the neck. Porcelain eyes are also popular, as are gold crosses and crucifixes.

In some parts of Palestine and Syria the evil eye is supposed to be the "baleful gift" of men who have light blue eyes, particularly if they are clean shaven. As an antidote against the awful influence of these blue-eyed monsters, the Palestinian and Syrian women decorate themselves with blue beads on the principle that *similia similibus curantur*, that is, like cures like. Caravan leaders do not dare set out on a journey unless every beast in their caravans is protected against the evil eye with a blue bead.*

The Arabs, who are also firm believers in the dangers of the evil eye, call it "ain al-hasad," or eye of envy. The prophet Mohammed was said to believe in the evil eye also, and Surah 113 of the Koran is

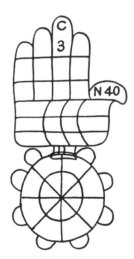

A diagram representing the Hand of Fatima, a most potent deterrent of the evil eye. Fatima was Mohammed's daughter, a woman reputed for all her virtues. In modern times there has been a great resurgence of this attractive amulet which is made in many forms, but most commonly in gold filigree.

---

* See George F. Kunz, *The Curious Lore of Precious Stones*, (New York, 1971).

often written on scrolls or cut on agates to protect against it. The Hand of Fatima, which is perhaps one of the most famous amulets against the evil eye, is of Arab origin.

Fatima was the daughter of the prophet Mohammed by his first wife Khadijah. Fatima was called Al-Zahra, meaning the "bright blooming," and Al-Batul, meaning "clean maid," or "Virgin." She retained these titles even after she married and gave birth to three children. The fingers of the hand of Fatima represent the whole religion of Islam and its fundamental duties, as follows: (1) to keep the fast of Ramadan; (2) to make the pilgrimage to Mekkah; (3) to give alms to the poor; (4) to destroy the unbelievers and (5) to perform daily the prescribed ablutions. The Hand of Fatima is always shaped as a right hand, as this is the hand of honor according to the Arabs. The left hand, which is used by the Arabs for all "unclean acts" is considered the hand of dishonor and many Muslims will not eat with it. According to Muslim law, one of the worst punishments that may be inflicted upon an individual is to cut off the right hand. This renders the person unable to eat and condemns that person to starvation or to eat the food directly with his or her mouth.

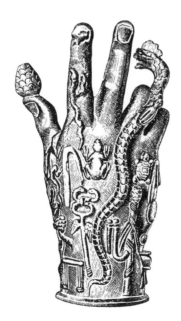

A bronze magic hand from Egypt, used to repel the evil eye. All the symbols engraved are said to be powerful deterrents of evil.

The hand as an amulet is common in many cultures. The Egyptians had a symbol known as "the Great Hand," which they saw as the supreme power who rules heaven and earth. In medieval pictures the deity is represented by a hand issuing from the clouds. One of the most miraculous prayers of the Catholic Church is dedicated to the All Powerful Hand, which is depicted as a gigantic hand in the clouds. Raising the hand is regarded as an invocation to God, and is commonly used as an oath in Europe and in the United States. During court procedures and during investiture ceremonies, one hand is placed on the Bible, while the other is raised in oath. This custom originated in Western Asia.

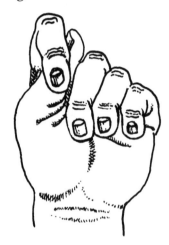

The figga or fico, a sign during which the thumb protrudes between the first two fingers. It is a well-known amulet against the evil eye. In Latin American countries, infants are often protected against the evil eye by a jet figga accompanied by a bit of coral, mounted in gold.

A closed hand with the first and second fingers outstretched, is an act of blessing. When only the first and fourth fingers are outstretched the hand symbolizes the horns of the devil and the powers of evil. Yet this symbol is often used as an amulet against the evil eye. The *figga* or *fico* is another very popular amulet against the evil eye. It depicts a closed hand where the thumb protrudes between the first and second fingers. The figga is said to symbolize the male genitals and is often used by witches to draw their magical circle when the traditional athame is not on hand for that purposes. In Latin American countries, the figgas made of ebony or jet are almost always worn by small children, to protect them against the evil eye.

The most vulnerable parts of the body and those most accessible to the evil eye are body orifices. The eyes, nose, ears, mouth and the anal and genital openings are all considered easy prey to the malevolent spirits attending the evil eye. Some extremely ingenious methods have been devised by people of different cultures and beliefs to protect these weak parts of the human anatomy. The Egyptians used malachite, a green carbonate of copper, as a base for their eye shadow, which they wore against the evil eye. Malachite has long been considered a powerful deterrent of all types of evil. Arab women use kohl to line their eyes. Even Arab children wear kohl around their eyes. The use of lipstick and all eye makeup can be traced to this attempt of the ancients to protect their eyes and mouths from the invasion of the spirits of the evil eye. The act of covering the mouth during a yawn was originally designed as a protective action rather than a polite one.

The invention of earrings and nose rings can also be linked to the fear of the evil eye. In primitive societies, bones are worn under the bridge of the nose, as are pieces of stones and pieces of elaborately carved metal. Hindu women of high social standing wear jewels on their nostrils, and sometimes one or more nose rings. Earrings are considered most effective when the ear has to be pierced to insert the earring. Only then are the evil spirits unable to enter the body through the ear.

Necklaces are also worn for amuletic purposes. The idea is to attract the looks of people to the necklace, thus warding off the mysterious and dangerous emanations of the evil eye. The necklace or its components are supposed to perform a similar service to that rendered by the lightning rod in diverting electrical discharges. Necklaces made of agate are particularly effective in repelling the evil eye. Brown or black agates with a ring in the center are the most popular stones for these necklaces. Combinations of black and white agates in a necklace are also believed to be powerful amulets against the evil eye.

Genital and anal orifices are protected in a variety of ways, such as written or woven charms, sacred life-attaching threads, girdles, and penis wrappers of painted palm leaves. Hindu boys always wear silver girdles around their genitals, and the codpiece worn by men in fourteenth and fifteenth century Europe was used as much for magical protection as for practical purposes.

Other protective devices against the evil eye range from fans and whistles to bells and mirrors. These latter are believed to be particularly effective because they reflect the gaze of the evil eye back to its sender.

Gypsies, perhaps the most superstitious of all human beings, use all of the preceding and more as amulets against the evil eye. The *Berufen,* or eye enchantment, is particularly dreaded by gypsy mothers who protect their children with the following remedy:*

---

* See C.G. Leland, *Gypsy Sorcery and Fortune Telling,* (New York, 1962).

(1) This necklace of carnelian beads from ancient Persia is an amulet against the evil eye. (2) A necklace of onyx beads, also a protection against the evil eye. From early Christian times.

A jar is filled with water from a stream, and it must be taken with, not against, the current as it runs. In it are placed seven coals, seven handfuls of meal, and seven cloves of garlic, all of which is put on the fire.When the water begins to boil it is stirred with a three-forked twig, while the wise woman repeats:

> "Miseç' yakha; tut dikhen,
> Te yon kathe mudaren!
> Te atunci efta; coka;

Te çaven miseçe yakhá;
Miseç' yakhá tut dikhen,
Te yon káthe mudáren!
But práhestař e yakha;
Atunci kores th'ávena;
Miseç' yakhá tut dikhen
Te yon káthe mudáren!
Pçábuvená pçábuvena;
Andre develeskero yakhá!

Evil eyes look on thee,
May they soon extinguished be!
And then seven ravens
Pluck out the evil eyes;
Evil eyes [now] look on thee,
May they soon extinguished be!
Much dust in the eyes,
Thence may they become blind,
Evil eyes now look on thee;
May they soon extinguished be!
May they burn, may they burn
In the fire of God!"

It has been speculated that the seven ravens mentioned in the spell are represented by the seven coals, while the garlic may symbolize lightning, a weapon of God and the plate of evil sprits. Garlic is one of the herbs most commonly used against the infernal machinations of evil spirits. Vampires are said to dread garlic because it poisons blood, the vampire's only means of sustenance.

Gypsies also treasure sea shells as amulets against the evil eye. Some of their more complex amulets are engraved in metal, and have a distinct Kabbalistic flavor. The snake, a symbol widely used in amulets from many cultures, is one of the most recurrent symbols in gypsy amulets.

The possession of the evil eye is not restricted to "wicked witches" or morally deformed people. Pope Pius IX, who died in 1878, was believed to have possessed the evil eye. Pope Leo XIII was also branded as a powerful "iettatore" and the deaths of many cardinals during his reign were dutifully laid at this feet. Napoleon III, Kaiser William II and Lord Byron were also feared as the possessors of the dreaded evil eye. George Bernard Shaw was very proud of the fact he could inflict death and destruction upon anyone by merely wishing it. He claimed that "a deadly but horrible emanation comes from the hater to his victim. All the people whom I have ever hated died."

One would imagine that with the formidable array of amuletic weapons at our disposal, humankind should have been able to dispose of the evil eye a long time ago. Yet, in spite of all our efforts to destroy it, we are still beset by this persistent plague. The reason for this failure is the persistent *belief* in the evil eye. Just as an amulet is empowered by the faith of its owner, so the evil eye is empowered by faith in its existence. The eradication of the evil eye will not come about with the use of spells or amulets, but rather with the determination to stop believing in it.

9 The Cross and the Star

THE CROSS IS PERHAPS THE OLDEST AMULETIC SYMBOL. Contrary to public opinion, this ancient symbol is not of Christian origin, and was in use among the pagan peoples of Europe and Western Asia long before the birth of Jesus Christ.

Early examples of crosses have been discovered and can be traced as far back as the Sumerians and the Assyrians. Most of these first crosses were equilateral or equal armed, and were often enclosed within a circle. Some were made entirely of circles or had a small circle within each of their four angles. The circle probably represented the earth, while the four arms of the cross were probably symbols of the four cardinal points and the four seasons.

Some Assyrian sculptures and inscriptions show what may be described as a solar or radiated cross, depicting a sun disk from which proceed four arms and four rays of light. Some authorities believe that the

The symbol known as the Cross of Atlantis, an ancient sign allegedly showing the three concentric walls of the Atlantean capital and the great waterway entering from the south. The ancient magic of Atlantis was said to have been inherited by the Egyptian priesthood, whose awesome feats of magic have never been equaled. Many of the world's most famous mystical societies, such as the Rosicrucians, the Masons, the Golden Dawn and the Ordo Templi Orientalis claim to descend from the Atlantean-Egyptian tradition.

four arms of this cross symbolized the four quarters of heaven over which the god Anu presided. The well-known Maltese or Coptic cross also dates from Assyrian times.

The first crosses were equal-arm crosses. Some were enclosed within circles to indicate the earth and the four seasons, while others were the Gammadions, formed of four Greek gammas placed in the form of a cross.

The Greek cross, which is a plain equilateral cross, was the one commonly in use among the pagans in the time before Christ. Examples of this cross have been found inscribed on pottery, vases, and bronze weapons from Scandinavia, Germany, Austria, France, and England. In the beginning, this cross symbolized heaven and its creative powers. Later on, it became an amulet believed to confer on its wearer the protection of heaven as well as prosperity, riches and a long life.

Columbus and his captains were amazed to find the equilateral cross in America, and immediately attributed its existence to the teachings of the apostle Thomas, who is said to have visited India where he worked as a carpenter. In any case, authorities on Peruvian and Mexican archaeology claim that the crosses found by Columbus have no connection with Christianity and were in fact "wind crosses." These wind crosses were used by the Indians as symbols of the four cardinal points; the four directions from which came the winds and rains. Later on, the crosses were given a solar or stellar character.

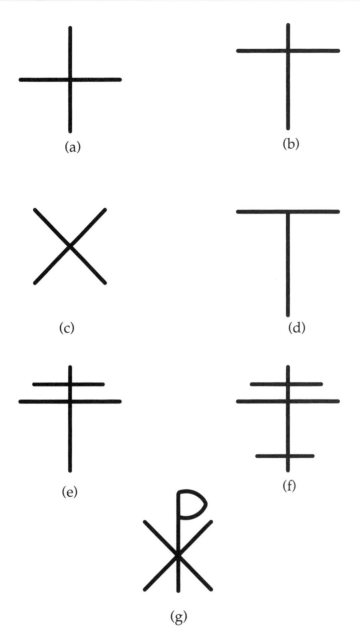

Various cross designs. (a) Equal-armed cross. (b) The Latin or Christian cross. (c) The cross of Saint Andrew, who asked to be crucified in this version of the cross, out of reverence for the cross where Jesus was crucified. (d) The Tau. (e) The cross of Lorraine. (f) Another version of the cross of Lorraine. (g) The monogrammatic symbol of Christ.

The Tau, or *crux commissa,* which is found in the catacombs of Rome and on early-Christian monuments, is also known as the "anticipatory cross," or the cross of the Old Testament.

Some writers believe that the Tau cross represents the hammer of Thor, the thunder god of Nordic mythology, but the swastika is probably the symbol most commonly accepted as Thor's hammer. Other scholars claim that the Tau is of Phoenician or Egyptian origin. Those advocating the latter theory believe that the Tau may be a form of one of the Egyptian hieroglyphics which represented the female organs of generation, and which was used to symbolize birth and life.

In the Old Testament, the prophet Ezekiel was commanded by God to go through Jerusalem and set a mark upon the foreheads of certain men, presumably to show they were to be exempt from judgment (Ezek. 9:4). The Hebrew word that is translated as "mark" is *hithwitha taw,* which has made many authorities think that the mark spoken of in Ezekial is the Tau cross. The mark made with the blood of the passover lamb on the houses of the Israelites before they left Egypt has also been identified with the Tau cross. But both these claims are largely speculative, and there is no real evidence to support their veracity. There is also no real evidence to support the view that both the Egyptian ankh and the nefer symbols were variations of the Tau cross.

The Tau is most commonly known as St. Anthony's cross. St. Anthony was a Copt hermit who used the Tau for the cure of inflammations of the skin and of erysipelas, which were called St. Anthony's fire, in his honor. The Brotherhood of Anthony wears a badge on the right shoulder with the Tau symbol and the word "Anthon." Across the centuries the Tau symbol became more elaborated, and today we often find it in the form of a triple Tau.

Four forms of the cross were used during the first centuries of our era: the Greek or equilateral cross; the *crux commissa* or Tau; the *crux decussata* or St. Andrew's cross; and the *crux immissa* or *crux capitata,* also known as the Latin cross. This latter was best known and most commonly used because it was believed to be the form of the cross on which Jesus was crucified. The Latin cross is sometimes called the *cross of Calvary* or the *passion cross.* The cross which is often seen in the hands of the resurrected Christ is known as the *cross of resurrection* and invariably has a small flag attached to it. Sometimes the Latin cross is represented in the form of a tree, and many Christian prayers make mention of Jesus Christ's death on "the tree of the cross."

The monogrammatic Cross was also very popular during the fifth century of our present era. This cross is a modification of the monogram formed by combining two Greek letters, the first two letters in the name of Christ. This device first appeared after the death of Constantine the Great, around A.D. 337. It shows a large letter X transfixed by an even larger letter P. These are the letters Chi (Ch) and Rho (P) of the Greek alphabet. χριστος is the name Christos in Greek. The Monogrammatic cross was cut on wood or stone and written or painted on parchment for amuletic purposes. It was believed to confer upon its wearer the almighty power of the blood of Jesus.

Monogram of the name of Christ engraved on an onyx gem. The letter X transfixed by a large P are the Greek letters Chi and Rho, the first two letters of the name Christos in Greek, meaning Messiah.
(From the "Cabinet de Pierres Antiques Gravées," by Gorlaeus, Paris, 1778.)

The cross did not become the acknowledged symbol of Christianity until the fourth century when the Empress Helena, mother of Constantine the Great, was said to have discovered the *true cross.* Historically, the true cross where Jesus died is believed to have been found during the reign of the Roman Emperor Tiberius, when St. James was bishop of Jerusalem. Therefore the Empress could only have rediscovered it, but according to the Coptic narrative that tells the legend, her excavations uncovered something which had never before been brought to light. She is said to have found three crosses instead of one, which presumably were the true cross and the crosses used to crucify the two thieves who died with Jesus. Since the Empress had no way to identify the cross where Jesus died, she had the body of a dead man brought to her. She placed the body first on one cross and then on another with no visible results, but when she placed the body on the third cross the body came back to life. This third cross, she concluded, was the true cross where Jesus was crucified.

The Empress sent a portion of the cross to her son Constantine and reburied the rest in the church which she had built over the side of Golgotha. Constantine sent a portion of the cross to the Pope, and this relic is still preserved in the Vatican.

The Latin cross is sometimes shown with two cross-pieces, instead of one. The second cross-piece, which is slightly smaller than the original one, symbolizes the scroll that was nailed to the cross giving Jesus' name and his title as King of the Jews. In this aspect, the Latin cross is known as the *cross of Lorraine* and of the *Knights Hospitallers*. Sometimes a third cross-piece is added to the cross of Lorraine around the area where the feet of Jesus were crucified.

The original scroll where the name of Jesus was inscribed in Hebrew, Greek and Latin is said to have been found by the Empress Helena, together with the nails used to crucify Jesus. These relics were discovered by accident in the church of St. Croce in Rome in A.D. 492. Almost immediately, Pope Alexander III published a Papal Bull or declaration certifying their authenticity.

The discovery of the true cross by Empress Helena and its acceptance by the Pope created an aura of added mysticism and supernatural power to the already revered symbol of the cross. It was immediately put into use as an amulet of great powers, believed to dispel the forces of evil and to surround its wearer with a protective shield of light.

The Empress herself, (who was later canonized by the Catholic church and hailed as St. Helena) was and is still used in magical spells, especially for love purposes. A very popular love spell calls for the use of four golden nails, a green silk handkerchief, the photograph of the loved one, and a small cardboard image of St. Helena. The photograph is nailed to the image of the saint and then it is tied with five knots in the green handkerchief. A special prayer is said in honor of St. Helena for nine days. At the end of this period, the spell is completed and the person desired will surrender to the one casting the spell.

The habit of making a cross over themselves became also a protective action among Christians, who used it particularly as a defensive measure against the powers of Satan. The prince of hell and his demonic hordes are said to live in abject terror of the cross, as are all creatures of darkness such as vampires and black witches. In the beginning of the Christian era, when Christians were still being persecuted by the Romans, they made the sign of the cross over themselves to make themselves known to other Christians.

The Christian churches did not encourage the use of the cross as an amulet, and insist to this day that the cross is purely a religious symbol, and should be seen strictly that way. But all their exhortations did not convince the Christian faithful that the cross had no miraculous powers. Undaunted by the assertions of the churches, Christians continued to inscribe the cross on the walls of their houses, on their persons and their property, including their cattle. Every conceivable metal and precious stone was used to create a variety of crosses in every size and for every possible purpose. Most commonly worn on a chain around the neck, the cross superseded its initial religious symbolism to become the best known and most potent amulet against evil. To all intent and purposes the cross carries with it the presence of Christ, and is in fact regarded as Christ himself by those who wear it. To wear the cross means to be accompanied by the spirit of Jesus every step of the way.

THE CRUCIFIX

Although the cross was engraved on tombs and monuments during the second and third centuries, it did not become a public symbol of Christianity until the Emperor Constantine removed the eagle from the shield of Roman soldiers and had it replaced by the Christian cross. This happened around the fourth century, after the Empress Helena claimed to have discovered the *true cross.*

The symbol of the crucifix did not come into being until the cross ceased to be a sign of agony and shame, and became instead an emblem of power and glory. Images of Christ on the cross existed as far back as the fifth century, but they did not appear in the churches until the seventh century. When they did, they invariably

A group of crosses and crucifixes in gold, steel and Limoges enamel. The cross on the upper right is inscribed with astrological signs of the zodiac. The one on the lower right is a crucifix version of the Russian Orthodox Cross.

depicted Jesus fully clothed. After the eleventh century clothing became less obvious until the present-day loin cloth was adopted.

The halo, which is often found on early scenes of the Crucifixion, and which later adorned the heads of all the saints, is of pagan origin like the cross. It seems to have been at first a symbol of power rather than of holiness. It probably represented the rays of the sun, a symbol of life and divinity in all ancient cultures. Later on, all powerful men (like Moses and Mohammed) were depicted with halos surrounding their heads. Although the first halos were circular and are still the preferred shape among religious artists, a square halo was introduced in the ninth century and a triangular one in the eleventh century. The halo that has a cross within it is always assigned to God.

Unlike the cross, the crucifix is not a very popular amulet for good luck and protection. The symbol seems to evoke a deep sense of sadness in its wearers and many people believe that although the crucifix is a powerful deterrent of evil, it brings tears and general unhappiness to those who wear it.

Greed and a crucifix were the undoing of one of my ancestors, several hundred years ago. The story is one of many colorful legends on my father's side of the family. It seems that early in the sixteenth century this particular ancestor of ours came from the ancient city of Salamanca in Spain to the island of Puerto Rico (then known as San Juan Bautista) with the hopes of replenishing with Caribbean gold his dwindling family fortunes. His name was Don Alonzo de Gonzaga, Count of Pezuela, and he arrived on the island with his younger brother Don Alvaro de Gonzaga. After some initial difficulties trying to find an appropriate Indian crew to aid them with their gold prospecting, the two brothers settled in the center of the island, near a village which was to be known later as the town of Lares. They were fairly successful with their gold mining and very soon they had accumulated a modest fortune in gold ore.

The downfall of the two brothers came one night when a stranger appeared at their door asking their help in digging up a large buried treasure. He promised the Spaniards two thirds of the treasure in exchange for their help. The offer was the sort of things dreams are made of as far as Don Alonzo and Don Alvaro were concerned, and they eagerly agreed to accompany the stranger.

They quickly arrived at the site where the treasure was supposed to be buried, a lonely promontory overlooking a precipice. The two brothers felt nervous and uneasy. Their strange companion answered all their questions laconically, and the velvety darkness of the tropical night was hardly dispelled by their oil lanterns. Before they started to dig, their companion told them that they could keep any part of the treasure that caught their fancy but that it had to be divided into three perfectly equal parts. Under no circumstances were they to speak as they dug, nor argue over any specific jewel.

All went fine for a while. They dug in silence until they reached the large trunk where the treasure was hidden. Barely managing to avoid crying out in exultation upon seeing the wooden casket, the two brothers pried it open and stared in fascination at the glittering jewels and gold doubloons within. But a severe glance from their companion brought them back to their senses, and they quickly set out to divide the treasure. They had no difficulty with the division until they arrived at the bottom of the trunk. There, semi-hidden among some remaining gold coins, was a large gold crucifix, so heavily encrusted with diamond, the figure of Jesus was hardly visible. The crown of thorns was made of emeralds and the blood on Jesus' wounds was made of rubies. So great was the brilliance of the gems that the gloomy surroundings seemed to brighten as daylight.

Don Alonzo stretched out a trembling hand to grasp the crucifix, but Don Alvaro's fingers closed firmly over his brother's wrist, stopping him from taking the jewel.The two brothers looked up at each other, their eyes black with greed and anger. Again, Don Alonzo reached for the crucifix, and again Don Alvaro stopped him. With a muffled oath, their vows of silence forgotten, the two brothers sprang to their feet and reached for the curved *machetes* that hung by their sides.

Like a sun that sinks suddenly behind the horizon, the crucifix and the rest of the treasure disappeared from view as if they had never existed. At the same time the light from the lanterns was extinguished and a hideous neighing echoed through the mountain side. Instantaneously the two brothers were lifted bodily and placed on the back of a headless mule whose hoofs drew forth sparks wherever they touched. For endless hours the two brothers sat paralyzed with terror on the back of their sinister mount, as it galloped ferociously across precipices and rocky crevices, the ghastly neighing issuing impossibly from the headless neck of the beast. And all during this time, the two brothers heard the curse that was to plague their family for five generations reverberate in the darkness around them. Thus they discovered that their fateful companion was a suicide who had killed himself after burying the treasure which they had found. His only hope for salvation was to find two brothers who would be so devoted to each other and so respectful of God's laws that they would be able to resist the temptation of the bejeweled crucifix without bickering over it. Because Don Alvaro and Don Alonzo had failed to help him, the spirit had to wait another hundred years before he could try to find two other brothers who might deliver before he could try to find two other brothers who might deliver him.

The punishment for their greed was never to return to their native Spain, and to live in poverty the rest of their lives. The curse was to extend to all their descendants through the next five generations.

According to the legend the curse proved to be very strong, and it took the Gonzagas and their aristocratic descendants several hundred years to overcome their ill fortunes. Finally, in desperation, my great-great grandfather decided to change his noble, but ill-starred name from Gonzaga to the more common Gonzalez, and immediately his luck changed as if by a miracle. When he died, at the ripe old age of 92, he was one of the wealthiest landowners in Puerto Rico. My grandfather, named Alonzo after our unfortunate ancestor, used to tell me this story with much relish when I was a little girl. The old family name was gone but my grandfather's lands, and the spacious country house we called our home, were part of an area known as Pezuelas, named after Don Alonzo de Gonzaga, the Count of Pezuelas.

This story stresses the holy aura that surrounds the crucifix and which makes it unsuitable both as an amulet or as a jewel. The sufferings of Jesus on the cross, so obviously manifest in the crucifix, are far too sacred to be the subject of anything but sadness and quiet grief. These are the very same characteristics that will surround a person who wears a crucifix, according to tradition.

THE SWASTIKA

The Nazis' unfortunate choice of the swastika as their especial emblem has cast a pall of shame and disgrace upon this symbol, which was always one of the most potent signs of power and glory of the ancients. The Nazi choice was not accidental, for Hitler and his followers were said to be deeply steeped in the practice of magic. They staged pagan revivals where young women dressed in earth-colored tunics carried symbols of the old religions, while flanked by large iron swastikas. Their involvement with magic is said to have extended to astrology, rune magic and satanism. Hitler's interest in Nordic mythology is said to have led him to choose the swastika as

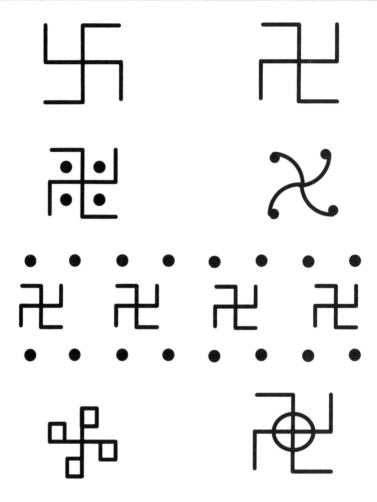

Different versions of the swastika, one of the most powerful magical symbols of antiquity.

the symbol of the Nazi party because it was said to represent Thor's hammer. Thor, the mighty god of thunder of the Nordic myths, was always depicted as a blue-eyed, golden-haired giant whose magic hammer gave him power over all the other gods. This heroic image must have appealed to Hitler as the embodiment of his dream of a superior, golden-haired Aryan race.

The primitive Aryans in all likelihood invented the swastika, which has also been called the *armed cross, gammadion, fylfot,* and *croix pattée.* The gammadion was a cross formed by four Greek gammas, placed in such a position that their angles formed a common center. Some of the early Christian mystics saw in the gammadion a symbol of Christ as the cornerstone of the church. But those who identified the gammadion with the swastika probably confused the equilateral cross used by the pagans with the swastika. In truth there is little or no similarity between the two symbols. In a similar instance, the fylfot, which has been described as "an equal-armed cross of which each arm is continued rectangularly, all clockwise or counterclockwise," is probably a version of the swastika, but not the swastika itself.

The early Christians used the swastika sometimes as the equivalent of the cross. As the symbol was often inscribed on the catacombs, it is possible the Christian's intention was to protect the dead by means of the swastika.

The Dance of Shiva, symbolized by the swastika. Shiva is the Lord of the Dance and his dancing creates the motions that bring about changes in the cosmos. The circle of fire which surrounds him symbolizes the life of the universe, while the flame in his hand signifies the fire with which he will destroy the world one day. Copper. South of India. Ca. A.D. 800. *(Victoria and Albert Museum.)*

Most modern scholars agree that the swastika is probably of Aryan origin, and the name itself comes from India. It is derived from the roots *su,* which means "well" and *asti,* which means "being." Therefore the overall meaning of the word is given as "fortunate" and "lucky."

There are two versions of the swastika. One of them, the version chosen by the Nazis, has arms pointing to the right. It represents the vernal sun. The second version is called the *sauvastika* and has arms that point to the left. It is a symbol of the autumnal sun and of total destruction. Some authorities identify the swastika with the god Ganesa and the male principle. The sauvastika, on the other hand, is identified with the goddess Kali and the female principle. Shiva's dance is also seen in the swastika, which is said to symbolzie the movement of the four seasons and the turn of the earth in the four cardinal points. Movement is believed to be the essence of life by most occultists. The circular movement, particularly, is seen as the power-generating motion. When they want to build their cone of power, witches move clockwise, holding hands and forming a circle. Dervishes whirl, indians swirl, shamans turn, all following Shiva's dance and the form of the swastika.

The Chinese also knew the swastika, which they called *Lei Wen,* meaning "thunder scroll." This name brings to mind the Nordic myth that indentifies the swastika as Thor's hammer, and Thor as the thunder god of mythical Aasgard. All of which underlines the universality of symbolic meanings among vastly different cultures.

The swastika was often engraved on the pedestals of Buddha statues and on the breasts of images and figures of Bodhisattvas, which is the name given to those who will someday become Buddhas. As a Chinese hieroglyphic, the swastika means prosperity, good luck and long life. It means the same in Japan and in most other ethnic societies. Although not commonly used as an amulet, the swastika is still an important magical symbol, very much in use in special magical rites, for both good and evil purposes.

THE STAR

From time immemorial the star has been a symbol of hope. There are many types of stars used for amuletic purposes, but the most popular are the pentagram, the Star of David or hexagram, and the octagon or eight-rayed star.

The eight-rayed star of Ishtar protects a boundary stone in ancient Babylonia.

The eight-rayed star is an attribute of Mars and is mostly used in talismanic magic to invoke the powers of that planet and to subjugate them to the will of the magician. But it has also been identified with the Star of the Magi, a symbol of hope, and with the *etoile flamboyante* or flaming star of Masonic symbolism. Another authority sees the eight-rayed star as a symbol of the law of equilibrium; the balance between spirit and matter, male and female, the inner and the outer bodies. It is the book of the apocalypse sealed with seven seals, and thus represents the inner realization and the outer realization, the birth of the soul and the birth of the body. The eight-rayed star is depicted clearly in The Star card, one of the Major Arcana of the Tarot deck. Its principle meaning is hope, and many knowledgeable occultists use the symbol for spiritual enlightenment and general protection.

The pentagram, as we mentioned earlier, can be of two types. The best known type has one point uppermost and is said to symbolize a person with outstretched arms and legs. It is a symbol of humanity's surrender to God's will and as such it represents white magic. The second version shows two points uppermost, and is a representation of Satan and black magic. But this is rather a

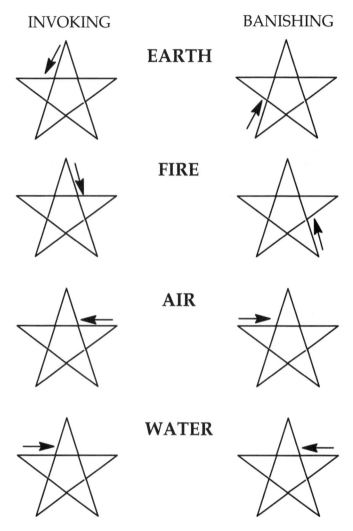

The various invoking and banishing pentagrams using the four elements in their directions.

simplification of the symbolism of the pentagram. In magic, its meaning is infinitely more complex.

The pentagram represents eternal spirit controlling the four elements—air, fire, water, and earth. The uppermost point symbolizes spirit, represented magically by a wheel. The upper left point symbolizes air, represented by the figure of a man. The upper right point symbolizes water, represented by the figure of an eagle. The lower left point symbolizes earth, represented by the figure of a bull. The lower right point symbolizes fire, represented by the figure of a lion. The four elements and their symbols are also identified with the four beasts of Ezekiel's vision and with the four zodiacal triplicities, represented by Aquarius, Scorpio, Taurus and Leo.*

The pentagram is often worn as a symbol by magicians, but usually the symbol is personally drawn by the one who is going to wear it, using certain determined colors and materials. Perhaps the most effective protective use that can be made of the pentagram is the Banishing Ritual, which is standard procedure among all witches and magicians before every major ceremony.** The ritual calls for the drawing of the pentagram in the air on the four cardinal points, starting on the east and moving clockwise within the circle. For banishing purposes, the pentagram is drawn beginning on the lower left point and moving from there to the uppermost point. The Banishing Ritual is said to rid the individual who conducts it from all forms of negative vibrations and also to purify the room where it is conducted. Many magicians recommend to occult students the practice of the Banishing Ritual every night as a protection against evil and against possible psychic attacks.

The companion of the Banishing Ritual is the Invoking Ritual which is basically the same, except the pentagram is drawn starting at the top and moving to the lower left point. Both these pentagrams belong to the element earth. The other three elements also have their own pentagrams, each drawn from a different point in the star.

The pentagram is often seen together with a crescent or half moon. This is a very ancient symbol, which was popular among the Himayarites and other peoples of Arabia, as well as among the Abyssinians and the Turks. It appears in many Arabic flags and is one of the traditional symbols associated with witchcraft. Today the pentagram and the crescent are so popular as amulets, they can be found in a variety of metals and with magical inscriptions. They appear in the form of rings, earrings, necklaces, bracelets, brooches, hair ornaments, and even key rings. Shirts, scarves, and even bumper stickers show the ancient symbols, loudly proclaiming a slow, but steady reawakening of old magical beliefs.

---

* See I. Regardie, *The Golden Dawn* (St. Paul, 1970.)

** See M.G. Wippler, *The Complete Book of Spells, Ceremonies and Magic* (New York, 1978) for a detailed description of the banishing and invoking pentagrams and their rituals.

The hexagram is formed of two triangles, which are shown interlaced most of the time. In this form it is known as the Star of David and the Seal of Solomon. This symbol is very important in ceremonial magic and in the preparation of talismans and amulets. The ancient Hebrews saw in the Star of David the union of fire and water, male and female, body and soul. It was also a symbol of God's love for humankind and humankind's love for God. But although the Star of David is considered the central symbol of Judaism today, the Jews did not invent the symbol. According to Robert Graves, the Egyptians used the two interlaced triangles as a fertility symbol depicting the sexual union between the Babylonian goddess Ashtaroth and the god Tammuz, later identified with Adonis.

The hexagram is also known as the signet of the macrocosm, and each angle is believed to project a radiation from the Deity. For this reason it is often called the six-rayed star. It is said to be under the presidency of the name Ararita, which is formed from the Hebrew initials of the sentence translated as: "One is his beginning. One is his individuality. His permutation is one."

'Each of the points of the hexagram, seen as the Star of David, is ascribed to one of the seven planets, with the sun residing within its center. An amulet can be made of the hexagrams, as of the penta-

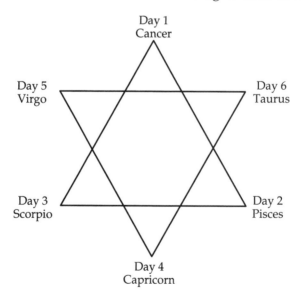

The Hexagram or Star of David illustrating the six days of the Creation and their connection with the signs of the zodiac.

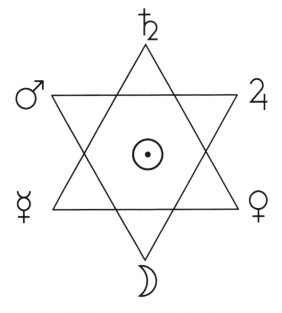

Attribution of the points of the hexagram to the planets.

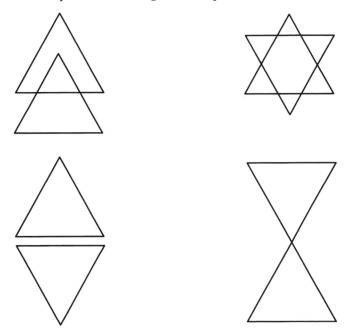

The four different ways in which the Hexagram can be used magically.

gram, using special colors on a black background. Like the pentagram, the hexagram also has a banishing and an invoking ritual which is not used for simple protection as the pentagram, but as an invocation of the forces of the Kabbalistic Tree of Life, as well as the forces of the seven planets. In the rituals of the hexagram the elements are not invoked, as these operations concern strictly the pentagram rituals. During the hexagram rituals each of the planets is invoked drawing the star from its appointed place at one of the six points.

The Star of David is not the only form that can be used for the hexagram. Three other forms are also commonly used in magic. In one of them, the two triangles are superimposed on each other, but both in the same upwards position, none of them inverted. In another version, one of the triangles points upwards and the other downwards, but they are not interlaced, rather their bases touch each other. In the third version, one of the triangles points upwards, while the other is inverted and balanced upon it, both upwards, while the other is inverted and balanced upon it, both tips touching. This latter form is also known as the prehistoric sign *diabolo*, a symbol of male/female sexuality.

A Hebrew amulet for good luck, using another version of the hexagram. From the Book of Raziel.

Like the pentagram, the hexagram, or Star of David, is a very powerful symbol in magic rituals, and is often inscribed or embroidered as a lamen on the breast of the magician's ceremonial robes. Because it is believed to possess the combined strength of all seven planets, it is considered a potent amulet for good luck in every aspect of life. It most extraordinary characteristic is that, like the cross, it is both a major religious symbol and a magical object. And if we look carefully at the various meanings ascribed to the cross and to the star (any form of star) we will find echoes of the same symbolism in both signs. The four elements, the four seasons, the four cardinal points, fertility, and especially life, are the continuing meanings attached to both symbols. All of these meanings translate themselves into creativity, energy, existence, being—all the characteristics that humankind ascribes to God, and which we constantly try to find in ourselves. When we wear the cross or the star we want more than protection, we want self-expression. For the extended arms of the cross, like the outstretched points of the star, are our arms.

PART II:

TALISMANS

Talismans
And How To Use Them

THE WORD *TALISMAN* IS DERIVED FROM THE GREEK ROOT *TELEO* WHICH means "to consecrate." And it is precisely the act of consecration which gives a talisman its alleged magical powers. For contrary to the amulet, which is usually an object naturally endowed with magical properties, the talisman must be "charged" with magical power by the person preparing it. Also, while the amulet is used for general purposes, such as averting evil or attracting good luck, the talisman is always prepared for a definite reason.

According to the famous Order of the Golden Dawn, a talisman is "a magical figure charged with the Force which it is intended to represent. In the construction of a talisman, care should be taken to make it, as far as is possible, so to represent the universal Forces that it should be in exact harmony with those you wish to attract, and the more exact the symbolism, the easier it is to attract the Force—other things coinciding, such as consecration at the right time, etc."*

The "Forces" referred to in the preceding definition are usually planetary or elemental forces, often called spirits, angels or intelligences, depending upon their manifestations. As we have already explained, these forces are concentrations of energy released by the human unconscious by means of a magical act. To aid in the proper channeling and use of the forces, they have been ascribed certain symbols, colors and seals. All this symbology is carefully taken into consideration by the magician during the preparation of a talisman. Chapter three gives some of the astrological correspondences of the planets, such as their colors, metals, and their spheres of influence. Ideally, talismans should be made of the metal ascribed to the planet whose influence is desired. When this is not possible parchment can be used instead, with the planetary or elemental colors taking

---

* I. Regardie, *The Golden Dawn* (St. Paul, 1969).

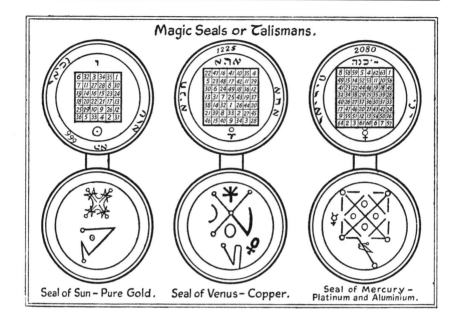

Seals or talismans of the Sun, Venus and Mercury.

the place of the metal. In other words, the parchment is painted with the color of the planet or the element used and all the various inscriptions are made either in black or in the complimentary planetary or elemental color, depending on whether planetary or elemental forces are used.

Chapter three gives the colors and metals of the planets, but we will repeat them here together with their complimentary colors for the magical inscriptions. Also the Kabbalistic number associated with each planet will be given for convenience. This number is important because many of the planetary talismans are made in geometric shapes corresponding to their Kabbalistic numbers. For instance, a Venusian talisman, whose number is seven, would be shaped like a heptagon; a Martian talisman, whose number is five, would be shaped like a pentagon, and so on (Table 3).

Again, chapter three gives a list of the planets and their spheres of influence. For example, Venus controls love and pleasures, Jupiter gives honors and riches, and so on. The seals and sigils of the various planetary spirits used in talismans are also given in chapter three.

Sometimes the magician decides to use the elemental forces,

TABLE 3
PLANETARY ATTRIBUTES FOR TALISMANS

Planet	Color	Number	Complementary Color	Metal
Saturn	Black	3	White	Lead
Jupiter	Blue	4	Orange	Tin
Mars	Red	5	Green	Iron
Sun	Yellow	6	Purple	Gold
Venus	Green	7	Red	Copper
Mercury	Orange	8	Blue	Quicksilver
Moon	Purple	9	Yellow	Silver

instead of the planetary. In this case he or she also uses colors and geometric forms for the preparation of the talisman, as shown in Table 4.

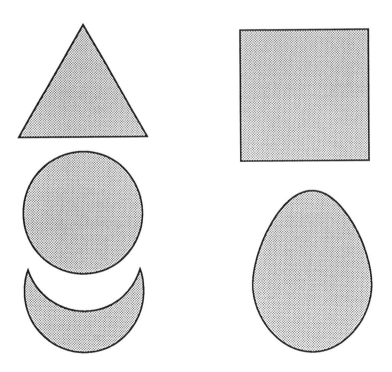

The geometric shapes of the elements.

TABLE 4
ELEMENTAL ATTRIBUTES FOR TALISMANS

Element	Tattwa	Color	Complementary Color	Shape
Earth	Prithivi	Yellow	Purple	Square
Air	Vayu	Blue	Orange	Circle
Water	Apas	Silver	Black	Crescent
Fire	Tejas	Red	Green	Triangle
Ether	Akasha	Black	Silver/White	Egg

Tattwa is the Sanskrit name given to each of the elements. The elements control the following human concerns:

Earth: Business, money, employment.
Air: Health, illnesses, troubles, arguments, disputes.
Fire: Power, dominion, authority, prestige.
Water: Love, marriage, pleasures, happiness, arts, fertility.
Ether: All spiritual matters.

TABLE 5
ELEMENTAL FORCES AND DIVINE ATTRIBUTES

Element	Divine Names	Archangel & Enochian King	Angel	Ruler	King
Earth — Gnomes	Adonai ha-Aretz EMOR DIAL HECTEGA	Auriel IC ZOD HEH CHAL	Phorlach	Kerub	Ghob
Air — Sylphs	Shaddai El Chai ORO IBAH AOZPI	Raphael BATAIVAH	Chassan	Ariel	Paralda
Water — Undines	Elohim Tzabaoth EMPEH ARSL GAIOL	Gabriel RA AGIO-SEL	Taliahad	Tharsis	Nichsa
Fire — Salamanders	YHVH (Jehovah) OIP TEAA PEDOCE	Michael EDL-PERNAA	Aral	Seraph	Djin
Ether — Spirit	Eheieh and Agla	EXARP HCOMA NANTA BITOM	ELEXARPEH COMANANU TABITOM	Yeheshuah and Yehovashah	

This table gives the elemental forces or spirits traditionally associated with the elements, the Divine names of God, the archangels, angels, rulers, and kings, all of which can be used in the preparation of talismans.

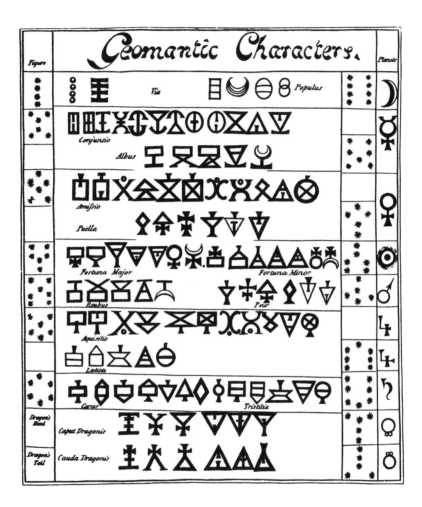

The Geomantic characters according the *The Magus* by Francis Barrett.

All the traditional magical schools recommend that a talisman be prepared by the person who intends to use it. They also advise that the person preparing a talisman become familiar with all the symbology attached to all the various planetary and elemental forces.

For example, in many of the medieval talismans, geomantic symbols were used in connection with the various planets. These symbols, which are commonly used in geomantic divination, also have alchemical connotations. The Minor Arcana of the Tarot, which is divided into the four elements of the ancients (the fifth—ether—represents Spirit and the Major Arcana), could also be used in the preparation of an elemental talisman. For instance, the symbology of the Ace of Cups, pertaining to love, fertility and pleasure, could be used in a love talisman. Of course, all the other Tarot cards could be similarly employed. Other magical correspondences, such as flowers, perfumes, Kabbalistic names and numbers, animals, and other designs can be incorporated in the preparation of a talisman, provided that they are all in harmony with the planetary or elemental force chosen to empower the talisman. Those readers interested in learning more about magical correspondences are directed to a superb treatise on the subject by Aleister Crowley, entitled *777*.

When most of the traditional symbolism attached to the planets and the elements has been understood, it is possible to add a personal touch to the talisman in the form of a favorite slogan or verse, a special design or inscription. The verse can range from a Biblical proverb to a Shakespearean sonnet. The inscriptions can be personal initials, magical symbols or a personalized scribble. The magician should at this point use all his or her creativity to encompass within the talisman all the feelings and the desires pertaining to that which he or she seeks. This will, of itself, invest the talisman with some of the energy it will need to bring about the results desired.

The first thing that must be done prior to making a talisman is to write down, *in one single sentence,* the exact objective pursued by means of the talisman. After this has been done, the magician must decide which planetary or elemental force will be of most help with this particular problem. It is at this point that he or she decides the type of talisman that will be used in order to achieve the goal. If he or she feels comfortable with the magical correspondences (and feels adventurous as well), it is a good idea to create an original design for the talisman, choosing a planet or element and then using all the

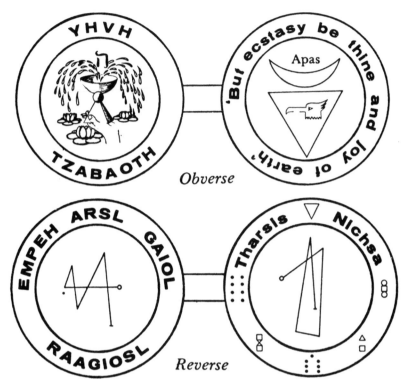

A specially designed talisman of the water element. Its purpose is to bring joy and pleasure to the wearer. All the symbols used in the talismans are ascribed to the element of water, which is the bringer of happiness and fertility according to the ancients.

traditional symbolism of the planet or element of choice. But if there is the slightest doubt about the symbolism to be used, the magician should abstain from designing the talisman him- or herself, and should instead make use of one of the many traditional talismans associated with the various planets and elements. This precaution is important because according to the ancient magicians, the slightest doubt connected with a magical ceremony can cause it to fail, or worse still, to backfire.

PENTACLES, SEALS AND TALISMANS

The word *pentacle* originated from the Latin *pentaculum*, meaning "a little painting." It usually referred to a painted or drawn talisman dedicated to one of the planetary forces. Because the five-pointed star or pentagram was often used in the preparation of pentacles and during the invocation of spirits, the terms pentacle and pentagram soon became identified with each other. Today both terms are used to denote five-pointed stars.

The term *seal* is generally used magically to denote the signature of concentration of a particular spiritual force. This can be planetary, elemental, angelic or demonic in essence. Both seals and pentacles are used as talismans, although sometimes a seal and a talisman are used in conjunction for a specific purpose.

Of all the ancient Grimoires purporting to teach the art of Talismanic Science, the two most famous are *The Greater Key of Solomon* and *The Lesser Key of Solomon*. Although both these treatises are said to have been written by the legendary King Solomon, most occult scholars doubt that claim, and date both volumes around the sixteenth century. *The Lesser Key*, also known as *Goetia*, is a treatise on the invocation of evil spirits. *The Greater Key*, which is the most popular and the most interesting of the two, is a veritable gold mine of information on the preparation of pentacles or planetary talismans. It is true that some of the instructions given on the consecration of the talismans are somewhat exaggerated (who is going to undertake the ritual sacrifice of an unblemished lamb to use its skin as virgin parchment?), but the pentacles themselves are perfect examples of the talismanic art, and could easily be used and consecrated in a less extravagant and yet equally reverent manner.

The languages used in most of the old talismans are Hebrew and Latin. And some of the symbology employed is so ancient that its meaning has been lost in the dust of the centuries. But it is not absolutely imperative for the magician to understand the inscriptions on these talismans. All he or she has to do is copy them as faithfully as possible and consecrate them according to established magical rules. If the instructions are followed carefully, the talismans will work in spite of his or her ignorance because they have been used again and again in the past for the same purposes, and are therefore closely linked to the collective unconscious of the human race.

The following talismans can be used by anyone, provided the instructions given with each talisman are carefully followed. It is good to remember that in the preparation of talismans, as in any other magical undertaking, we are attempting to channel our own psychic energies in a predetermined course. It is therefore wise to adhere to the well-tried methods of the ancient magicians who were, in many ways, more skilled than modern psychologists in reaching the deeper levels of the human unconscious.

THE PENTACLE OF RABBI SOLOMON THE KING

The Pentacle of Rabbi Solomon the King.

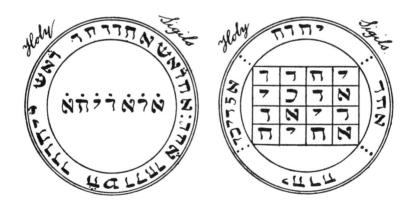

The Most Sacred Seals of Rabbi Solomon the King

This pentacle can be made any day of the week except Saturday. It is said to be a most necessary talisman for the evocation of spirits and very efficacious "for all good." Evil spirits cannot injure the wearer at any time. This pentacle must be worn with the corresponding Seals of Solomon to ensure its efficacy. If both seals cannot be worn with the pentacle, then the first seal alone must accompany the pentacle.

The pentacle can be worn by different types of people and for different purposes. The purpose, however, determines which day the talisman and seals should be made or cut. The following is a list of the days of the week (except Saturday), and when they should be used for the preparation of the talisman.

Sunday should be used by those who occupy authoritative positions or who desire to influence people in authority. If made on this day the talisman should be made of gold.

Monday should be used by people in administrative positions, who both take and give orders. The talisman should be made of silver if cut on this day.

Tuesday should be used by doctors and surgeons, nurses and all others who administer to the general health of others, for Tuesday is ruled by Mars and this is the planet of Medicine, surgery and all associated activities. For those who wish to make the talisman, the mental iron should be used.

Wednesday should be used by those who are concerned with mental health; also manipulative healers such as chiropractors, osteopaths, and psychic healers. In addition, all those whose activities embrace the giving of practical advice for the good and benefit of other people can cut out or make this particular talisman on this day. In making it, silver, platinum or aluminum should be used.

Thursday should be used by all associated with religion and with any form of missionary work, as well as with charitable and philanthropic interests. Sometimes legal interests (where the effort, advice and action are associated with welfare and kindred matters) can be influenced by the making of the talisman and seals on this day, or if the talisman is cut out on this day. The metal used should be tin.

Friday should be used where financial interests associated with the arts and pleasures are concerned. Alternatively it is a day when matters specifically connected with women can be influenced, for the planet Venus has rule over this day and Venus is a feminine planet. If the talisman is actually made, the metal used should be copper.

A TALISMAN AND SEAL FOR THE FRUITS OF THE EARTH

This talisman should be made on a Saturday, when Saturn is in conjunction with Jupiter or Venus, or in a good aspect to Mercury. It is said to be a splendid talisman for farmers, cattle dealers, estate agents, and poultry farmers. The corresponding seal should be worn with this talisman.

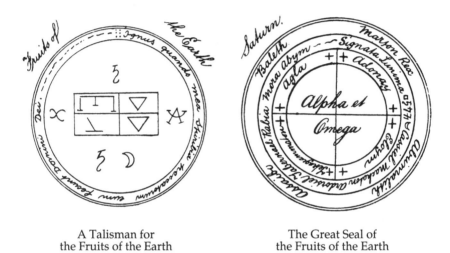

A Talisman for
the Fruits of the Earth

The Great Seal of
the Fruits of the Earth

For those who desire to actually make this talisman, the metal used should be lead which comes under the influence of the planet Saturn. It can be made during the first, eighth, fifteenth or twenty-second hours of the day.

If, instead of making it, the reader wishes to cut this talisman and seal out of the book (or to photocopy it and then cut it out) then that should be done only on a Saturday in one of the hours specified.

In addition, all persons who are in any way connected with mining (coal-mining in particular) irrespective of their actual position in the industry, can use this talisman for the furthering of their interests.

A TALISMAN AND SEAL TO SECURE ELOQUENCE

This talisman with its seal should be made on a Wednesday; of silver, platinum, or aluminum; in either the first, eighth, fifteenth or twenty-second hours of the day.

Those readers who wish to cut out the talisman and seal and place them in a silken bag for safe carrying, should do so on a

A Talisman to Secure Eloquence   The Seal of Eloquence

Wednesday, in one of the hours specified.

The talisman will assist all those who wish to become writers, journalists, or orators and/or who may desire to develop latent abilities for radio, television, stage or screen.

Concentration upon this talisman will intensify natural inspiration and assist in the writing of books and plays, poetry or short stories.

In addition to the characteristics already listed, wearing this talisman will help to promote safety in travel and will protect all those who work on the railway, in the air or who have any connection whatsoever with transportation.

A TALISMAN AND SEAL FOR HONORS, RICHES AND PROSPERITY

This talisman, together with the seal of great prosperity, should be made on a Sunday and, if the use of metal is desired, it should be made of gold. Those readers wishing to cut out the talisman and seal should do so on a Sunday in the first, eighth, fifteenth, or twenty-second hour, placing them in a silken bag.

All those who wish to further their ambitions should certainly carry this talisman and seal, as its influence will enable them to achieve their desires and will help to lift them from mediocrity to relative eminence.

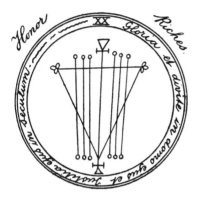

A Talisman for Honor and Riches

The Seal of Great Prosperity

For those who already occupy high positions, this talisman and seal will ensure continuity of their established place and safeguard against the attacks of open or secret enemies.

This talisman and seal are designed for all who desire honor and riches in whatever sphere of activity they may find themselves.

A TALISMAN FOR HEALTH

This talisman should be made or cut out of the book on a Sunday. The metal should be gold. Sunday is chosen because this day is ruled by the Sun, and this luminary governs vitality and the life force. It should be made or cut out in the first, eighth, fifteenth, or twenty-second hour of the day.

Not only is this a very powerful talisman for the preservation of good health, it is also extremely helpful for all persons who are associated with the art of healing.

Doctors, surgeons, and nurses should wear it for it will assist them in their work. It will also aid those who follow natural healing methods, and spiritual healing, as its possession will help both diagnosis and practice.

As an alternative, doctors, physicians, and nurses can make or cut out this talisman on a Thursday, for this day comes under the influence of Jupiter, which is the healing planet. The same hours should be used as were used for Sunday.

Soldiers, surgeons, dentists and veterinary surgeons can use Tuesday as an alternative, as this day is ruled by Mars, the planet that rules any form of surgery, as well as war. If made of metal, it should be made of Iron. The same hours as for Sunday should be used.

The seal to be used with this talisman is the seal of Great Prosperity. Both should be cut or made on the same day.

A Talisman for Health

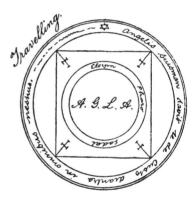

A Talisman for Traveling By
Land or Sea

TALISMAN FOR TRAVELING BY LAND OR SEA

This talisman does not require an accompanying seal. It should be made on a Monday, of silver, or cut out from the book on a Monday, during the first, eighth, fifteenth, or twenty-second hours of the day.

The talisman can be made for the purpose of general travel or for a specific journey and is very helpful if a long journey is contemplated.

It does not matter what particular walk of life a person may be in or what his occupation is, this talisman will be helpful in smoothing out difficulties in travel arrangements. It will help ease the journey so that it is safe and pleasant, and it will also bring contacts with traveling companions of a helpful and cheerful nature.

TALISMANS FOR ALL KINDS OF PROSPERITY

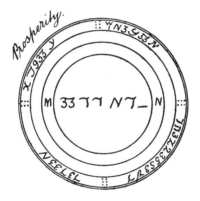

A Talisman for
All Kinds of Prosperity

A Talisman for Trade

The Seal of Trade and Hazard

This talisman, although designed more specifically for business people, can be worn by persons in other endeavors in order to increase their general prosperity.

Those who wish to make the talisman and its seal should do so on a Sunday. It should be made of gold; those who wish to cut the talisman and seal out of the book should also do so on a Sunday, in either the first, eighth, fifteenth or twenty-second hour.

The seal to be used with this talisman is the Seal of Great Prosperity.

TALISMAN AND SEAL FOR TRADE OR BUSINESS

This talisman and its seal should be made or cut of tin on a Thursday. It is said to be helpful to those engaged in any type of business, particularly in those of a speculative nature, such as investment, banking, gambling and sports.

The accompanying seal, also known as the Seal of Jupiter, is said to be one of the greatest assets that anyone engaged in business can possibly have.*

THE GREATER KEY OF KING SOLOMON

The pentacles discussed in this section are from the most famous of all talismanic treatises, *The Greater Key of Solomon.* Like those in the preceding section, these talismans are based on the magical correspondences of the planetary forces. They are to be made on the day ascribed to each planet, and consecrated with the appropriate rituals.

A word of caution is needed here for the reader who may be thinking of making and using these talismans to create magic. To use the talismans properly you must follow a number of complex rituals involving knowing the proper time of the year, the day, and

---

* The talismans and seals given in this section, together with their descriptions, are from *The Book of Charms and Talismans* by Shepharial (London, n.d.).

the hour; how the planets are aspected, etc. Otherwise, you will not attract the proper cosmic vibrations. Unless you are an expert, do not attempt it.

The Greater Key is said to be Solomon's Testament, made in favor of his son Roboam, to whom he speaks in the following excerpts:

> Treasure up, O my son Roboam! the wisdom of my words, seeing that I, Solomon, have received it from the Lord.
>
> Then answered Roboam, and said: How have I deserved to follow the example of my father Solomon in such things, who hath been found worthy to receive the knowledge of all living things through (the teaching of) an Angel of God?
>
> And Solomon said: Hear, O my son, and receive my sayings, and learn the wonders of God. For, on a certain night, when I laid me down to sleep, I called upon that most holy Name of God, IAH, and prayed for the Ineffable Wisdom, and when I was beginning to close mine eyes, the Angel of the Lord, even Homadiel, appeared unto me, spake many things courteously unto me, and said: Listen, O Solomon! thy prayer before the Most High is not in vain, and since thou hast asked neither for long life, nor for much riches, nor for the souls of thine enemies, but hast asked for thyself wisdom to perform justice. Thus saith the Lord: According to thy word have I given unto thee a wise and understanding heart, so that before thee was none like unto thee, nor ever shall arise.
>
> And when I comprehended the speech which was made unto me, I understood that in me was the knowledge of all creatures, both things which are in the heavens and things which are beneath the heavens; and I saw that all the writings and wisdom of this present age were vain and futile, and that no man was perfect. And I composed a certain work wherein I rehearsed the secret of secrets, in which I have preserved them hidden, and I have also therein concealed all secrets whatsoever of magical arts of any masters; any secret or experiments, namely, of these sciences which is in any way worth being accomplished. Also I have written them in this Key, so that like as a key openeth a treasure-house, so this (Key) alone may open the knowledge and understanding of magical arts and sciences . . .*

Solomon then proceeds to instruct his beloved son in all the

---

* From Add. Mss. 10862, "The Key of Solomon, translated into Latin from the Hebrew idiom," British Museum.

magical arts. Among the instructions are painstaking directions on how to prepare the magical instruments; what perfumes and incenses to use during the various rituals; which prayers, invocations, curses, and conjurations to employ in coercing the spirits to carry on commands; and how to prepare and use planetary pentacles and pentagrams. To Solomon, both white and black magic were excusable as long as the intention and the soul of the magician were kept impeccably pure. For this reason, the Key abounds with exhortations on the importance of observing God's laws, of not taking His name in vain, and of fasting and abstaining from impure acts for several days before any major magical ceremony. The idea was that the purer the intention, the less accessible the magican would be to the attacks of evil spirits. The following excerpt typifies this attitude:

CONCERNING THE DIVINE LOVE WHICH OUGHT TO PRECEDE THE ACQUISITION OF THIS KNOWLEDGE

SOLOMON, the Son of David, King of Israel, hath said that the beginning of our Key is to fear God, to adore Him, to honour Him with contrition of heart, to invoke Him in all matters which we wish to undertake, and to operate with very great devotion, for thus God will lead us in the right way. When, therefore, thou shalt wish to acquire the knowledge of Magical Arts and Sciences, it is necessary to have prepared the order of hours and of days, and of the position of the Moon, without the operation of which thou canst effect nothing; but if thou observest them with diligence thou mayest easily and thoroughly arrive at the effect and end which thou desirest to attain.

The days, hours and order of the planets were also of great importance:

OF THE DAYS, AND HOURS, AND OF THE VIRTUES OF THE PLANETS

When thou wishes to make any experiment or operation, thou must first prepare, beforehand, all the requisites which thou wilt find described in the following Chapters: observing the days, the hours, and the other effects of the Constellations which may be found in this Chapter.

It is, therefore, advisable to know that the hours of the day and of the night together, are twenty-four in number, and that each hour is governed by one of the Seven Planets in regular order, commencing at the highest and descending to the lowest. The order of the Planets is as follows: ShBThAI,

Shabbathai, Saturn; beneath Saturn is TzDQ, Tzedeq, Jupiter; beneath Jupiter is MADIM, Madim, Mars; beneath Mars is ShMSh, Shemesh, the Sun; beneath the Sun is NVGH, Nogah, Venus; beneath Venus is KVKB, Kokav, Mercury; beneath Mercury is LBNH, Levanah, the Moon, which is the lowest of all the Planets.

It must, therefore, be understood that the Planets have their dominion over the day which approacheth nearest unto the name which is given and attributed unto them—viz., over Saturday, Saturn; Thursday, Jupiter; Tuesday, Mars; Sunday, the Sun; Friday, Venus; Wednesday, Mercury; and Monday, the Moon . . .

Note that each experiment or magical operation should be performed under the Planet, and usually in the hour, which refers to the same. For example:—

In the Days and Hours of Saturn thou canst perform experiments to summon the Souls from Hades, but only of those who have died a natural death. Similarly on these days and hours thou canst operate to bring either good or bad fortune to buildings; to have familiar Spirits attend thee in sleep; to cause good or ill success to business, possessions, goods, seeds, fruits, and similar things, in order to acquire learning; to bring destruction and to give death, and to sow hatred and discord.

The Days and Hours of Jupiter are proper for obtaining honours, acquiring riches; contracting friendships, preserving health; and arriving at all that thou canst desire.

The Key then proceeds to give detailed instructions on the preparation of pentacles:

CONCERNING THE MEDALS OR PENTACLES, AND THE MANNER OF CONSTRUCTING THEM

As we have already made mention of the Pentacles, it is necessary that thou shouldest understand that the whole Science and understanding of our Key dependeth upon the operation, Knowledge, and use of Pentacles.

He then who shall wish to perform any operation by the means of the Medals, or Pentacles, and therein to render himself expert, must observe what hath been herein before ordained. Let him then, O my Son Roboam, know and understand that in the aforesaid Pentacles he shall find those Ineffable and Most Holy Names which were written by the finger of God in the Tables of Moses; and which I, Solomon, have received through the Ministry of an Angel by Divine Revelation. These then have I collected together, arranged, consecrated, and kept, for the benefit of the human race, and the preservation of Body and of Soul.

The Pentacles should then be made in the days and hours of Mercury, when the Moon is in an aerial* or terrestrial sign; she should also be in her increase, and in equal number of days with the Sun.**

It is necessary to have a Chamber or Cabinet specially set apart and newly cleaned, wherein thou canst remain without interruption, the which having entered with thy Companions, thou shalt incense and perfume it with the odours and perfumes of the Art. The sky should be clear and serene. It is necessary that thou shouldest have one or more pieces of virgin paper prepared and arranged ready, as we shall tell you more fully later on, in its place.

Thou shalt commence the writing or construction of the Pentacles in the hour aforesaid. Among other things, thou shalt chiefly use these colours: Gold, Cinnabar or Vermilion Red, and celestial or brilliant Azure Blue. Furthermore, thou shalt make these Medals or Pentacles with exorcised pen and colours, as we shall hereafter show thee . . .

The Pentacles being finished and completed, take a cloth of very fine silk, as we shall hereafter ordain thee, in the which thou shalt wrap the Pentacles. After which thou shalt take a large Vessel of Earth filled with Charcoal, upon the which there must be put frankincense, mastic, and aloes, all having been previously conjured and exorcised as shall hereafter be told thee. Thou must also be thyself pure, clean, and washed, as thou shalt find given in the proper place. Furthermore, thou shouldest have the Sickle or Knife of Magical Art, with the which thou shalt make a Circle, and trace within it an inner circle, and in the space between the two thou shalt write the Names of God, which thou shalt think fit and proper. It is necessary after this that thou shouldest have within the Circle a vessel of earth with burning coals and odoriferous perfumes thereon; with the which thou shalt fumigate the aforesaid Pentacles; and, having turned thy face towards the East, thou shalt hold the said Pentacles over the smoke of the Incense, and shalt repeat devoutly the following Psalms of David my Father: Psalms viii., xxi., xxvii., xxix., xxxii., li., lxxii., cxxxiv.

After this thou shalt repeat the following Oration:—

---

* That is, in Gemini, Libra, Aquarius, Taurus, Virgo, or Capricorn.
** The Moon should be waxing, that is, between New and Full Moon.

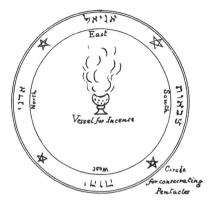

Circle of Solomon to be used for the consecration of Pentacles.

THE ORATION

O ADONAI most powerful, EL most strong, AGLA most holy, ON most righteous, the ALEPH and the TAU, the Beginning and the End; Thou Who hast established all things in Thy Wisdom; Thou Who has chosen Abraham Thy faithful servant, and has promised that in his seed shall all nations of the earth be blessed, which seed Thou hast multiplied as the Stars of Heaven; Thou Who hast appeared unto Thy servant Moses in flame in the midst of the Burning Bush, and hast made him walk with dry feet through the Red Sea; Thou Who gavest the Law to him upon Mount Sinai; Thou Who hast granted unto Solomon Thy Servant these Pentacles by Thy great Mercy, for the preservation of Soul and of Body; we most humbly implore and supplicate Thy Holy Majesty, that these Pentacles may be consecrated by Thy power, and prepared in such manner that they may obtain virtue and strength against all Spirits, through Thee, O Most Holy ADONAI, Whose Kingdom, Empire, and principality remaineth and endureth without end.

The Key gives a specific number of pentacles in their traditional order, since there are so many, I have selected a few of each as examples.

HERE FOLLOW THE HOLY PENTACLES, EXPRESSED IN THEIR PROPER FIGURES AND CHARACTERS, TOGETHER WITH THEIR ESPECIAL VIRTUES: FOR THE USE OF THE MASTER OF ART.

THE ORDER OF THE PENTACLES

(1) Seven Pentacles consecrated to Saturn = Black.
(2) Seven Pentacles consecrated to Jupiter = Blue.
(3) Seven Pentacles consecrated to Mars = Red.
(3) Seven Pentacles consecrated to the Sun = Yellow.
(4) Five Pentacles consecrated to Venus = Green.
(5) Five Pentacles consecrated to Mercury = Mixed Colours.
(6) Six Pentacles consecrated to the Moon = Silver.

SATURN

The First Pentacle of Saturn. This Pentacle is of great value and utility for striking terror into the Spirits. Wherefore, upon its being shown to them they submit, and kneeling upon the earth before it, they obey.

PENTACLES OF SATURN

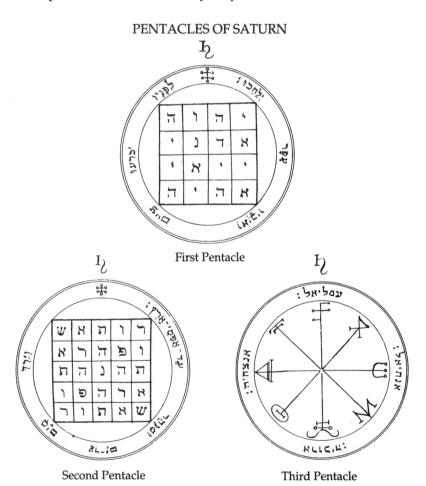

First Pentacle

Second Pentacle   Third Pentacle

*Editor's Note:** The Hebrew letters within the square are the four great Names of God which are written with four letters: IHVH, Yod, He, Vau, He; ADNI, Adonai; IIAI, Yiai (this Name has the same Numerical value in Hebrew as the Name EL); and AHIH, Eheieh. The Hebrew versicle which surrounds it is from Psalm lxxii. 9: "The Ethiopians shall kneel before Him, His enemies shall lick the dust."**

The Second Pentacle of Saturn. This Pentacle is of great value against adversities; and of especial use in repressing the pride of the Spirits.

Editor's Note: This is the celebrated

```
S A T O R
A R E P O
T E N E T
O P E R A
R O T A S,
```

the most perfect existing form of double acrostic, as far as the arrangement of the letters is concerned; it is repeatedly mentioned in the records of medieval Magic; and, save to very few, its derivation from the present pentacle has been unknown. It will be seen at a glance that it is a square of five, giving twenty-five letters, which, added to the unity, gives twenty-six, the numerical value of IHVH. The Hebrew versicle surrounding it is taken from Psalm lxxii, 8: "His dominion shall be also from the one sea to the other, and from the flood unto the world's end." This passage consists also of exactly twenty-five letters, and its total numerical value (considering the final letters with increased numbers), added to that of the name Elohim, is exactly equal to the total numerical value of the twenty-five letters in the Square.

The Third Pentacle of Saturn. This should be made within the Magical Circle, and it is good for use at night when thou invokest the Spirits of the nature of Saturn.

Editor's Note. The characters at the ends of the rays of the Mystic Wheel are Magical Characters of Saturn. Surrounding it are the Names of the Angels: Omeliel, Anachiel, Arauchiah, and Anazachia, written in Hebrew.

---

* The "editor" in these notes is S. Liddell MacGregor Mathers, one of the founders of the famous occult society, *The Golden Dawn.*

** The translations of Biblical passages in this work differ from the King James' version of the Bible, and are probably MacGregor Mathers' own translation of the scriptures. But since MacGregor Mathers was an accomplished Biblical scholar, his translation was based on careful research.

JUPITER

The First Pentacle of Jupiter. This serveth to invoke the Spirits of Jupiter, and especially those whose Names are written around the Pentacle, among whom Parasiel is the Lord and Master of Treasures, and teacheth how to become possessor of places wherein they are.

This Pentacle is composed of Mystical Characters of Jupiter. Around it are the Names of the Angels: Netoniel, Devachiah, Tzedeqiah, and Parasiel, written in Hebrew.

PENTACLES OF JUPITER

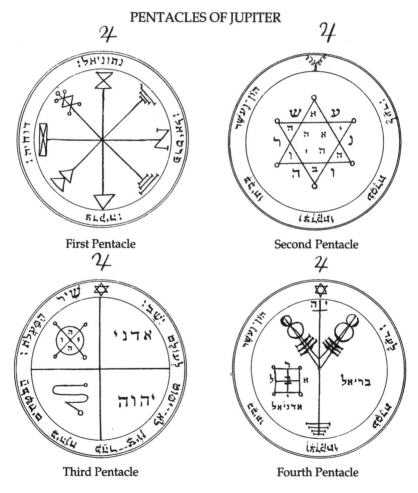

First Pentacle   Second Pentacle

Third Pentacle   Fourth Pentacle

The Second Pentacle of Jupiter. This is proper for acquiring glory, honours, dignities, riches, and all kinds of good, together with great tranquillity of mind; also to discover Treasures and chase away the Spirits who preside over them. It should be written upon virgin paper or parchment, with the pen of the swallow and the blood of the screech-owl.

Editor's Note. In the centre of the Hexagram are the letters of the Name AHIH, Eheieh; in the upper and lower angles of the same, those of the Name AB, the Father; in the remaining angles those of the Name IHVH. I believe the letters outside the Hexagram in the re-entering angles to be intended for those of the first two words of the versicle, which is taken from Psalm cxii. 3: "Wealth and Riches are in his house, and his righteousness endureth for ever."

The Third Pentacle of Jupiter. This defendeth and protecteth those who invoke and cause the Spirits to come. When they appear show them this Pentacle, and immediately they will obey.

Editor's Note. In the upper left corner is the Magical Seal of Jupiter with the letters of the Name IHVH. In the others are the Seal of the Intelligence of Jupiter, and the Names Adonai and IHVH. Around it is the versicle from Psalm cxxv. 1: "A Song of degrees. They that trust in IHVH shall be as Mount Zion, which cannot be removed, but abideth for ever."

The Fourth Pentacle of Jupiter. It serveth to acquire riches and honour, and to possess much wealth. Its Angel is Bariel. It should be engraved upon silver in the day land hour of Jupiter when he is in the Sign Cancer.

MARS

The First Pentacle of Mars. It is proper for invoking Spirits of the Nature of Mars, especially those which are written in the Pentacle.

Editor's Note. Mystical Characters of Mars, and the Names of the four Angels: Madimkiel, Bartzachiah, Eschiel, and Ithuriel written in Hebrew around the Pentacle.

The Second Pentacle of Mars. This Pentacle serveth with great success against all kinds of diseases, if it be applied unto the afflicted part.

Editor's Note. The letter Hé, in the angles of the Hexagram. Within the same the Names IHVH, IHSHVH Yeheshuah (the mystic Hebrew Name for Joshua or Jesus, formed of the ordinary IHVH with the letter SH placed therein as emblematical of the Spirit), and Elohim. Around it is the sentence, John i. 4: "In Him was life, and the life was the light of man." This *may* be adduced as an argument of the greater antiquity of the first few mystical verses of the Gospel of St. John.

The Third Pentacle of Mars. It is of great value for exciting war, wrath, discord, and hostility; also for resisting enemies, and striking terror into rebellious Spirits; the Names of God the All Powerful are therein expressly marked.

Editor's Note. The letters of the Names Eloah and Shaddai. In the Centre is the great letter Vau, the signature of the Qabalistic microprosopus. Around is the versicle from Psalm lxxvii. 13: "Who is so great a God as our Elohim?"

PENTACLES OF MARS

First Pentacle

Second Pentacle

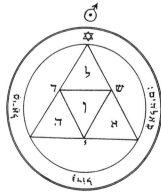

Third Pentacle

THE SUN

The First Pentacle of the Sun. The countenance of Shaddai the Almighty, at whose aspect all creatures obey, and the Angelic Spirits do reverence on bended knees.

Editor's Note. This singular Pentacle contains the head of the great Angel Methraton or Metatron, the vice-regent and representative of Shaddai, who is called the Prince of Countenance, and the right-hand masculine Cherub of the Ark, as Sandalphon is the left and feminine. On either side is the Name "El Shaddai." Around is written in Latin:— "Behold His face and form by Whom all things were made, and Whom all creatures obey."

PENTACLES OF THE SUN

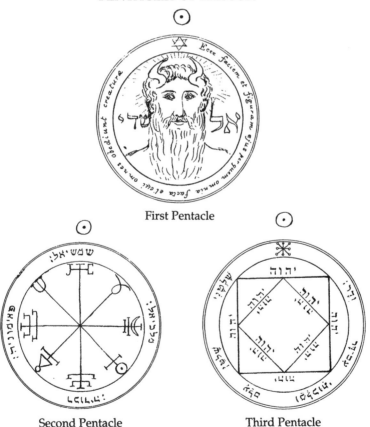

First Pentacle

Second Pentacle   Third Pentacle

The Second Pentacle of the Sun. This Pentacle, and the preceding and following, belong to the nature of the Sun. they serve to repress the pride and arrogance of the Solar Spirits, which are altogether proud and arrogant by their nature.

Editor's Note. Mystical characters of the Sun and the Names of the Angels: Shemeshiel, Paimoniah, Rekhodiah, and Malkhiel.

The Third Pentacle of the Sun. This serveth in addition (to the effects of the two preceding) to acquire Kingdom and Empire, to inflict loss, and to acquire renown and glory, especially through the Name of God, Tetragrammaton, which therein is twelve times contained.

Editor's Note. The Name IHVH, twelve times repeated; and a versicle somewhat similar to Daniel iv. 34: "My Kingdom is an everlasting Kingdom, and my dominion endureth from age unto age."

VENUS

The First Pentacle of Venus. This and those following serve to control the Spirits of Venus, and especially those herein written.*

Editor's Note. Mystical Characters of Venus, and the Names of the Angels: Nogahiel, Acheliah, Socodiah (or Socohiah) and Nangariel.

The Second Pentacle of Venus. These Pentacles are also proper for obtaining grace and honour, and for all things which belong unto Venus, and for accomplishing all thy desires herein.

Editor's Note. The letters round and within the Pentagram form the Names of Spirits of Venus. The versicle is from Canticles viii. 6: "Place me as a signet upon thine heart, as a signet upon thine arm, for love is strong as death."

The Third Pentacle of Venus. This, if it be only shown unto any person, serveth to attract love. Its Angel Monachiel should be invoked in the day and hour of Venus, at one o'clock or at eight.

Editor's Note. The following Names are written within the Figure: IHVH, Adonai, Ruach, Achides, AEgalmiel, Monachiel, and Degaliel. The versicle is from Genesis 1, 28: "And the Elohim blessed them, and the Elohim said unto them, Be ye fruitful, and multiply, and replenish the earth, and subdue it."

The Fourth Pentacle of Venus. It is of great power, since it compels the Spirits of Venus to obey, and to force on the instant any person thou wishest to come unto thee.

---

* The First Pentacle of Venus is not included in the illustration.

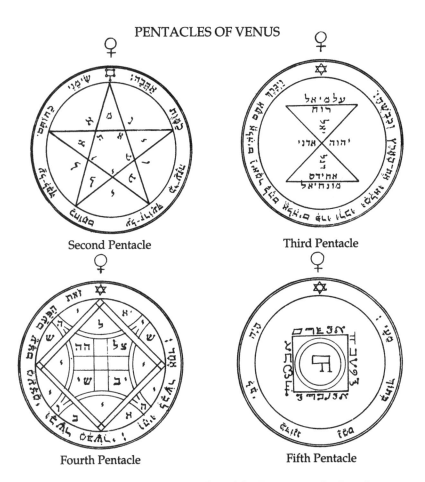

PENTACLES OF VENUS

Second Pentacle

Third Pentacle

Fourth Pentacle

Fifth Pentacle

Editor's Note. At the four Angles of the Figure are the four letters of the Name IHVH. The other letters form the Names of Spirits of Venus, e.g.: Schii, Eli, Ayib, etc. The versicle is from Genesis ii. 23;24: "This is bone of my bones, and flesh of my flesh. And they two were one flesh."

The Fifth and Last Pentacle of Venus. When it is only shown unto any person soever, it inciteth and exciteth wonderfully unto love.

Editor's Note. Around the central Square are the Names Elohim, El Gebil, and two other Names which I cannot decipher, and have, therefore, given them as they stand. The characters are those of the "Passing of the River." The surrounding versicle is from Psalm xxii. 14: "My heart is like wax, it is melted in the midst of my bowels."

MERCURY

The First Pentacle of Mercury. It serveth to invoke the spirits who are under the Firmament.

Editor's Note. Letters forming the names of the Spirits Yekahel and Agiel.

The Second Pentacle of Mercury. The Sprits herein written serve to bring to effect and to grant things which are contrary unto the order of Nature; and which are not contained under any other head. They easily give answer, but they can with difficulty be seen.

PENTACLES OF MERCURY

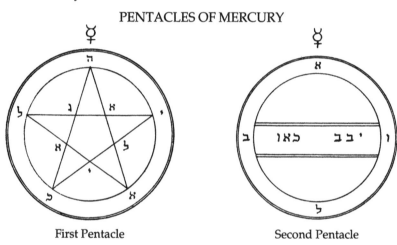

First Pentacle   Second Pentacle

THE MOON

The First Pentacle of the Moon. This and the following serve to call forth and invoke the Spirits of the Moon; and it further serveth to open doors, in whatever way they may be fastened.*

Editor's Note. The Pentacle is a species of hieroglyphic representation of door or gate. In the centre is written the Name IHVH. On the right hand are the Names IHV, IHVH, AL, and IHH. On the left hand are the Names of the Angels: Schioel, Vaol, Yashiel, and Vehiel. The versicle above the Names on either side is from Psalm cvii. 16: "He hath broken the Gates of brass, and smitten the bars of iron in sunder.'

The Second Pentacle of the Moon. This serveth against all

---

* The First Pentacle of the Moon is not included in the illustrations.

perils and dangers by water, and if it should chance the Spirits of the Moon should excite and cause great rain and exceeding tempests about the Circle, in order to astonish and terrify thee; on showing unto them this Pentacle, it will all speedily cease.

Editor's Note. A hand pointing to the Name EL, and to that of the Angel Abariel. The versicle is from Psalm lvi. II: "In Elohim have I put my trust, I will not fear, what can man do unto me?"

The Third Pentacle of the Moon. This being duly borne with thee when upon a journey, If if be properly made, serveth against all attacks by night, and against every kind of danger and peril by water.

PENTACLES OF THE MOON

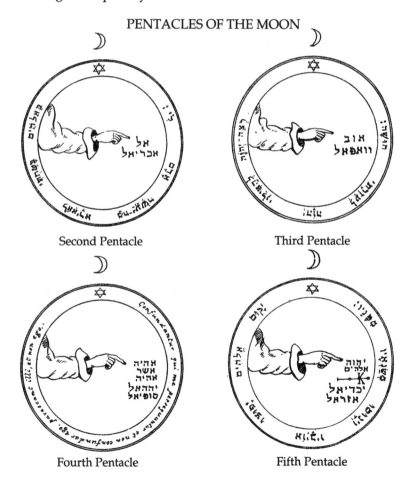

Second Pentacle

Third Pentacle

Fourth Pentacle

Fifth Pentacle

Editor's Note. The Names Aub and Vevaphel. The versicle is from Psalm xl. 13: "Be pleased O IHVH to deliver me, O IHVH make haste to help me."

The Fourth Pentacle of the Moon. This defendeth thee form all evil sorceries, and from all injury unto soul or body. Its Angel, Sophiel, giveth the knowledge of the virtue of all herbs and stones; and unto whomsoever shall name him, he will procure the knowledge of all.

Editor's Note. The Divine Name Eheieh Asher Eheieh; and the Names of the Angels Yahel and Sophiel. The versicle is: "Let them be confounded who persecute me, and let me not be confounded; let them fear, and not I."

The Fifth Pentacle of the Moon. It serveth to have answers in sleep. Its Angel Iachadiel serveth unto destruction and loss, as well as unto the destruction of enemies. Thou mayest also call upon him by Abdon and Dalé against all Phantoms of the night, and to summon the souls of the departed from Hades.

Editor's Note. The Divine Names IHVH and Elohim, a mystical character of the Moon, and the Names of the Angels Iachadiel and Azarel. The versicle is from Psalm lxvii, 1: "Let God arise, and let His enemies be scattered; let them also who hate Him flee before Him."

These excerpts and illustrations from *The Key of Solomon* were provided to give the reader a taste of one of the most famous of all magical text books, and to give some examples of very powerful talismans.

THE BLACK PULLET

Another talismanic treatise of great popularity is the *Black Pullet*. It purports to be still another legacy from an old man to his son; this time an adopted son. Though largely discredited by many occult scholars and branded as a spurious and rather unfelicitous work, the *Black Pullet* has an undeniably large selection of talismans and magic rings from which to choose. None of the talismans or rings are of a planetary nature, and much of the symbolism is rather obscure, but the designs are unusual and attractive, and some modern magicians claim to have achieved some results with them.

Arthur Edward Waite, one of the foremost scholars of the occult in modern times, had this to say about the Black Pullet.*

> The *Black Pullet* is far the most curious of its class and there is indeed sufficient individuality in its narrative to lift it much above the paltry impostures with which it connects. Its chief occult interest centres in the series of talismanic rings which it incorporates with the text, itself a species of magical romance. It makes no claim to antiquity, except that it embodies its wisdom, and it does not appeal to Solomon. In a book of Black Magic, as it certainly is, though the Goetic intention is disguised, such modesty makes for virtue. Many of the Talismans seem to be original devices; at least they connect with nothing in occult symbolism known to the present writer. At the same time they are constructed in accordance with the rules laid down by the Fourth Book attributed to Cornelius Agrippa as regards infernal signatures.
>
> The *Black Pullet* reappeared during its own period at various dates, with slight alterations—once as the *Treasure of the Old Man of the Pyramids*, when it was followed by a sequel or companion under the title of the *Black Screech Owl*. It has been reprinted within recent years at Paris in an edition intended for bibliophiles but bearing no indications of bibliographical research. Though modest in the claims which have been specified, the title of the original edition is portentous enough, namely, "The Black Pullet, or the Hen with the Golden Eggs, comprising the Science of Magical Talismans and Rings, the Art of Necromancy and of the Kabalah, for the Conjuration of Arial and Infernal Spirits, of Sylphs, Undines and Gnomes, serviceable for the acquisition of the Secret Sciences, for the Discovery of Treasures, for obtaining power to command all beings and to unmask all Sciences and Bewitchments. The whole following the doctrines of Socrates, Pythagoras, Zoroaster, Son of the Grand Aromasis, and other philosophers whose works in MS. escaped the conflagration of the Library of Ptolemy. Translated from the Language of the Magi and that of the Hieroglyphs by the Doctors Mizzaboula-Jabamia, Danhuzerus, Nehmahmiah, Judahim, and Eliaeb. Rendered into French by A.J.S.D.R.L.G.F." The place of publication is Egypt, which probably stands for Rome, and the date is 740, meaning 1740, which, however, is untrue, as we shall see. It may be said at once that there is no pretense in

---

* See A.E. Waite *The Book of Black Magic and of Pacts* (London, 1898).

the text to fulfill the magnificent assurances of the title.

The work, it has been said, is a romance, and the first thing which it makes clear is that even the addition of a thousand years to the date in the title is insufficient. It is the narrative of a man who "formed part of the expedition to Egypt," and was "an officer in the army of the genius." The reference is, of course, to Napoleon and at best the date of composition is little more than a century ago. While in Egypt, the narrator was sent upon an expedition to the Pyramids, accompanied by some mounted chasseurs. They lunched under the shadow of the "grand colossus," when they were attacked by a horde of Arabs of the desert; the comrades of the writer were slain and even he was left for dead upon the ground. On returning to consciousness, he surrendered himself to mournful reflections in the immediate anticipation of his end and delivered a valedictory address to the setting sun, when a stone was rolled back in the Pyramid, and a venerable man issued forth, who was proclaimed to be a Turk by his turban. This personage did not fail to discover the corpses which strewed the desert, nor to identify their nation. When the officer in his turn was examined, he manifested life by kissing the hand of the ancient man, who, superior to all prejudices which might have been dictated to the ordinary Mussulman by patriotism or religion, took pity on him, revived him by a wonderful cordial which put the wounded man upon his feet, and he followed his preserver into the Pyramid, wherein was the home of the ancient man and a mighty house of Magic. There were vast halls and endless galleries, subterranean chambers piled with treasures, apparitions of blazing lamps, ministering spirits innumerable, magic suppers; above all things there was the Black Pullet. In a word, diurnal life was illustrated throughout by the supernatural; it was a methodised version of Aladdin with an inner meaning by Astaroth. The sage himself proved to be the sole heir of the Magi and the makers of those Egyptian hieroglyphics which are the "despair of the learned," while, not least, he was himself in quest of an heir, for he felt that he was about to pass away. In fine, the French officer, having acquired the Turkish language by means of a grammar which had its root in sorcery, and being thus enabled to converse with his protector, which on the whole seems superfluous, seeing that his protector possessed a talisman which communicated immediate proficiency in all tongues, was instructed in the powers and wonders of twenty-two talismanic figures and the rings cor-

responding to these, as well as in the secret of the manufac-
ture of the Black Pullet, which possessed more skill in gold-
finding than the divining rod in the discovery of water. After
these instructions, in spite of many prayers, and the minis-
tries of the genius Odous, the just man expired upon a sofa,
while the fortunate kinsman in philosophy swooned at the
feet of his benefactor. In due course, accompanied by the genius who has been transferred to his service, the French officer
managed to depart from Egypt, laden with treasures, and
with the ashes of the sage in a costly urn. He took ship for
Marseilles, stilled a tempest on the voyage and returned to
his native country. He made his abode in Provence, spending
his days in experiments with the Black Pullet, or in study,
meditation and rambling.

The twenty talismans and rings of the Black Pullet, as well as
their descriptions, are given here:

I. Serves for the conjuration of celestial and infernal powers. It should be embroidered in silver upon sky-blue
satin. The evoking words are SIRAS, ETAR, BE-
SANAR, at which multitudes of spirits will appear.

II. Gives the love and complaisance of the entire female
sex. It should be embroidered in silver on black satin.
The evoking words are NADES, SURADIS,
MANINER, pronounced with the ring—which should
be on the middle finger of the left hand—pressed
against the lips. This conjuration ensures the manifestation of a genius with rose-colored wings, who, if addressed with the words SADER, PROSTAS, SOLAS-
TER, will traverse all space to transport you to the lady
of your heart . . .

III. Discovers all treasures and ensures their possession.
The figure of the talisman should be embroidered in
gold upon green satin. The words ONAIM,
PERANTES, RASONASTOS, will cause the appear-
ance of seven genii *au teint bazané*, each of who will pour
out golden ducats from great bags of hide at the feet of
the sorcerer, the operations of this Grimoire being performed upon a huge scale. *Item*, a black-hooded bird,
will be perched upon the shoulder of each spirit.

IV. Discovers the most hidden secrets and enables its possessor to penetrate everywhere unseen. The talisman
should be of violet satin, with the figures embroidered

Talisman I

The characters should be graven on
the inner side of the ring.

Talisman II

The characters should be graven on
the inner side of the ring.

Talisman III

The characters should be graven on
the inner side of the ring.

Talisman IV

The characters should be graven on the outer side of the ring.

Talisman V

The characters should be graven on the outer side of the ring.

Talisman VI

The characters should be graven on the outer side of the ring.

Talisman VII

The characters should be graven on the inner side of the ring.

in silver. It must be held in the left hand, on which also the ring should be worn, and should be placed close to the ear, pronouncing the words NITRAE, RADOU, SUNANDAM, when a distinct voice will utter the desired mystery.

V.   Will make the most tactiturn man unbosom himself to its possessor, whose enemies will also be forced to confess all their machinations. The talisman should be of gold-coloured satin with the figures embroidered in gold. By placing the ring on the little finger of the left hand, the talisman against the right ear, and by pronouncing the words NOCTAR, RAIBAN, the most discreet man—as I have indicated—will be compelled to unveil his utterly secret thoughts. The addition of the word BIRANTHER will force the enemies of the possessor to declare their projects aloud.

VI.   Sets to work enough genii for the immediate achievement of any work which the possessor may desire to undertake, and for the stoppage of any which may oppose him. The talisman should be of lilac satin with the figures embroidered in shaded silk. the magical words are ZORAMI, ZAITUX, ELASTOT.

VII.   Has the power to destroy everything; to cause the fall of hail, thunderbolts and stars from heaven; to occasion earthquakes, storms and so forth. At the same time it preserves the friends of the possessor from accidents. The figure of the talisman should be embroidered in silver upon poppy-red satin. The magical words are: (1) DITAU, HURANDOS, for works of destruction; (2) RIDAS, TALIMOL, to command the elements; (3) ATROSIS, NARPIDA, for the fall of hail; (4) HISPEN TROMADOR, for hurricanes and storms; (6) PARANTHES, HISTANOS, for preservation of friends.

VIII.   Gives invisibility, even to the eyes of genii, so that God alone shall witness the actions of the possessor. It is accompanied by the power of penetrating everywhere and passing through brick walls. The magical words are BENATIR, CARARKAU, DEDOS, ETINARMI. For each operation the ring must be placed upon a different finger of the right hand. The talisman is of yellow satin embroidered with black silk.

IX.   Transports the possessor to any part of the world, and

Talisman VIII

The characters should be graven on
the outer side of the ring.

Talisman IX

The characters should be graven on
the inner side of the ring.

Talisman X

The characters should be graven on
the outer side of the ring.

Talisman XI

The characters should be graven on
the outer side of the ring.

Talisman XII

The characters should be graven on
the inner side of the ring.

Talisman XIII

The characters should be graven on
the outer side of the ring.

Talisman XIV

The characters should be graven on
the outer side of the ring.

Talisman XV

The characters should be graven on
the outer side of the ring.

that without danger. The potent words are RADITUS, POLASTRIEN, TERPANDU, OSTRATA, PERI-CATUR, ERMAS. The talisman is of puce-coloured satin embroidered with gold.

X. Opens all locks at a touch, whatever precautions have been taken to secure them. The magical words are SARITAP, PERNISOX, OTTARIM. The talisman is of deep blue satin embroidered with silver.

XI. Sets the possessor in any desired house without the preliminary of entering and reads the thoughts of all persons, so that they can be helped or harmed at pleasure. The talisman is of light grey satin embroidered with gold. To know thoughts, place it on your head, breathe upon the ring, and say: O TAROT, NIZAEL, ESTARNAS, TANTAREZ. To serve those who are worthy: NISTA, SAPER, VISNOS, and they will forthwith enjoy every kind of prosperity. To punish your enemies or evil persons: XATROS, NIFER, ROXAS, TORTOS, and they will be immediately delivered to frightful torments.

XII. Destroys all projects formed against the possessor and compels rebellious spirits. The talisman is of rose-coloured satin embroidered with silver. It should be placed upon a table, the left hand imposed upon it; the ring should be on the middle finger of the right hand, and the operator, with bent head, should repeat in a low voice the words: SENAPOS, TERFITA, ESTAMOS, PERFITER, NOTARIN.

XIII. Endows the possessor with every virtue and talent, as well as with the desire to do good. All substances of evil quality can be rendered excellent by means of it. For the first advantage, it is sufficient to raise up the talisman, having the ring upon the first joint of the third finger of the right hand, and to pronounce the words: TURAN, ESTONOS, FUZA. For the second, say: VAZOTAS, TESTANAR. The talisman should be of saffron-coloured satin embroidered with silver.

XIV. Gives the knowledge of all minerals and vegetables, with their virtues and properties; gives also the universal medicine and the faculty of healing all sick persons. The talisman is of orange-coloured satin embroidered with silver. It should be worn upon the breast and the ring in a locket (kerchief) round the neck, secured by

Talisman XVI

The characters should be graven on
the outer side of the ring.

Talisman XVII

The characters should be graven on
the inner side of the ring.

Talisman XVIII

The characters should be graven on
the inner side of the ring.

Talisman XIX

The characters should be graven on
the outer side of the ring.

means of a ribbon of flame-coloured silk. The operative words are: RETERREM, SALIBAT, CRATARES, HISATER.

XV. Gives immunity from the most ferocious animals; gives the means of overcoming them; gives the knowledge of their language; and drives mad animals away. The talisman should be of deep green satin embroidered with gold. For the first three objects, say: HOCATOS, IMORAD, SURATER, MARKILA. For the last: TRUMANTREM, RICONA, ESTUPIT, OXA.

XVI. Gives discernment for the good or bad intentions of any person. The talisman is of black satin embroidered with gold. It should be placed upon the heart and the ring on the little finger of the right hand. The words are: CROSTES, FURINOT, KATIPA, GARINOS.

XVII. Gives all talents and a profound knowledge of every art, so that the possessor will outshine the toil-worn experts—though unqualified by scholarship. Hereof are the advantages of an art which—speaking generally concerning it—is nothing except practical and the quality of its claims is not strained. The talisman, which must be carried on the person, should be of white satin embroidered with black silk. The operative words are: RITAS, ONALUN, TERSORIT, OMBAS, SERPITAS, QUITDATHAR, ZAMARATH, specifying the art which it is desired to possess.

XVIII. Gives good fortunes in any lottery. The talisman is of cerise-coloured satin embroidered in gold and silver. It should be bound upon the left arm by means of a white ribbon, and the ring must be on the little finger of the right hand. The words are: ROKES for a winning number, PILATUS, for an ambes-ace, ZOTOAS for a denary, TULITAS for a quaternary, XATANITOS for a quinary, being careful to pronounce all the words at the quine—an instruction which I do not quite grasp, but if the art or science of the lottery is followed at this day under the old laws, I commend the question to those who are experts therein. This is one of the lesser mysteries of occultism. At cards the same potent formula should be repeated when shuffling for self or partner. Before beginning, touch your left arm with your right hand in the neighborhood of the talisman, and kiss the ring. These little contrivances can be effected, says the honest Grimoire, without exciting the notice of your opponent.

XIX. Gives the power of directing all the infernal hosts against the enemies of its possessor. The talisman is of greyish-white satin, shaded. It may be worn in any manner, and the words are: OSTHARIMAN, VISANTIPAROS, NOCTATUR.

XX. Gives the knowledge of the counsels Infernus (the hierarchy of hell) and the means of rendering its projects abortive, but whether for the ultimate health and weal of the operator's soul there is no guarantee offered. The talisman is of red satin, with the centre embroidered in gold, the border in silver and the figures in black and white silk. It should be worn upon the breast and the ring on the first joint of the little finger of the left hand. The words are: ACTATOS, CATIPTA, BEJOURAN, ITDAPAN, MARNUTUS.

Talisman XX

The characters should be graven on the outer side of the ring.

KAMEAS OR MAGIC SQUARES

The traditional magical squares or *kameas*, the sigils and the hierarchical names that form part of talismanic magic, have come down to us through the works of the Abbot Trithemius, Peter de Abano and Cornelius Agrippa. Most of these were reprinted in the famous treatise by Francis Barrett, *The Magus,* which is perhaps one of the most poetically beautiful books ever written on the subject of magic.

The magical squares of the planets are an important part of the science of talismanic magic. To each planet belongs the number of the Kabbalistic sephira to which it corresponds, as well as the other

TABLES OF THE PLANETS

The Table of
Saturn

4	9	2
3	5	7
8	1	6

The Table of
Jupiter

4	14	15	1
9	7	6	12
5	11	10	8
16	2	3	13

The Table of Mars

11	24	7	20	3
4	12	25	8	16
17	5	13	21	9
10	18	1	14	22
23	6	19	2	15

The Table of the Sun

6	32	3	34	35	1
7	11	27	28	8	30
19	14	16	15	23	24
18	20	22	21	17	13
25	29	10	9	26	12
36	5	33	4	2	31

The Table of Venus

22	47	16	41	10	35	4
5	23	43	17	42	11	29
30	6	24	49	81	36	12
13	31	7	25	43	19	37
38	14	32	1	26	44	20
21	39	8	33	2	27	45
46	15	40	9	34	3	28

The Table of Mercury

8	58	59	5	4	62	63	1
49	15	14	52	53	11	10	56
41	23	22	44	48	19	18	45
32	34	38	29	25	35	39	28
40	26	27	37	36	30	31	33
17	47	46	20	21	43	42	24
9	55	54	12	13	51	50	16
64	2	3	61	60	6	7	57

The Table of the Moon

37	78	29	70	94	62	13	54	5
6	38	79	30	71	22	63	14	46
47	7	39	80	31	72	23	55	15
16	48	8	40	81	32	64	24	56
57	17	49	9	41	73	33	65	25
26	58	18	50	1	42	74	34	66
67	27	59	10	51	2	43	75	35
36	68	19	60	11	52	3	44	76
77	28	69	20	61	12	53	4	45

numbers, which are the sum of the various horizontal and vertical rows of the square. For example, Jupiter is a planetary symbol of the sphere of Chesed in the Tree of Life, whose number is 4. Thus the square of Jupiter has four boxes or divisions, both horizontally and vertically, resulting in sixteen individual units, each line adding up to 34, with a grand total of 136. In other words, all the squares total the same number on each vertical and horizontal row. See, for example, the square of Mars, which represents the fifth sephira of the Tree of Life, Geburah. Each side has 5 units for a total of 25 squares, each line totaling 65, vertically and horizontally.

The Kabbalah teaches that it is possible to impose a sigil, or graphic representation of any name, on the *kameas* or squares. This can be done by ascertaining the numerical values of a name according to the Hebrew alphabet and then tracing a line connecting these numbers on the kamea. This connecting line is what is known as a *sigil.** After the sigil of a name has been found, it can be used either on the squares or by itself for some other magical reason. It is possible, for example, to learn the sigil of somebody's name in any of the planetary squares and then to control him in the particular human endeavor controlled by the planet of the square. To get money from somebody, for example, one might learn this person's sigil on the planetary square of Jupiter or the Sun. For love, one would use the Venus square.

---

* A sigil or seal is a magic diagram that comprises the essence of the name of either a person or a spirit.

Most of the names of the spirits have been discovered through their numbers in the squares, proving once more the tremendous relevance that numbers have in the Kabbalah.

When one tries to find the numerical value of a name and some of the numbers have one or more zeros, the first zero should always be removed. Thus, if a letter in a name has a numerical value of 30, this is reduced to 3, if its value is 300, the number is brought down to 30. Each letter in a name must be transformed into its numerical equivalent in order to find its sigil in the proper square. Please note the two sigils in the next squares to understand this concept well.

4	14	15	1
9	7	6	12
5	11	10	8
16	2	3	13

The name *Vincent* on the square of Jupiter.

V I N C E N T
4 9 5 3 5 5 2

6	32	3	34	35	1
7	11	27	28	8	30
19	14	16	15	23	24
18	20	22	21	17	13
25	29	10	9	26	12
36	5	33	4	2	31

The name *Vincent* on the square of the Sun. (From Israel Regardie's *How to Make and Use Talismans*.)

For those readers who find the Hebrew alphabet difficult to manipulate, we offer the Western alternative in the modern system of numerology, where the letters have the following evaluation:

1	2	3	4	5	6	7	8	9
A	B	C	D	E	F	G	H	I
J	K	L	M	N	O	P	Q	R
S	T	U	V	W	X	Y	Z	

Talismans are best made of the metal ascribed to each of the planetary forces, or of virgin parchment. The symbols are usually inscribed within a circle, which represents the universe as well as humanity. The colors, numbers, perfumes, and other attributes of the force being invoked through the talisman are carefully observed by the magician, as are the day and planetary hour corresponding to the planet that rules the talisman.

The magic square of a planet is often incorporated into its talisman or seal. Some magic squares are made with letters instead of numbers and often the letters form words that read equally both horizontally and vertically. Perhaps the most famous of these squares is the one using the words SATOR, AREPO, TENET, OPERA, ROTAS, which appear in one of the pentacles of Saturn in the Greater Key of Solomon. According to the Key, the pentacle and therefore the words, are of value in adversity and serve to repress the pride of evil spirits. Some people use this square indiscriminately for many diverse purposes, such as gaining love and affection or to acquire riches. This is a mistaken use of the square, as it belongs to the planet Saturn, a negative force evoking feelings of sorrow and restriction. Another authority* however has changed the square slightly to read SALOM, AREPO, LEMEL, OPERA, MOLAS, and in this version the square is used to obtain love and the favor of others.

S	A	T	O	R
A	R	E	P	O
T	E	N	E	T
O	P	E	R	A
R	O	T	A	S

S	A	L	O	M
A	R	E	P	O
L	E	M	E	L
O	P	E	R	A
M	O	L	A	S

The well-known SATOR, AREPO, TENET, OPERA, ROTAS. It is a square of 25 squares, with the following meanings: SATOR = The Creator; AREPO = slow-moving; TENET = maintains; OPERA = His creation; ROTAS = as vortices.

The meaning of the second square is as follows: SALOM = Peace; AREPO = He distills, LEMEL = unto fullness; OPERA = upon the dry ground; MOLAS = in quick motion, or stirring it up into quickness, i.e. life.

The famous magical treatise known as *The Sacred Magic of Abramelin the Mage,* from which the second version of the preceding square originated, gives a variety of magic squares for a multitude of purposes. The use of the squares is accompanied by

---

* See *The Book of the Sacred Magic of Abramelin the Mage,* trans. S.L. MacGregor-Mathers, (Chicago, 1948).

MAGIC SQUARES FOR LOVE

(1)

D	O	D	I	M
O				
D				
I				
M				

(2)

R	A	I	A	H
A				
I	G	O	G	I
A				
H	A	I	A	H

(3)

M	O	D	A	H
O	K	O	R	A
D				
A				
H				

(4)

S	I	C	O	F	E	T
I						
C	E	N	A	L	I	F
O	R	A	M	A	R	O
F						
E						
T						

Magic squares for love and affection.
>   (1) To be loved by one's husband or wife.
>   (2) For some special love.
>   (3) To be loved by a relation.
>   (4) For the love of a single girl.

MAGIC SQUARES FOR SECRETS

(1)

M	E	G	I	L	L	A
E						
G						
I						
L						
L						
A						M

(2)

S	I	M	B	A	S	I
I						
M	A	R	C	A	R	A
B						
A						
S						
I						

(3)

M	A	A	B	H	A	D
A						
A						
B						
H						
A						
D						

(4)

M	I	L	C	H	A	M	A	H
I								
L								
C								
H								
A	D	I	R	A	C	H	I	
M								
A							I	
H				E	L	I	M	

(5)

C	E	D	I	D	A	H
E						
D						
I						
D	E	R	A	R	I	D
A						
H	A	D	I	D	E	C

Magic squares to know the secrets of any person.

(1) To know the secrets of letters.
(2) To know the secrets of words.
(3) To know secret operations.
(4) For the military secrets of a Captain.
(5) To know the secrets of love.

MAGIC SQUARES FOR ILLNESSES

(1)

T	S	A	R	A	A	T
S	I	R	A	P	L	A
A						
R						
A						
A						
T						G

(2)

M	E	T	S	O	R	A	H
E	L	M	I	N	I	M	A
T	M	A	R	O	M	I	R
S	I	R	G	I	O	N	O
O	N	O	I	G	R	I	S
R	I	M	O	R	A	M	T
A	M	I	N	I	M	L	E
H	A	R	O	S	T	E	M

(3)

R	E	C	H	E	M
E	R	H	A	S	E
C	H	A	I	A	H
H	A	I	A	H	C
E	S	A	H	R	E
M	E	H	C	E	R

Magic squares to cure illnesses.
      (1) To cure leprosy.
      (2) To heal ulcers.
      (3) To heal pestilential diseases.

the invocations of the proper spirits at the proper time and place. Like *The Greater Key of Solomon*, this treatise advises fasting and general purification of the body before the undertaking of any magical ceremony. The book suggests a period of six months as the minimum time required for purification and the study of the squares. The aspiring magician is also advised to live alone during this period, to abstain from impure acts and to meditate constantly on his spiritual aims. The purpose of this discipline is to acquire the knowledge of the "Holy Guardian Angel," by means of the squares. Great magical powers are said to develop as a result of the proper observance of this technique.

MAGIC SQUARES FOR GOLD & SILVER

(1)

S	E	Q	O	R
E	Q	A	M	O
Q		S		Q
O			Q	
R		Q		

(2)

K	E	S	E	R
E				
S				
E				
R				K

Magic squares to have as much gold and silver as one may wish, both to provide for one's needs and to live in opulence.

(1) To have coined gold.

(2) To have coined silver.

Because the magic squares are so numerous in this volume, only some of them could be reproduced here, but the interested reader is directed to further reading of this treatise, which is one of the most fascinating and truly mysterious of all occult literature.

ON THE CONSECRATION OF TALISMANS

Although some of the ancient magicians recommended complicated ceremonies of consecration for the proper "charging" of a talisman, in reality the one necessary step that must be taken for this purpose is the concentration of mental power on the talisman. It is, however, important to make the talisman on the day and hour as-cribed to the planet ruling it. The incenses or perfumes used should also be those corresponding to the planet (Table 6). The actual cere-mony can be carried out as follows:

1. Once prepared, the talisman should be placed on a silk cloth the color of the planet. A large sphere of light of the same color should be visualized over the talisman.

2. Read aloud the purpose of making the talisman, which should be written down in one sentence. Be strong and deter-mined that the talisman should succeed.

3. Consecrate the talisman with the element *Water* by sprinkling it with the liquid water. Say "I consecrate this talisman with the element of Water so that it will accomplish my every wish and hope."

4. Pass the talisman through the smoke of the incense as many times as the number ascribed to the planet. For example, four times for Jupiter, six times for the Sun, seven times for Venus. Say "I consecrate this talisman with the element of *Fire* so that it will accomplish my every wish and hope."

5. Breathe upon the talisman the same amount of time as the number ascribed to the planet. Say "I consecrate this talisman with the element *Air* so that it will accomplish my every wish and hope."

6. Sprinkle the talisman with salt and say, "I consecrate this tal-isman with the element of *Earth* so that it will accomplish my every wish and hope."

7. As you consecrate the talisman, visualize the sphere above it becoming smaller, more intense and brighter.

8. Gather all your mental power and direct it towards the sphere, which you then visualize descending upon the talis-man and becoming one with it. This is the fifth and final con-secration in the element of *Ether* (spirit). It is recommended that in order to make the link between the magician and the talisman stronger, the latter should be anointed with a drop of the magician's blood.

9. After the talisman is consecrated it should be wrapped in the same cloth where it laid during the ritual and kept always near the owner. Some magical treatises suggest that the talis-

man be kept in a small silk bag and carried around constantly, always in close contact with the skin. It is also important that the owner of the talisman does not think about it after its consecration because it is said that constant worry and conjectures interfere with the success of a talisman.*

TABLE 6
OF THE COMPOSITION OF SOME PERFUMES APPROPRIATED TO THE SEVEN PLANETS**

THE SUN

We make a suffumigation for the sun in this manner:
Take of saffron, ambergris, musk, lignum aloes, lignum balsam, the fruit of the laurel, cloves, myrrh, and frankincense; of each a like quantity; all of which being bruised, and mixed together, so as to make a sweet odour, must be incorporated with the brain of an eagle, or the blood of a white cock, after the manner of pills or troches.

THE MOON

For the moon, we make a suffume of the head of a frog dried, and the eyes of a bull, the seed of white poppies, frankincense, and camphire, which must be incorporated with menstruous blood, or the blood of a goose.

SATURN

For Saturn, take the seed of black poppies, henbane, mandrake root, loadstone, and myrrh, and mix them up with the brain of a cat and the blood of a bat.

JUPITER

Take the seed of ash, lignum aloes, storax, the gum Benjamin, the lapis lazuli, the tops of peacocks' feathers, and incorporate with the blood of a stork, or swallow, or the brain of a hart.

---

* See F. King, and S. Skinner, *Techniques of High Magic*, (New York, 1976).

** From *The Magus* by Francis Barrett. The "Suffumigations" referred to in this famous treatise have proven too overpowering for most modern magicians, who have settled for less complicated recipes for their incenses. Thus, myrrh or civet are usually burned during Saturn rituals; cedar is used for Jupiter; tobacco for Mars; olibanum and laurel for the Sun; benzoin, rose; or red sandal for Venus; Storax or cinnamon for Mercury; jasmine or ginseng for the Moon; and Ditanny of Crete for the Earth.

MARS

Take uphorbium, bedellium, gum armoniac, the roots of both hellebores, the loadstone, and a little sulphur, and incorporate them altogether with the brain of a hart, the blood of a man, and the blood of a black cat.

VENUS

Take musk, ambergris, lignum aloes, red roses, and red coral, and make them up with sparrow's brains and pigeon's blood.

MERCURY

Take mastich, frankincense, cloves, and the herb cinquefoil, and the agate stone, and incorporate them all with the brain of a fox, or weasel, and the blood of a magpie.

The talismans discussed in this chapter are only a small cross section of the vast treasure house of talismans gathered in countless treatises and grimoires, some dating from thousands of years before Christ. Most of these treatises were written during the Middle Ages, but the sources upon which they were based are so old, they are practically impossible to trace. The *Greater Key of Solomon*, for example, although of fairly recent scholarship, is said to have originated in Solomon's magical practices. In the first century of our era,the Jewish historian Josephus mentioned a book ascribed to Solomon, containing incantations for summoning spirits.

All the medieval magicians, like Agrippa, Albertus Magnus, Paracelsus, and Peter de Abano, among many others, made use of talismanic magic in their occult practices. They believed that talismans were among the most successful methods to contact spirits and to force them to do the will of the magician.

Today talismans and amulets are no longer seen as points of contact with the spiritual world. They are worn mostly for general good luck, and sometimes even as conversation pieces. But as long as they are worn, humans are expressing their faith and hope for the future, and the survival of the human race.

Bibliography

Anon. *The Black Pullet*. New York, 1972.
Anon. *The Book of Raziel*. London, n.d.
Aquinas, T. *Summa Theologiae*. New York, 1976.
Bardon, F. *The Key to the True Quabbalah*. Germany, 1971.
—— *The Practice of Magical Evocation*. Germany, 1971.
Baroja, J.C. *The World of Witches*. London, 1964.
Barrett, F. *The Magus*. London. 1965.
Baxter, R. *The Certainty of the Worlds of the Spirits*. London, 1961.
Bayley, H. *The Lost Language of Symbolism*. London, 1912.
Beadsworthy, P. Trans. *Larousse World Mythology*. London, 1965.
Berne, E. *Transactional Analysis*. New York, 1975.
Bhattacharya, A.K. *Gem Therapy*. Calcutta, 1976.
Binder, P. *Magic Symbols of the World*. London, 1976.
Binder, V.; Binder, A.; and Remland, B.; *Modern Therapies*. New Jersey, 1975.
Birdsell, J. B. *Human Evolution*. Chicago, 1972.
Blavatsky, H. P. *Isis Unveiled*. London, 1967.
—— *The Secret Doctrine*. London, 1966.
Boyd, R.T. *A Pictorial Guide to Biblical Archeology*. New York, 1974.
Breger, L. *From Instinct to Identity*. New Jersey, 1975.
Brennan, J.H. *Experimental Magic*. New York, 1972.
—— *Astral Doorways*. New York, 1973.
Briggs, K.M. *Pale Hecate's Team*. London, 1962.
Brookes, A. *Dictionary of Judaism*. London, 1959.
Buber, M. *The Way of Response*. New York, 1977.
Buckland, R. *Witchcraft from Inside*. Minnesota, 1971.
—— *The Tree*. New York, 1974.
Budge, E. A. Wallis. *Amulets and Superstitions*. New York, 1978.
—— *The Egyptian Book of the Dead*. New York, 1967.
—— *Egyptian Magic*. New York, 1971.
—— *A History of Ethiopia*. London, n.d.
—— *Tutankhamen*. New York, 1975.
Burland, C. A. *Myths of Life and Death*. New York, 1975.
Butler, E. M. *The Myth of the Magus*. London, 1952.
—— *Ritual Magic*. Cambridge, 1949.
Butler, W. E. *Apprenticed to Magic*. London, 1962.
—— *How to Read the Aura*. New York, 1971.
—— *Magic and the Qabbalah*. London, 1964.
—— *Magic, Its Ritual, Power and Purpose*. New York, 1970.
—— *The Magician, His Training and Work*. London, 1959.

Calvani, V. *Lost Cities*. New York, 1972.

Carrington, H. *Your Psychic Powers and How to Develop Them*. New York, 1973.

Cavagnaro, D. *This Living Earth*. New York, 1977.

Cavendish, R. *The Black Arts*. New York, 1967.

—— Ed. *Man, Myth and Magic*. London, 1971.

Christian, P. *The History and Practice of Magic*. New Jersey, 1972.

Clark, G. *The Stone Age Hunters*. New York, 1967.

Conway, D. *Magic*. New York, 1972.

Crow, W. B. *Precious Stones*. New York, 1968.

—— *A History of Magic, Witchcraft and Occultism*. New York, n.d.

Crowley, A. *Book 4*. Texas, 1972.

—— *Book of the Law*. New York, 1967.

—— *Book of Thoth*. New York, n.d.

—— *Magick in Theory and Practice*. New York, n.d.

—— *777*. New York, 1970.

—— *The Confessions of Aleister Crowley*. Edited by J. Symonds and K. Grant, New York, 1971.

Dale-Green, P. *The Cult of the Cat*. New York, 1975.

Dalton, M. *Discovery of Witches*. London, 1618.

David-Neel, A. *Magic and Mystery in Tibet*. New York, 1958.

Davidson, G. *A Dictionary of Angels*. New York, 1967.

Day, H. *The Study and Practice of Yoga*. New York, 1955.

De Givry, E. G. *Illustrated Anthology of Sorcery, Magic and Alchemy*. New York, 1973.

Denning, M. and Phillips, O. *The Magical Philosophy*. 5 vols., Minnesota, 1974.

De Plancy. *Dictionnaire Infernal*. Paris, 1852.

Deren, M. *Divine Horseman: The Living Gods of Haiti*. London, 1953.

Dogigli, J. *The Magic of Rays*. New York, 1965.

Douglas, N., Ed. *Tibetan Tantric Charms and Amulets*. New York, 1978.

Einstein, A. *Ideas and Opinions*. New York, 1954.

Eliade, M. *Rites and Symbols of Initiation*. New York, 1971.

Eliot, R. M. V. *Runes*. Manchester, 1959.

Elworthy, F. T. *The Evil Eye*. London, 1895.

Encyclopedia Judaica. New York, 1971,

Epstein, I. *Judaism*. London, 1960.

Evans-Wenz, W. Y., Ed. *The Tibetan Book of the Dead*. London, 1927.

Farrar, S. *What Witches Do*. New York, 1972.

Ferro, R. and Grumley, M. *Atlantis, the Autobiography of a Search*. New York, 1960.

Fortune, D. *Applied Magic*. London, 1962.

—— *Cosmic Doctrine*. London, 1966.

—— *The Mystical Qabalah*. London, 1951.

Frazer, J. G. *Folk-Lore in the Old Testament*. London, 1919.

—— *The Golden Bough*. 13 vols. New York, 1980.

Freud, S. *The Interpretation of Dreams*. New York, 1961.

—— *Totem and Taboo*. New York, 1960.

Frost, G., and Frost, Y. *The Witch's Bible*. California, 1972.

—— *A Witch's Guide to Life*. Arizona, 1978.

Gaer, J. *How the Great Religions Began*. New York, 1956.

Galilei, G. *Dialogue Concerning the Two Chief World Systems*. California, 1977.

Gamache, H. *Mystery of the Long Lost 8th, 9th, and 10th Books of Moses*. New York, 1967.

Gandee, L. R. *A Strange Experience*. New Jersey, 1976.
Gardner, G. *High Magic's Aid*. London, 1949.
—— *Witchcraft Today*. London, 1954.
Gaster, T. H. *The Dead Sea Scriptures*. New York, 1976.
Gennep, A. V. *The Rites of Passage*. London, 1960.
Ginsberg, C. D. *The Kabbalah*. London, 1956.
Gonzalez-Wippler, M. *The Complete Book of Spells, Ceremonies and Magic*. St. Paul, 1988.
—— *A Kabbalah for the Modern World*. St. Paul, 1987.
—— *Santeria, African Magic in Latin America*. New York, 1973.
—— Ed. *Sixth and Seventh Books of Moses*, New York, 1982.
Goodman, L. *Sun Signs*. New York, 1968.
Goodman, M. C. *Modern Numerology*. New York, 1945.
Graves, R. *The Greek Myths*. 2 vols. New York, 1962.
Gray, E. *The Complete Guide to the Tarot*. New York, 1971.
Gray, W. *Ladder of Lights*. London, 1968.
—— *Magical Ritual Methods*. London, 1969.
—— *Seasonal Occult Rituals*. London, 1970.
Green, A. and Holtz, B. W., Eds. *Your Word is Fire*. New York, 1977.
Gregor, A. S. *Amulets, Talismans, and Fetishes*. New York, 1975.
Gunther, M. *Wall Street and Witchcraft*. New York, 1972.
Haining, P. *The Warlock's Book*. New York, 1973.
Hansen, C. *Witchcraft at Salem*. London, 1970.
Harding, M. E. *Woman's Mysteries*. New York, 1972.
Hartmann, F. *Magic, White and Black*. London, 1969.
Hayes, C. J. H., and Hanscom, J. H. *Ancient Civilizations*. New York, 1968.
Heindl, M. *Simplified Scientific Astrology*. California, 1928.
Herm, G. *The Celts*. New York, 1975.
—— *The Phoenicians*. New York, 1976.
Heussenstamm, K. *Reflections of a Universal Idealist*. Madras, 1968.
Hittleman, R. *Guide to Yoga Meditation*. New York, 1973.
Hoebel, E. A. *Anthroplogy: The Study of Man*. New York, 1970.
Hopper, R. J. *The Early Greeks*. New York, 1975.
Howard, M. *The Runes and Other Magical Alphabets*. New York, 1978.
Howells, W. *The Heathens*. New York, 1918.
Huebner, L. *Power Through Witchcraft*. California, 1969.
Hughes, P. *Witchcraft*. London, 1969.
Hurston, Z. *Voodoo Gods*. London, 1939.
Huson, P. *Mastering Witchcraft*. New York, 1971.
Jahada, G. *The Psychology of Superstition*. London, 1969.
Janov, A. *The Primal Revolution*. New York, 1976.
Johann, B. *Vestitus Sacerdotum Hebraeorum*. Amsterdam, 1680.
Jonas, D., and Jonas, D. *Other Senses, Other Worlds*. New York, 1976.
Josephus, Flavius. *Complete Works of Josephus*. 4 vols. Michigan, 1960.
Jung, C. G. *Dream Analysis*. Princeton, 1972.
—— *Two Essays on Analytical Psychology*. New York, 1971.
—— Ed. *Man and His Symbols*. New York, 1971.
Kaplan, S. R. *Tarot Classic*. New York, 1974.
Kilemen, P. *Art of the Americas, Ancient and Hispanic*. New York, 1972.
King, F. *The Rites of Modern Occult Magic*. New York, 1970.

King, F., and Skinner, S. *Techniques of High Magic*. New York, 1976.
Klossowski de Rola, S. *Alchemy, The Secret Art*. New York, 1977.
Knight, G. *A Practical Guide to Qabalistic Symbolism*. London, 1969.
Kravitz, D. *Who's Who in Greek and Roman Mythology*. New York, 1975.
Kunz, G. F. *Curious Lore of Precious Stones*. New York, 1971.
LaFay, H. *The Vikings*. New York, 1972.
Larsen, K. *History of Norway*. Princeton, 1972.
Leadbeater, C. W. *The Chakras*. Madras, 1968.
—— *Man, Visible and Invisible*, Illinois, 1969.
Leek, S. *Cast Your Own Spell*. New York, 1970.
—— *Diary of a Witch*. New Jersey, 1970.
Leland, C. G. *Aradia, Gospel of the Witches*. New York, 1975.
—— *Gypsy Sorcery and Fortune Telling*. New York, 1962.
Levi, E. *The Key of the Mysteries*. London, 1969.
—— *Transcendental Magic*. London, 1958.
Levi-Strauss, C. *Totemism*. New York, 1975.
Lilly, J. *The Center of the Cyclone*. New York, 1971.
Lippman, D. and Colin, P. *How to Make Amulets, Charms and Talismans*. New York, 1974.
Lissner, I. *Man, God and Magic*. London, 1961.
Llewellyn, M. *Initiation and Magic*. London, 1965.
McCarroll, T. *Exploring the Inner World*. New York, 1974.
MacGregor-Mathers, S. L., Trans. *The Key of Solomon the King*. New York, 1976.
—— *The Book of the Goetia of Solomon the King*. New York, 1973.
—— *The Book of the Sacred Magic of Abramelin, the Mage*. Chicago, 1948.
Magnus, Albertus, Trans. *Egyptian Secrets*. 3 vols. Germany, n.d.
Magus Incognitdo. *The Secret Doctrine of the Rosicrucians*. Chicago, 1949.
Malchus, M. *The Secret Grimoire of Turiel*. London, 1960.
Malinowski, B. *Magic, Science and Religion*. New York, 1976.
Martello, L. *Witchcraft: The Old Religion*. New Jersey, 1975.
Michelet, J. *Satanism and Witchcraft*. New Jersey, 1967.
Middleton, J. *Magic, Witchcraft and Curing*. New York, 1967.
Montagu, A. *Man, His First Million Years*. New York, 1972.
—— *Man's Most Dangerous Myth, the Fallacy of Race*. Oxford, 1971.
Moore, G. *Numbers Will Tell*. New York, 1973.
Mueller, C. G., et al., *Light and Vision* (Life Science Library), New York.
Murray, M. *The God of the Witches*. London, 1967.
—— *Magical Rites and Rituals*. London, 1975.
Neal, J. H. *Jungle Magic*. New York, 1971.
Neumann, E. *The Great Mother*. Princeton, 1975.
Newell, V. *The Encyclopedia of Witchcraft and Magic*. New York, 1974.
Norvell, A. *Cosmic Magnetism*. New York, 1971.
Ophiel. *The Art and Practice of Cabala Magic*. California, 1976.
—— Ouseley, S. G. J. *Colour Meditations*. London, 1949.
Ouspensky, P. D. *In Search of the Miraculous*. New York, 1949.
Pachter, H. M. *Pracelsus*, New York, 1951.
Panchadasi, Swami. *The Astral World*. New York, n.d.
Papus (Gerald Encausse). *Tarot of the Bohemians*. New York, 1965.
Pauwels, L., and Bergier, J. *The Morning of the Magicians*. New York, 1960.

Pearce, J. C. *The Crack in the Cosmic Egg.* New York, 1972.
Pelton, R. *Voodoo Secrets from A to Z.* New York, 1973.
—— *Complete Book of Voodoo.* New York, 1972.
Petrie, W. F. *Amulets.* London, 1914.
Plinius, S. C. (Pliny). *Natural History.* London, 1964.
Powell, A. E. *The Etheric Double.* New York, 1969.
Ptolemy, C. *Tetrabiblos.* Cambridge, 1940. (F.E. Rabban, Ed.)
Randolph, V. *Ozark Superstitions.* New York, 1947.
Regardie, I. *The Golden Dawn,* 4 vols. St. Paul, 1969.
—— *How to Make and Use Talismans.* New York, 1972.
—— *Tree of Life.* New York, 1969.
—— *The Art of True Healing.* London, 1970.
—— *The Art and Meaning of Magic.* London, 1971.
Reik, T. *The Creation of Woman.* New York, 1967.
Rigaud, M. *Veve.* New York, 1974.
—— *Secrets of Voodoo.* New York, 1970.
Robbins, R. H. *The Encyclopedia of Witchcraft and Demonology.* New York, 1959.
Rose, S. *The Conscious Brain.* New York, 1976.
Rubinstein, A., Ed. *Hasidism.* Jerusalem, 1975.
Ruchlis, H. *The Wonder of Electricity.* New York, 1962.
St. Clair, D. *Drum and Candle.* New York, 1971.
Salzmann, Z. *Anthropology.* New York, 1969.
Schaya, L. *The Universal Meaning of the Kabbalah.* New Jersey, 1971.
Schiller, J. C. *Philosophical Letters.* London, 1929.
Scholem, G. G. *Major Trends in Jewish Mysticism.* New York, 1941.
—— *On the Kabbalah and its Symbolism.* New York, 1970.
Sepharial. *The Book of Charms and Talismans.* London, n.d.
Shah, I. *Oriental Magic.* London, 1956.
—— *The Serect Lore of Magic.* London, 1957.
Shirer, W. *The Challenge of Scandinavia.* Massachusetts, 1963.
Smith, B. *Meditation: The Inward Art.* New York, 1976.
Spence, L. *The History of Atlantis.* New York, 1974.
—— *Encyclopedia of Occultism.* New York, 1965.
Summers, M. *The History of Witchcraft and Demonology.* New York, 1956.
Thomas, P. *Hindu Religion, Customs, and Manners.* Bombay, 1960.
Thompson, R. C. *Devils and Evil Spirits.* London, n.d.
Thoreau, H. *On Man and Nature.* New York, 1977.
Torrens, R. G. *The Golden Dawn, Its Inner teachings.* London, 1969.
Trachtenberg, J. *Jewish Magic and Superstition.* New York, 1961.
Waite, A. E. *A New Encyclopedia of Free Masonry.* New York, 1970.
—— *The Holy Kabbalah.* New York, 1960.
—— *The Pictorial Key to the Tarot.* New York, 1970.
—— *The Book of Black Magic and of Pacts.* London, 1898.
Watts, A. *Tao: The Watercourse Way.* New York, 1975.
Wedeck, H. E. *Treasury of Witchcraft.* New York, 1960.
Weiner, H. *Nine and a Half Mystics: The Kabbalah Today.* New York, 1969.
White, J. *Frontiers of Consciousness.* New York, 1973.
Williams, C. A. S. *Outlines of Chinese Symbology and Art Motives.* New York, 1960.
Wilson, J. A. *The Culture of Egypt.* Berkeley, 1951.
Woddin, G. B. *Popular Superstitions.* New York, 1970.

Wooley, Sir Leonard. *Excavations at Ur.* New York, 1965.
—— *The Sumerians.* New York, 1965.
Worth, V. *The Crone's Book of Words.* St. Paul, 1971.
Yates, F. A. *Giordano Bruno and the Hermetic Traditions.* Chicago, 1970.
Yeterian, D. *Exploring Psychic Reality.* New York, 1975.

INDEX

Free Catalog

Get the latest information on our body, mind, and spirit products! To receive a **free** copy of Llewellyn's consumer catalog, *New Worlds of Mind & Spirit,* simply call 1-877-NEW-WRLD or visit our website at www.llewellyn.com and click on *New Worlds.*

☾ LLEWELLYN ORDERING INFORMATION

Order Online:
Visit our website at www.llewellyn.com, select your books, and order them on our secure server.

Order by Phone:
- Call toll-free within the U.S. at 1-877-NEW-WRLD (1-877-639-9753). Call toll-free within Canada at 1-866-NEW-WRLD (1-866-639-9753)
- We accept VISA, MasterCard, and American Express

Order by Mail:
Send the full price of your order (MN residents add 6.5% sales tax) in U.S. funds, plus postage & handling to:

Llewellyn Worldwide
2143 Wooddale Drive, Dept. 978-0-87542-287-9
Woodbury, MN 55125-2989

Postage & Handling:

Standard (U.S., Mexico, & Canada). If your order is:
$24.99 and under, add $3.00
$25.00 and over, FREE STANDARD SHIPPING

AK, HI, PR: $15.00 for one book plus $1.00 for each additional book.

International Orders (airmail only):
$16.00 for one book plus $3.00 for each additional book

Orders are processed within 2 business days.
Please allow for normal shipping time. Postage and handling rates subject to change.

THE COMPLETE BOOK OF
SPELLS,
CEREMONIES
& MAGIC

Migene González-Wippler

The Complete Book of Spells, Ceremonies & Magic

Migene González-Wippler

This book is far more than a historical survey of magical techniques throughout the world. It is the most complete book of spells, ceremonies, and magic ever assembled. It is the spiritual record of humanity.

Topics in this book include magical spells and rituals from virtually every continent and every people. The spells described are for love, wealth, success, protection, and health. Also examined are the theories and history of magic, including its evolution, the gods, the elements, the Kabbalah, the astral plane, ceremonial magic, famous books of magic, and famous magicians.

You will learn about talismanic magic, exorcisms and how to use the I Ching, how to interpret dreams, how to construct and interpret a horoscope, how to read Tarot cards, how to read palms, how to do numerology, and much more.

Included are explicit instructions for:

- love spells and talismans
- spells for riches and money
- weight-loss spells
- magic for healing
- psychic self-defense
- spells for luck in gambling

. . . and much more.

No magical library is complete without this classic text of magical history, theory, and practical technique. The author is known for her excellent books on magic. Many consider this her best. Includes over 150 rare photos and illustrations.

0-87542-286-1, 400 pp., 6 x 9, illus.   **$14.95**

Dreams

and What they Mean to You

Migene González-Wippler

Everyone dreams. Yet dreams are rarely taken seriously—they seem to be only a bizarre series of amusing or disturbing images that the mind creates for no particular purpose. Yet dreams, through a language of their own, contain essential information about ourselves which, if properly analyzed and understood, can change our lives. In this fascinating and well-written book, the author gives you all of the information needed to begin interpreting—even creating—your own dreams.

Dreams and What They Mean To You begins by exploring the nature of the human mind and consciousness, then discusses the results of the most recent scientific research on sleep and dreams. The author analyzes different types of dreams: telepathic, nightmares, sexual, and prophetic. In addition, there is an extensive dream dictionary that lists the meanings for a wide variety of dream images.

Most importantly, Gonzalez-Wippler tells you how to practice creative dreaming—consciously controlling dreams as you sleep. Once a person learns to control his dreams, his horizons will expand and his chances of success will increase!

0-87542-288-8, 240 pp. $5.99

What Happens After Death

Scientific & Personal Evidence for Survival

Migene González-Wippler

What does science tell us about life after death? How do the different religions explain the mystery? What is the answer given by the strange mystical science known as Spiritism? These and other questions about the life beyond are explored in *What Happens After Death*.

The first part of the book is an objective study of the research about life after death. The second part is a personal narrative by a spirit guide named Kirkudian in which he explains his various incarnations. While the two sections could be considered two separate books, they simply express the same concepts in uniquely different ways.

Experience for yourself one soul's journey through the afterlife, and discover the ultimate truth: that every soul is created in union with all other souls, and that we are all manifestations of one purpose.

1-56718-327-1, 256 pp., 5 3/16 x 8 $7.95

Santeria

The Religion

Migene González-Wippler

When the Yoruba of West Africa were brought to Cuba as slaves, they preserved their religious heritage by disguising their gods as Catholic saints and worshiping them in secret. The resulting religion is Santería, a blend of primitive magic and Catholicism now practiced by an estimated five million Hispanic Americans.

Blending informed study with her personal experience, González-Wippler describes Santería's pantheon of gods (orishas), the priests (santeros), the divining shells used to consult the gods (the Diloggún), and the herbal potions prepared as medicinal cures and for magic (Ewe) as well as controversial ceremonies—including animal sacrifice. She has obtained remarkable photographs and interviews with Santería leaders that highlight aspects of the religion rarely revealed to non-believers.

This book satisfies the need for knowledge of this expanding religious force that links its devotees in America to a spiritual wisdom seemingly lost in modern society.

1-56718-329-8, 400 pp., 6 x 9, photos $17.95

Egyptian Scarab Oracle

deTraci Regula
Art by Kerigwen

Do you dream of Egypt? The *Egyptian Scarab Oracle* emerged in a very Egyptian way—through a magical dream that deTraci Regula had one night after studying ancient Egyptian writings.

The Egyptian alternative to rune stones, this oracle is simple to learn, easy and fun to use, and also serves as an introduction to the gods, goddesses, and religious concepts of ancient Egypt.

1-56718-561-4, Boxed kit includes 30 scarab pieces, drawstring pouch, and 240-pp., 6 x 9 book

$34.95

Egyptian Paganism for Beginners

Jocelyn Almond and Keith Seddon

Practice a modern form of Paganism based on an ancient Egyptian religion with Egyptian Paganism. People are turning to the ancient Egyptian deities in increasing numbers. Pagan organizations, especially the International Fellowship of Isis (with 20,000 members), have stimulated this growing interest.

For solitary practitioners who want to perform daily devotions, this straightforward guide contains genuine invocations and prayers for each of the main deities, as well as a general overview of the deeper spiritual and magical aspects. There are translations of authentic religious texts along with practical instructions for creating a shrine, casting a circle, consecrating statues, and invoking deities.

0-7387-0438-5, 288 pp., 5 3/16 x 8 $12.95

Did you know . . . Many of Migine González-Wippler's books are available in Spanish—From Llewellyn Español!